Fairleigh Dickinson University Library
Teaneck, New Jersey

THE GRAMMAR
OF JUSTICE

Elizabeth H. Wolgast

CORNELL UNIVERSITY PRESS

ITHACA AND LONDON

First published 1987 by Cornell University Press.

International Standard Book Number (cloth) 0-8014-2081-4
International Standard Book Number (paper) 0-8014-9402-8
Library of Congress Catalog Card Number 87-47608
Printed in the United States of America
Librarians: Library of Congress cataloging information
appears on the last page of the book.

The paper in this book is acid-free and meets the guidelines
for permanence and durability of the Committee on Production
Guidelines for Book Longevity of the Council on Library Resources.

F O R

_____

Norman Malcolm
Abe Melden
Wallace Matson

Contents

Preface

What is justice? When is a punishment fitting? What makes majority rule fair? How can a government morally represent its citizens? Such large and abstract questions enter familiarly into our political debates and discussions of policies, questions about who to vote for and what taxes are justified, for example. With policy decisions riding on their votes, citizens of democracies seem to need to make decisions that are philosophically sound and illuminated by a theoretical vision of justice. They seem to need a general picture of justice and the concepts linked to it, a picture with form and coherence.

But experience shows that when hard decisions are to be made, we often begin without a preferred theory, even with many theories. We begin by recognizing that a practice or deed is unjust and that something must be done about it, and in the face of that urgency we dig around for a theory that shows *why* the deed is unjust and what, if anything, should be done.

It is my belief that when we theorize about social good and justice, we do so after we have confronted problematic facts rather than in advance. Our thinking begins with particular occasions, and then we try to connect cases and priorities into a picture of general principles, fashioning for ourselves a satisfying rational scheme. This procedure is similar to the one Plato describes when he says that it is our distress about contradictions and conflicts that makes us reach for a higher theoretical level of understanding. For practical reasons, dilemmas pave the way for theory.[1] With Peter Winch and Ludwig Wittgenstein and Alasdair MacIntyre, I take moral philosophy and its debates as occurring not in a vacuum but at a particular place and time, with cultural traditions and practices already in place. As we lack an absolute theoretical beginning, so we can't see things *sub specie aeternitatis* (from the viewpoint of eternity), as Spinoza would have us do, but must reason from here and now. We consider crucial ideas as generally as possible, detach ourselves from many circumstances, take as abstract a view as we can, and wrestle with our limitations. But even as we reason, we look over our shoulders to see whether our argument squares with our intuitions about what practices are right and with our concrete understanding of a good human life and acceptable human behavior. In such ways our moral experience informs and limits what we can formulate abstractly.

These essays are "grammatical" in Wittgenstein's sense of that term. In that sense the grammar of a term includes a wide variety of practices connected with its use and the criteria and background conditions that govern its normal application. Thus it is part of the grammar of "chair," Wittgenstein says, that *this* is what it is to sit on one.

But if background conditions are important in regard to right and justice, it follows that we necessarily lack an absolute and neutral beginning, some fixed Archimedean point from which to derive a true moral or political theory. Instead it may be that reasoning and values form a circle, and that the way we are brought up shapes both our ideas about what is good and our notion of what reasoning (even about good) is sound. In that case, we shouldn't suppose, for instance, that people made an original social contract out of pure rational conviction; rather they learned about contracts and obligations and how to act and live in society in the same way they learned the meanings of right. We all learned them as children, and learned then how to reason about such things too. Thus there are crucial links between culture and rea-

---

[1]Plato, *Republic*, trans. Paul Shorey, in *The Collected Dialogues of Plato*, ed. Edith Hamilton and Huntington Cairns (Princeton: Princeton University Press, 1961), 523a–525a; see also my *Paradoxes of Knowledge* (Ithaca: Cornell University Press, 1977), p. 18.

soning and learning one's native language, links that indicate that language is something other than a scientific instrument of communication. These links make us ask how we took in morality as we grew up and when—how—we came to grasp its awesome seriousness. How did this aspect of life dawn on us?

On this grammatical approach we need not assume that all rational people should be convinced by the arguments that convince us—for example, about the nature of a good life, the form that a society should take, and what its laws and policies should be. Instead it is possible to acknowledge an area where political and ethical theory, understood as abstract disciplines, cannot argue further. At that point we can only present a moral anthropology in which personal biography, history, and abstract reasoning all have their place but none is isolatable or fundamental or theoretically prior to the others.

In view of this approach, it should not be surprising that some of the essays in this book are peculiar to the American tradition while others are more general, taking as their framework Western culture. The citizen spoken of is generally American, and the tradition that citizen consults began to develop in the seventeenth century from roots established by English and European philosophers. Among the terms vital to American thinking are social contract, respect, individual rights, freedom, majority rule, political representation; and each of these concepts has its philosophical background. The first four chapters are especially concerned with such ideas. Chapter 1 explains the model I call "social atomism," which entered philosophy during the Enlightenment and put its indelible stamp on American political thinking from the beginning. Its consequences can be spelled out and examined, and although it is pervasive in our thought, in the end we can question our thoroughgoing commitment to it.

Chapter 2 takes up one consequence of the model: the singular emphasis we put on individual rights as a way of addressing injustices. While atomism makes this approach seem ennobling, I argue that it is sometimes inappropriate. Chapter 3 considers self-government as an aspect of social atomism and explores the conditions required if majority rule is to be, as we commonly imagine it to be, a morally superior form of government. It concludes that atomism makes poor moral sense of majority rule; and this conclusion raises again the question whether the atomistic model serves us well.

Chapter 4 looks from an ethical perspective at the conception of action by a representative, any representative. It asks in particular whether a government can carry out good deeds in the name of its constituents. And if not, how should citizens view the role of government vis-à-vis their own ethical standards?

Chapter 5 focuses on a contemporary issue, control of pornography. Looking at the issue in the light of the atomistic traditions of freedom and respect, one sees that conflicting conclusions are drawn from the same premises. What can help us decide such an issue? Here the engagement of the demand for justice and expressions of moral objection can be seen in their everyday working clothes.

Chapter 6 takes up the more abstract question of what kind of concept justice is. Is it a positive ideal from which injustice is a departure, as philosophers often imply? I argue that it is not, and that the grammar of justice is intimately connected with the invocation of justice when we object to wrong. Such a connection reveals justice as playing an ambiguous role, as a term that signifies some morally satisfying response to wrong without pointing to what that might be.

The next two chapters deal with punishment. Chapter 7 asks why punishment seems so necessary, so mandatory in response to wrong. The answer it offers forces us to look at the role of abhorrence and passionate objection in the grammar of such terms as "wrong," "unjust," and "intolerable." Chapter 8 takes a different approach, taking the punishment of children by conscientious parents as a paradigm. What light does this practice shed on the punishment of criminals and the role of the society that condemns them?

Chapter 9 considers how passionate feelings about injustice can be reconciled with the idea that justice is to be reasoned about and not merely felt. This discussion brings us back to Wittgenstein by pointing to the notion "form of life" as important for both ethical and political concepts. Only in the context of a human life, a life of a certain kind with certain complexity, can questions about these concepts have any sense.

The goal of these essays is to get a clearer view of how our moral reasoning works and how it in turn illuminates political judgments. Through a variety of arguments related to justice I seek a perspective that will permit us to view our dearest convictions from some philosophical distance, so that we may see where they conflict and some places where they trip up our thinking.

The reader I imagine is someone curious and interested in political ideas, who wonders why we are often unable to address real problems in ways that square with our ethical values, who realizes these questions are important and that they have deep philosophical roots. Is something wrong with our values? Is something amiss with our reasoning? These were my own questions, and they prompted these philosophical diggings.

Many people influenced this book as it developed. Albert Borgmann's comments and references on atomism were invaluable, as were Newton Garver's on the sense of injustice. Abe Melden helped in all stages, but particularly in criticisms of my argument on rights. Rush Rhees, Renford Bambrough, and Páll Árdal all influenced the argument on retributivism. I owe a particular debt to Christine Littleton on the pornography argument, as well as a debt to Rita Manning and Michael Krausz. Karen Wiederholt improved that argument too and gave the entire manuscript a thoughtful and discriminating editing. I also thank John Ackerman of Cornell University Press for his continuing encouragement and interest and Barbara Salazar for her judicious editing.

Earlier versions of some essays have appeared in journals, and permission to use them by the journals is hereby acknowledged: "Intolerable Wrong and Punishment" appeared in *Philosophy* in April 1985, copyright © 1985 by Cambridge University Press; "Sending Someone Else" in *Philosophical Investigations* in April 1986; and "Wrong Rights" in *Hypatia* in Winter 1987. "Why Justice Isn't an Ideal" was part of a symposium on justice and equality sponsored by the Center for Ethics and Social Policy at the Pacific School of Religion.

ELIZABETH H. WOLGAST

Berkeley, California

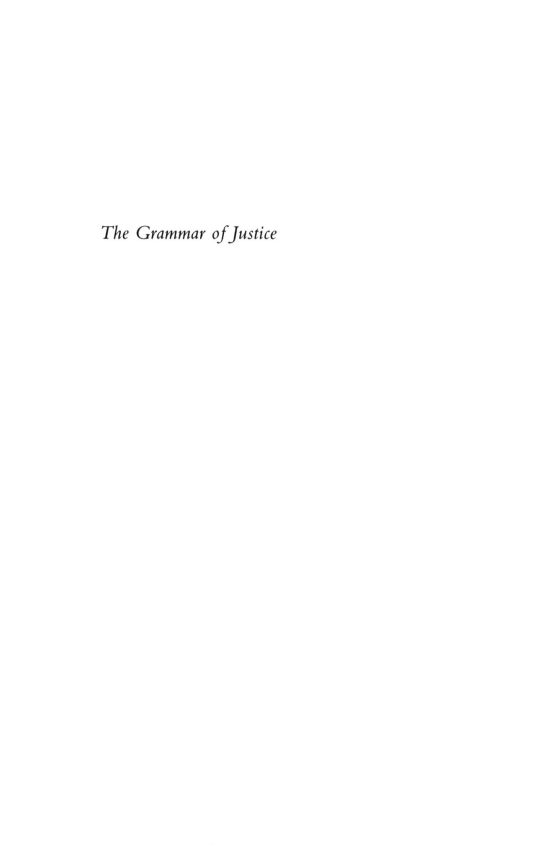

The Grammar of Justice

1

A World of Social Atoms

We call on the ideas of social atomism when we reason about political and ethical issues, but, perhaps because they are so familiar, we don't often examine them critically.[1] Here we look at the logic and interconnections of ideas of social atomism and at some of their historical sources.

I

In the seventeenth century a new fashion in thought appeared, one whose motivation was to challenge traditional authorities in a variety of dimensions. René Descartes, for instance, challenged the church's claim to authority on matters concerning God, the soul, and the world God presumably made. Thomas Hobbes and John Locke challenged the traditional grounds given for political authority. In that enlightened time government could not be based on divine right or on natural heredity or paternalism; it needed some more rational basis. David Hume, Thomas Reid,

---

[1]Atomism has come under increasing criticism. See, for instance, Alasdair MacIntyre, *After Virtue* (Notre Dame: University of Notre Dame Press, 1981); Robert N. Bellah et al., *Habits of the Heart: Individualism and Commitment in American Life* (New York: Harper & Row, 1985); and my own *Equality and the Rights of Women* (Ithaca: Cornell University Press, 1980).

and Immanuel Kant in turn took up the question of the foundation of morality; why should we accept what anyone says about what is right and morally justifiable?

Standing against the old authorities required a secure point, an Archimedean point from which to strike.[2] So it happened that in a variety of fields—science, theology, political theory, morality— such a point was located in the autonomous, unconnected, rational human individual. Starting with this person and his or her inherent abilities, requirements, and values, one got a neutral and detached perspective on any claim to authority. Thus a new kind of moral, political, and epistemological justification came into being, one that derived from the natural, free, rational, and morally autonomous individual. It was an unbinding of the inquiring spirit; it was a new premise for shedding a critical light on old orthodoxies.

Contemporary American social and moral theories and our political arguments bear the mark of this bold anti-authoritarianism. The new ideas of the Enlightenment became unshakable American principles. Nonetheless, new problems followed upon this advance, and we face them still.

II

Descartes's anti-authoritarianism appears in his claim that men are equal in their reason. No one is distinguished by intelligence, rather "good sense is of all things in the world the most equally distributed . . . [and] the power of forming a good judgment and distinguishing the true from the false . . . is naturally equal in all men."[3] One finds it astonishing that an indisputable and not very modest genius should say such a thing if one neglects its importance for the challenge he took up in theology and sci-

---

[2]Though the reference to Archimedes was first made by Descartes in this connection, it reappears in recent political theory, in the works of John Rawls and Robert Nozick, for example. Their views are discussed later in this chapter and in chap. 3.

[3]René Descartes, "Discourse on Method," in *The Philosophical Works of Descartes*, trans. Elizabeth Haldane and G. R. T. Ross, vol. 1 (Cambridge: Cambridge University Press, 1967), p. 81.

ence. For if all people are alike in their ability to learn and know, and there are no experts, then a person who wants to understand God or the soul or the universe doesn't need anyone else. We can all figure it out for ourselves.

Along with this intellectual individualism Descartes proposed a method for investigating problems, a method universally applicable to theology, mathematics, physiology, morals, and every other subject. Its use, he proposed, would guarantee that all attainable human knowledge would be within the reach of everyone. The fruits of the method would be considerable: "Nothing more useful can be accomplished in philosophy than once for all to seek with care for the best of these reasons [concerning God and the soul] and to set them forth in so clear and exact a manner, that it will henceforth be evident to everybody that they are veritable demonstrations." Deductive demonstrations require nothing from outside a person, they do not call on a specialized knowledge, and so "all that which can be known of God may be made manifest by means which are not derived from anywhere but from ourselves."[4] This was something new, a do-it-yourself science and theology. Thus in the end it is Descartes's egalitarianism that provides the power that drives his rational anti-authoritarianism.

Descartes's English contemporary Thomas Hobbes used the autonomous individual in a very different way—to give a novel justification for government. From the Archimedean point of such individuals Hobbes believed he could justify the existence of government—of any form—in a way that anyone would have to accept. His justification would not appeal to natural, divine, or hereditary right but only to human nature and human rationality. A government comes into existence through a contract, he proposed, a covenant that free and independent individuals make with one another. The resulting government is then a kind of artifact.

Before there was government, Hobbes's theory said, people managed to exist, but not well and not peacefully. For in that presocial state men separately governed their activities, that is to say, each pursued his own interest and depended entirely upon himself for protection. People in this condition were roughly

[4]Ibid., p. 134.

equal, Hobbes held: "Nature hath made men so equall, in the faculties of body, and mind . . . [that] when all is reckoned together, the difference between man and man, is not so considerable, as that one man can . . . claim to himselfe any benefit, to which another may not pretend, as well as he. For as to the strength of body, the weakest has strength enough to kill the strongest. . . . And as to the faculties of the mind . . . I find yet a greater equality amongst men, than with strength." Equality of people both mentally and physically, combined with desires and motives of self-interest, yielded competition as a natural way of life, competition that was unrelenting, harsh, deadly.

> From this equality of ability, ariseth equality of hope in the attaining of our Ends. And therefore if any two men desire the same thing, which neverthelesse they cannot both enjoy, they become enemies; and . . . endeavour to destroy, or subdue one an other. . . . If one plant, sow, build, or possesse a convenient Seat, others may probably be expected to come prepared with forces united to dispossesse, and deprive him, not only of the fruit of his labour, but also of his life, or liberty.

This natural state was consequently barren of the goods of civilization: "There is no place for Industry; because the fruit thereof is uncertain: and consequently no Culture of the Earth, no Navigation . . . no Knowledge of the face of the Earth; no account of Time; no Arts; no Letters; no Society; and which is worst of all, continuall feare, and danger of violent death; And the life of man, solitary, poore, nasty, brutish, and short."[5]

In Hobbes's picture of equal autonomous agents, people can be likened to molecules of gas bouncing around inside a container. Each molecule proceeds independently, is free to go its own way, although it occasionally bumps into others in its path. As molecules have their energy, people are driven by their passions, and their relations with one another reflect both their "love [of] Liberty, and [love of] Dominion over others."[6] No atom helps or moves aside for another; that wouldn't make sense. They are a collection of unrelated units. This fundamental picture I call "so-

---

[5]Thomas Hobbes, *Leviathan* (New York: Everyman, 1947), pp. 63–65.
[6]Ibid., p. 87.

cial atomism," for it shows society as a simple collection of independent, self-motivated units.

In Hobbes's view, government is justified as an instrument by which people further their security and thus their self-interest. It is the people's creation, and its irreplaceable function is to create a state of peace and security in which the human atoms can pursue their interests without fear. That function and that alone justifies government's existence; therefore it cannot have interests that are not ultimately reducible to the interests of its members. So Hobbes reserved for citizens the right to disobey their government in the face of threats to their lives or security. Insofar as government was a creation of the people who were to live under it, this was a do-it-yourself political theory.

Atomism need not be associated with such a dismal account of human nature as Hobbes's. Another social atomist of this period, John Locke, held a more generous view. For him people are generally sociable and not naturally at war; only a few create problems: "Were it not for the corruption and viciousness of degenerate men, there would be no need" for a contract or government. Human nature did not generally need restraint by government, and the value people placed on liberty, property, and political equality needed to be respected by government. Still the autonomous, independent individual is the central motif. "Men being . . . by nature all free, equal, and independent, no one can be put out of this estate and subjected to the political power of another without his own consent. The only way whereby any one divests himself of his natural liberty, and puts on the bonds of civil society, is by agreeing with other men to join and unite into a community for their comfortable, safe, and peaceable living one amongst another, in a secure enjoyment of their properties, etc."[7] Individuals have the power to keep or give away authority over them. Therefore at bottom of political authority is the idea of individual independence and autonomy: the authority one has over oneself.[8]

---

[7]John Locke, *Second Treatise on Civil Government*, in *Two Treatises on Government*, ed. Thomas I. Cook (New York: Hafner, 1966), chap. 9, p. 185; chap. 8, pp. 168–69.

[8]I treat autonomy as a primitive notion. Other authors have interpreted the term differently; e.g., Joel Feinberg includes a Kantian moral dimension in it and thus

For Locke a contract is optional rather than a matter of survival, and any number of people may contract with one another to join together while leaving the rest in the state of nature. When they do so contract, they have formed a community: "When any number of men have, by the consent of every individual, made a community, they have thereby made that community one body, with a power to act as one body."9

While Hobbes's and Locke's views of men's nature and the form of government that's "natural" for them differ, their views of the contract on which government is based are similar. Both see it as being made voluntarily and rationally, out of people's natural, self-oriented desires and their recognition of their limitations; and should people be thrown into the state of nature again, both see the rational course as being to make another contract of the same kind. Without claiming to represent the historical origins of society, this conception came to have a profound effect on the understanding Americans have of the relation holding between government and citizens.10

In the following century another form of atomism was developed by Kant, Hume, Shaftesbury, and Reid: its concern was morality. These philosophers held that the source of moral authority lay in the individual—in one's conscience, moral sense, or reason. This conception of moral autonomy sets the stage for the proper treatment of others, and it gives force to the idea that political authority must have its moral source in such individuals.11 For these philosophers, the justification of moral precepts must derive from an individual conceived without the imprint of society. The single individual is the ground of moral principles. This is do-it-yourself moral theory.

finds autonomy compatible with social regulation (*The Moral Limits of the Criminal Law* [New York: Oxford University Press, 1986], 3: chap. 18, esp. pp. 40–41), while Robert Paul Wolff sees autonomy and regulation as in total conflict (*In Defense of Anarchism* [New York: Harper & Row, 1970]).

9Locke, *Second Treatise*, p. 71. Locke adds that the will shall be "by the majority." Chap. 3 discusses majority rule and Locke's justification of it.

10Some of the consequences for the relation of democratic citizens to their government are discussed in chap. 3.

11A contrasting view of the relation of individual autonomy to society is given in Jean Piaget, *The Moral Judgment of the Child*, trans. Marjorie Gabain (New York: Macmillan, 1965). Piaget argues that moral autonomy is a late achievement of children and therefore a product of social development; see particularly pp. 105–7.

Ethical atomism combined with Hobbes's and Locke's social atomism supplies some of the most important and characteristic features of American political theory, and the imprint of these ideas is evident and fixed in the Constitution.[12] It is from Hobbes, for example, that we derive the idea that no one should be forced to give evidence against himself and threaten his own security—the essence of the Fifth Amendment. From Locke we have a picture of man as a solid citizen, conscientious and property-owning, and the right of such citizens to monitor the actions of their government. From him, too, we have emphasis on the sanctity of property. From the ethical atomists we derive the need to respect expressions of conscience, since conscience is tied to moral autonomy; it follows that the authority of government must be qualified by the moral authority of the governed.

Such timeless theoretical foundations give Americans a vocabulary and a framework for discussing social problems, and at the same time they define avenues for addressing such problems. If its implications fail to square with our moral judgment, then—by ethical atomism's own premise of individual authority—it is subject to serious criticism.

III

In form, social atomism appears scientific, and its analogues in science are easy to recognize. For we understand what physical compounds are when we know what they're made of. A wall of bricks is understood as an assemblage of separate bricks. A molecule of water is made up of separable atoms, and to understand what water is you must know about those atoms. Often we talk about compounds in terms of their parts; why not apply the same method to a society? Thus we can understand a society if we know what it's made of. The resulting theory of society can then claim a truth that is abstracted from historical contexts, can claim

[12]See Garry Wills, *Inventing America* (Garden City, N.Y.: Doubleday, 1978), for an excellent account of the moral background of the Constitution. Wills argues that the Constitution bears the imprint of the Scottish moralists even more than of Locke, but both influences are clearly reflected in it.

the lasting and objective validity of physics or chemistry.[13] It will include the features that a society not only has but must of necessity have. In giving social theory this foundation, Hobbes became one of the founders of political and social "science."

In contemporary political thought the idea is expressed by Robert Nozick, who says that although the political realm can be "understood" by various means, a nonpolitical explanation is the only means that "promises full understanding . . . and stands as the . . . most desirable and complete kind of explanation of a realm."[14] A complete understanding of the political requires us to begin with the nonpolitical, and Nozick's starting point, like Hobbes's and Locke's, is the single human individual. This is their Archimedean point.

Dividing a thing into its parts was also recommended by Descartes, one of whose principles was to "reduce involved and obscure propositions step by step to those that are simpler, and then starting with the intuitive apprehension of all those that are absolutely simple, attempt to ascend to the knowledge of all others by precisely similar steps."[15] To get clear about anything complex, he says, first break it down into its simplest units. Following this advice, we should understand a society as a collection of persons; Descartes's advice applies in a straightforward way.

It may seem self-evident that one way to understand a thing is to take it apart, but notice what this idea assumes. It assumes that a part will be a discrete thing with its own nature, and that if we know the component parts, we will understand the whole. But not every compound or complex thing can be understood by this means. Take a machine: it is not just a collection of parts, but a collection of parts assembled in accordance with a particular design

[13]For an interesting argument against this conception, see Alasdair MacIntyre, "Is a Science of Comparative Politics Possible?" in *Against the Self-Images of the Age: Essays on Ideology and Philosophy* (London: Duckworth, 1971); also reprinted in *Philosophy, Politics, and Society*, ed. Peter Laslett, W. G. Runciman, and Quentin Skinner (Oxford: Blackwell, 1972). MacIntyre argues that Machiavelli was right when he saw politics as partly a creature of chance, and that Hobbes was led astray by his desire for a scientific theory of society.

[14]Robert Nozick, *Anarchy, State, and Utopia* (Cambridge: Harvard University Press, 1977), p. 6.

[15]Descartes, "Rules for the Direction of the Mind," in *Philosophical Works of Descartes*, 1:14.

and in a particular order. If we have only the assorted parts or a list of them, we may altogether fail to understand how the assembled parts function. We still need a diagram or design, a conception of how the machine works, maybe an idea of its eventual purpose. Then are the design and purpose *parts of* the machine? Hardly. But if the machine is not understandable without the design and can't be assembled without it, how can the machine be understood in terms of parts? Or take a cake: it's a collection of ingredients, but not ingredients assembled any which way. It needs a method or recipe, or else it can't be accounted for; putting the same ingredients together at random may yield a disaster. Then is the recipe *part of* the cake? No. Nonetheless, the cake cannot be understood in terms solely of its parts or ingredients.

Consider the following argument, then. Some things cannot be understood in terms of simple units, units that exist originally in isolation; an understanding even of the parts may depend on their being in an appropriate context and related within a whole. Take part of a flower, a pistil, for instance. What is it? It's part of a particular flower, with a function in the life of the plant and the generation of new plants, a function in a whole pattern of the plant's growth and its relation to other things. It is the pistil of that flower, functioning with respect to it; that is what it is. The same problem applies to some parts of machines. Think of finding an odd-looking piece of metal in the road; how does one describe or identify it? Most commonly, perhaps, as a part of some kind of machine, a piece that has a characteristic place and function in various mechanisms. Some fairly standard parts—bolts, screws, wheels—are describable individually because, like atoms and bricks and marbles, they are interchangeable and their functions standardized. But in any case they are identified as things with a certain function in a larger whole. Therefore while an atomistic approach works to explain some things, we can't assume it will provide an adequate understanding of society, though it will certainly press out a crisp and simple theory.

Among those who have held anti-atomistic views were the ancient Greeks.[16] Aristotle, for instance, believed that a man is a

---

[16]Werner Jaeger traces in detail the importance of the community in the Greeks'

particular individual only in the context of his community. To understand the individual, then, we must begin with the community he or she belongs to, "for the whole must be prior to the part. Separate hand or foot from the whole body, and they will no longer be hand or foot except in name, as one might speak of a 'hand' or 'foot' sculptured in stone." Moreover, without a state, a man is without family, heritage, and home, for these things have reality only within a political community. More: "he is mad on war: he is a non-cooperator like an isolated piece in a game of draughts."[17] The community is the right place for a person, and humans need to be seen in that context if we want to understand them.

For Aristotle a person *is* the legal child of So-and-so, the husband of So-and-so, the father of So-and-so, the owner of such land, the person who trades in such goods, the one who holds such office and votes under such-and-such name. These social properties and relationships define a person. They do so by referring to other people, some of them closely related, others more distant, others who are fellow citizens, and eventually to the community itself. The individual is nothing without these relationships, has no importance, is nobody; for it is in this framework that he is credited and counts as an individual.[18] The whole makes the part comprehensible.

Not everyone accepts atomism's assumption that separate units provide understanding of a compound, or the related claim that "since society consists only of individuals, it cannot have a character different from that of the individuals who compose it." Emile Durkheim, for example, answers with different analogies:

---

idea of human perfection in *Paideia: The Ideals of Greek Culture* (New York: Oxford University Press, 1945), particularly vol. 1, chaps. 1–6. Alasdair MacIntyre also contrasts the modern view of the self with that of ancient societies in *After Virtue*, pp. 33–34.

[17]Aristotle, *Politics*, trans. T. A. Sinclair, rev. Trevor Saunders (New York: Penguin, 1981), p. 60. In this connection see Plato's representation of the laws as parents, who bring a citizen into the world and rear and educate him (*Crito*, 51b–e). See also MacIntyre, *After Virtue*, esp. p. 220.

[18]It is important not to overemphasize the "priority" of the community to Aristotle. For while he sometimes speaks of the "natural" need of humans for a society, at other times he speaks of the best life for a man as a contemplative, asocial one.

Experience demonstrates in a thousand ways that a combination of elements presents new properties that do not characterize any of the elements in isolation. The combination is then something new. . . . In combining tin and copper, basic elements that are soft and malleable, one gets a new substance with an altogether different property. It is bronze, which is hard. A living cell consists entirely of inanimate, mineral molecules. But by the sheer fact of their combination the qualities characteristic of life emerge—the capacity for self-nourishment and reproduction.

The case is the same for society, he argues. "Because men live together rather than separately, individual minds act upon one another; and as a result of the relationships thus established there appear ideas and feelings that never characterized these minds in isolation. . . . Thus it is that human groups have a way of thinking, of feeling, and of living differing from that of their members when they think, feel and live as isolates."[19] Such views encourage the suspicion that atomism may not be the only or best way to understand human society.[20] Whether it is even a reasonable one needs reflection as well, for insofar as we take a theory of society seriously, our choice of a model is crucial.

IV

The question of what a society is made up seems to many to have an obvious answer: It's made up of individual people, as bricks in a wall, as molecules in a substance. What else is there besides individuals?

To explain a community in terms of these units is to imply that people are complete in themselves, that they are self-contained, independent, self-motivated, energized from within—by passions and desires, Hobbes would say. They are complete and real, each

[19]Emile Durkheim, *Moral Education,* trans. Everett K. Wilson and Herman Schnurer (New York: Crowell-Collier, 1961), pp. 61–62.

[20]See also Michael Sandel, who speaks of community as *constitutive* and thus as giving identity to persons: *Liberalism and the Limits of Justice* (Cambridge: Cambridge University Press, 1982), chap. 4. He argues that individualism cannot give an adequate account of community or morality.

in him- or herself, and their autonomy is related to a certain independence. As Joel Feinberg writes of self-reliance: "The morally independent person does not bind himself to others any more than he can help . . . does not rely on the commitments of others to him. In certain areas of his life, at least, he doesn't need others, and dispensable needs he doesn't want."[21]

Starting with these units, we naturally see society as deriving from their individual interests. In its favor is Occam's razor, which says that you should make only the minimum assumptions, nothing more. Social atomism needs nothing besides the individual units with their individual interests. It needs no glue to bind people together; self-interest will account for the society in what Nozick calls an "invisible hand" explanation, accounting for laws and institutions as the natural result of individual choices. Rationality enters here, for on this account we are rational if we recognize our self-interest and act accordingly. Because it is formed to serve people's self-interests, government can be seen as just; it represents only what the people *chose*.

V

Given the starting point of separate and self-interested individuals, it is clear that those individuals must be equal. They must be equal to satisfy the anti-authoritarian mission of the theory, but also because this analysis is meant to derive a just society from a universal theory of human nature, a theory that represents humans as alike. People's distinguishing characteristics, the superior talents and skills of some, differences of personality, age, sex, and ability to contribute to the community—all these elements must drop out if the analysis is to work. The atoms must be equal. The historian J. R. Pole writes of the connection between atomism or individualism and equality in American thought: "The individualist principle dissociates people from the context of family, religion, class, or race and when linked with the idea of equality . . . it assumes the coordinate principle of interchangeability."

[21]Feinberg, *Moral Limits of the Criminal Law*, 3:42.

Bricks are interchangeable and so are molecules of water; interchangeability goes with our understanding of such units. But in fact people are in many ways not alike, and then how can it be fair to treat them as interchangeable? Pole gives this explanation: "The interchangeability principle . . . means simply that, if the requisite training and experience were given [them], . . . a white and a black, a Protestant and a Roman Catholic, a Jew and a gentile, as well as a peasant and a nobleman, could take each other's places in work, in sport, in intellectual discourse, and in the respect their personal bearing could command from others."[22]

The theoretical role of the interchangeability principle is clear, but its application is not; in particular its application to differences of sex is, as Pole realizes, problematic. How it can be just to treat people alike when their needs and situations differ?

Answers to this question are notoriously involved and difficult. Some people say that justice presupposes equality, but equality doesn't mean similarity; people can be treated equally but differently. People's equality is something more general, a matter of meriting equal respect, and not any specific treatment or specific rights.[23] Others have called a prejudice our tendency to characterize *any* fair arrangement as one of equality, to argue that "because an inequality may be just or justified, it is really an equality after all."[24]

How can the model's egalitarianism be squared with a society that accords respect to different kinds of individuals? Perhaps the most ingenious answer is John Rawls's conception of an "original position" and the "veil of ignorance" that characterizes it. Rawls believes that the basic principles of a fair society can be founded upon a kind of blind egalitarianism, a philosophical starting point

[22]J. R. Pole, *The Pursuit of Equality in American History* (Berkeley: University of California Press, 1978), p. 293.

[23]This answer can be found in Gregory Vlastos, "Justice and Equality," in *Social Justice,* ed. Richard Brandt (Englewood Cliffs, N.J.: Prentice-Hall, 1962). Some of the turnings of the debate are traced in Wolgast, *Equality and the Rights of Women,* pp. 34–35.

[24]Hugh Bedau, "Egalitarianism and the Idea of Equality," in *Nomos IX: Equality,* ed. J. R. Pennock and J. W. Chapman (New York: Atherton, 1967), p. 13. Also see Peter Westen, "The Empty Idea of Equality," 95 *Harvard Law Review* 537 (1982); and Wolgast, *Equality and the Rights of Women,* chaps. 1, 2, and 6.

at which people are ignorant of their own characteristics and therefore of what would serve their advantage.[25] In this position one would not know one's sex, financial situation, education, talents, weaknesses, abnormalities. Not to know these things is not to know whether one is in a strong or weak position vis-à-vis others who are parties to the contract. Thus in the original position one will be careful to accept only principles that *will not* be prejudicial to oneself if one's real position turns out to be weak. For it is assumed that people will take advantage of one another *unless* they imagine themselves similarly vulnerable. From this position, Rawls believes, people will come to agree on principles that are fair to everyone.

The original position is a philosophical device whose purpose is to make plausible the adoption of fair principles as people move from an unorganized existence to membership in a community. The resulting community, moreover, is one in which their conflicts of interest are resolved through a commonly accepted conception of justice. What guarantees people's agreement to a single conception is that each will look at his own position in terms of all the possible positions, which will include those of others as well as his own, and come to a decision that will be both his own and hypothetically that of others.[26]

It is important to distinguish the sense in which Rawls means a person to "put himself in the place of another" and the sense in which a white person, for instance, may "put himself in the place of" a black person when he considers racial issues. The latter projection is an exercise in sympathy with the lot of others. But Rawls's original position doesn't depend on sympathy or feeling of humanity. It doesn't ask the original parties imaginatively to take the point of view of others, projecting sympathy or empathy in the manner of Butler or Shaftesbury while they know that their own positions are secure. On the contrary: to evaluate the justice of a principle, one needs to look at its implications from a *self*-interested point of view, to consider all possible situations *as if they*

[25]John Rawls, *A Theory of Justice* (Cambridge: Harvard University Press, 1971), pp. 138–39.

[26]The best criticism of the self that must make such a judgment is Sandel's in *Liberalism*, esp. chap. 2.

might really be one's own. Thus self-interest serves to define for Rawls a *dis*interested point of view; and such a view he considers the key to justice.[27]

Rawls's derivation of a just state from self-interest is part of a long, ongoing tradition of attempts to derive moral rules or principles of justice from self-interest, of attempts to show that being moral must in some way be reducible to doing what is to one's benefit.[28] What I attempt here is to understand why such projects seem plausible.

VI

In a container of gas all molecules are free to move where they want. But the freedom they enjoy is to move randomly in space; what does the metaphor mean as applied to human beings? If we ask whether people act freely in a real community, the answer is most certainly no. Most of them, adults and children, act a good deal of the time according to fixed rules and responsibilities, according to promises and needs, not to mention the constraints of laws. What does it mean to say that nonetheless they are free? This remark signifies that we are looking through the grid of the model. Just as one cannot imagine molecules being restricted by invisible bonds, people must be free and independent, for only in this way can they satisfy the features of the model.

Autonomy, Rawls emphasizes, is closely connected with freedom, since everyone needs "equal liberty to pursue whatever plan of life he pleases" within broad limits. "The main idea is that a person's good is determined by what is for him the most rational long-term plan of life given reasonably favorable circumstances. A

[27]Sandel rightly asks, "Assuming . . . that the parties to the original position really would choose the principles Rawls says they would, why does *this* give us reason to believe that these principles are just?" (ibid., p. 104). The answer Rawls gives, that justice is defined this way, is clearly unsatisfactory.

[28]Among the philosophers who have tried this kind of justification are Kurt Baier, *The Moral Point of View: A Rational Basis of Ethics* (Ithaca: Cornell University Press, 1958). For a criticism of this justification from the side of an ethical egoist, see David Gauthier, "Morality and Advantage," in *Morality and Rationality,* ed. Gauthier (Englewood Cliffs, N.J.: Prentice-Hall, 1970).

man is happy when he is more or less successful in the way of carrying out this plan."[29] But what does this mean for a real human life: from what position does one make his or her long-range plans? Is there an absolute beginning from which all possible life plans can be arrayed?[30] Our real beginnings seem full of influences and training, and our plans change all the time. Is there undue interference with our free choice? And is it really so bad that some plans are frustrated while others fall of their own defects? Making and fulfilling our long-range plans might be crucial for happiness if happiness depended on our plan's fulfillment, and if we knew at some very early age what would make us happy and what kind of life we wanted. But these are large qualifications.

The autonomy of individuals and their self-interest are connected with the use of contract to explain human connections and institutions.[31] Consider the explanation of marriage as a contract made by two parties for their mutual self-interest. A sensible person has to wonder: a contract for what and concerning what? A contract involves specific conditions, and failure to carry out any one of them breaches the contract. Imagine, then, that a couple at their wedding are making a legally enforceable agreement regarding the exchange of goods or services, some kind of fair agreement based on mutual self-interest. What are the conditions of the contract? Does one promise to love and honor? The first is impossible to promise, the second is demeaning to free, autonomous agents. Other conditions mentioned are to stay together for better or worse, for richer or poorer, in sickness and in health—eventualities as risky as they are vague. And how long does the contract run? Until death. Besides

[29]Rawls, *Theory of Justice,* pp. 94, 92–93.

[30]See Sandel, *Liberalism,* chap. 2, on the choice of an "unencumbered self" in Rawls; see also Michael Sandel, "The Procedural Republic and the Unencumbered Self," *Political Theory* 12 (February 1984): 81–96.

[31]Anthropologists and philosophers have long played a speculative game to explain human arrangements. Perhaps the latest manifestation of this tendency is Robert Axelrod, *The Evolution of Cooperation* (New York: Basic Books, 1984), which derives cooperative behavior from the rational self-interest of opponents in a game. His account entirely fails to explain, however, the cooperation of a group to accomplish some *joint* enterprise; in the end he has only egoists making and confirming their calculations of self-interest. Mary Midgley observes some of the limitations of such theories in *Beast and Man* (Ithaca: Cornell University Press, 1978), chap. 6.

the wonder that any rational being would engage in such a deal, there is the fact that such a contract could not be validly enforced. No performances are specified, no term is mentioned, much is specifically left to chance; how could such a contract be binding? And of course such "contracts" aren't enforced.

Marriage *is* a legal relationship, voluntarily entered into, and in that way it is like a contract. But the commitment to weather unknown exigencies is a feature that no contract can tolerate.[32] On the other side, if marriage had to be construed as a contract, one might argue that there would be nothing resembling marriage at all.

The reduction of such human relationships to contracts is forced upon us by a picture, the picture of atomism, and the problems it creates suggest that the picture cannot be right.

Nonetheless, society was also thought to rest on a contract. As Ronald Dworkin observes, the "contract device" is one that "supposes each individual to pursue his own interest and gives each a veto on the collective decision. . . . It is designed to produce the distribution that each individual deems in his own best interest, given his knowledge under [the contract]." Dworkin believes, however, that the relation of man in the state of nature to his role as citizen needs more explication. The claim that a society founded on a contract will be just is not self-evident; other fundamental requirements are needed, in particular the theory of natural rights. Thus he argues that "the deep theory behind the original position . . . must be a theory that is based on the concept of rights that are *natural,* in the sense that they are not the product of any legislation, or convention, or hypothetical contract."[33]

My claim is that the "deep theory" here goes even deeper than a

---

[32]Rawls acknowledges in his *Theory of Justice* that a contract can't explain the bond of marriage, but he seems very confused about what other account works better; see particularly pp. 525–26, 573. Also see my *Equality and the Rights of Women,* pp. 144–45.

[33]Ronald Dworkin, *Taking Rights Seriously* (Cambridge: Harvard University Press, 1977), pp. 174, 177. Dworkin's use of "natural right" here is mainly negative: a natural right is one that's *not* dependent on government. Founding a political theory on natural rights, as if the existence of such rights were clear and self-evident, is a hazardous move, as Dworkin recognizes, but he believes it is better than no ground at all.

theory of natural rights. At bottom is a theory of people's natural discreteness, and from this theory an account of their relations to one another and to society has somehow to be derived. In that picture society arises only from some individual-based reason. For such creatures communal life has to result from rational self-interest, and even then the adjustments required may be awkward and uncomfortable.[34] If we take this picture as the "deep theory," then, it is obvious why, as Dworkin observes, "rights-based theories" "place the individual at the center . . . [and] are concerned with the independence . . . of individual action. They presuppose and protect the value of individual thought and choice. . . . The man at [the center of such a theory] is the man who benefits from others' compliance, not the man who leads the life of virtue by complying himself."[35] In this tradition the individual always *was* at the center—his freedom to act, to express himself and pursue his interests entail his reluctance to be governed at all. He is at heart an anarchist and accepts government as a necessary evil.[36]

Connected with individual freedom is the importance of competition. Just as molecules in a container bounce around in their competition for space, so the social molecules compete for the satisfaction of their needs and desires. In the state of nature competition was perfectly free but threatening; in a society it can be made orderly and peaceful, and thus it becomes the normal mode of human interaction.[37]

But when this picture is applied to society, anomalies appear. In such a society the elderly and frail must compete with the young and strong, men compete with their childbearing wives, the handi-

---

[34]Inasmuch as people must sacrifice some precious freedom to get a community while guarding it in the community, their situation is, as Alasdair MacIntyre says, paradoxical (*After Virtue*, p. 66).

[35]Dworkin, *Taking Rights Seriously*, p. 172.

[36]Or does not accept it at all, as Wolff refuses to do (*In Defense of Anarchism*). The consequence that the atomistic person is mistrustful of his government, no matter how democratic, is explored in chap. 3, below.

[37]While Milton Friedman and others argue, atomistically, for an ideal of free competition, Friedrich Hayek argues persuasively that perfectly free competition is a fiction, that what we need is for society to guarantee the conditions for *orderly* competition; see Friedman, *Free to Choose* (New York: Harcourt Brace Jovanovich, 1979); Hayek, *Individualism and Economic Order* (Chicago: University of Chicago Press, 1948), chaps. 5 and 6.

capped compete with the well endowed. Correspondingly, the economy of the community is seen as an *n*-person game in which each player plays against all others to maximize his advantage. The problems of this picture have not deterred social and economic thinkers from using it, even though it is at center a picture of ruthless egoism and unconcern for others.

VII

Through Hobbes and Locke the political implications of the model profoundly influenced the framers of the Constitution, who sharply appreciated its anti-authoritarian force. They viewed the founding of a new constitutional government as a new beginning, a chance to follow and act out the tenets of the contract theory, and as they were no longer united with England, they could assume the role of a collection of people who could choose and form their government as they wanted. Insofar as all the colonies had to ratify it, the Constitution could be thought of as a voluntary contract among all the people.

Much of the language of the Constitution, and the constitutions of the states, comes from social contract philosophers, especially Locke. The constitution of Virginia states, for example, "that all men are by nature equally free and independent, and have certain inherent rights, of which, when they enter into a state of society, they cannot by any compact deprive or divest their posterity: namely, the enjoyment of life and liberty, with the means of acquiring and possessing property, and pursuing and obtaining happiness and safety." The Alabama Declaration of Rights declares "that all *freemen,* when they form a social compact, are equal in rights." And the Connecticut Declaration of Rights pronounces "that all men, when they form a social compact, are equal in rights, and that no man or set of men are entitled to exclusive public emoluments or privileges from the community."[38] Sometimes it was the states rather than individuals that were viewed as

[38]Quoted in David Ritchie, *Natural Rights* (London: Allen & Unwin, 1952), pp. 5, 245, 246.

the independent parties to the contract.[39] But throughout the early American state papers appears language suggesting that a contract is the proper foundation for government.

The model's claim to be scientific was also an important virtue. The framers did not, however, adopt Hobbes's materialism and its deterministic consequences. Hobbes conceived man as a kind of machine, subject to natural forces within himself, just as objects are subject to the force of gravity, and his actions as much the result of such forces as a stone's fall. A man on this view could no more exercise self-restraint than he could fly. While human nature was in part mechanical, the colonists would agree, and physical causes explained some of its workings—the workings of the heart and liver and brain, for instance—man was more than this.[40] For them the account of Sir Walter Raleigh was closer to the truth: "And wheras God created three sorts of living natures, (to wit) Angelicall, Rationall, and Brutall; giving to Angels an intellectuall, and to Beasts a sensual nature, he vouchsafed unto man both the intellectuall of angels, and sensitive of Beasts, and the proper rationall belonging unto man; and therefore—man is the bond and chaine which tieth together both natures."[41] The emphasis on a human's ability to reason and so to understand himself became associated later with the philosophy of John Locke.

Man was not to be seen only in terms of intellect and animal functions; he also had a moral side. But how could a moral nature be reconciled with the self-interest of atomism? The moral philosophers Francis Hutcheson, Thomas Reid, and Anthony Shaftesbury gave answers that showed man as a divided creature, a creature who was on one side moral, and who, regardless of intellect and education, was endowed with a moral sense. Hutcheson put the alternative to selfish egoism like this: "We have not only self-love, but benevolent affections also toward others, in various degrees,

[39]For example, the Virginia Resolutions, December 24, 1798, reproduced in *The People Shall Judge*, ed. The Staff, Social Sciences 1, College of the University of Chicago (Chicago: University of Chicago Press, 1949), 1:439.

[40]On the fascination early Americans felt with the mechanical workings of humans, see Wills, *Inventing America*, *esp. pp. 96–97*.

[41]Walter Ralegh, *History of the World*, ed. C. A. Patrides (Philadelphia: Temple University Press, 1972), p. 126.

making us desire their happiness as an ultimate end . . . we have a moral sense or determination of our mind to approve every kind of affection either in ourselves or others . . . without our having a view to our own private happiness in our approbation of these actions." This moral sense, which makes "publicly useful actions and kind affections grateful to the agent and to every observer," is common to all men, Hutcheson proposes.[42] Reid sounds a similar note: "The testimony of our moral faculty, like that of the external senses, is the testimony of nature, and we have the same reason to rely upon it," he writes. No great intellect is required to understand morality: "The truths immediately testified by our moral faculty, are the first principles of all moral reasoning," and such reasoning is practiced by "all men come to years of understanding."[43] Both Reid and Hutcheson picture a moral egalitarianism, a moral democracy in which each person is competent to make good judgments and to be fully responsible for decisions. This vision had a profound influence on Jefferson, among others.[44]

But this moral view seems to be inconsistent with the social contract's assumption of the primacy of self-interest and the natural unconnectedness of people. Indeed, it has some of the ring of Aristotle. Jefferson was clear about the conflict between the two forms of atomism, and comes down firmly on the side of Reid and Hutcheson against Hobbes. Here he sides with Hutcheson against one critic: "I gather . . . that he [the critic] adopts the principle of Hobbes, that justice is founded in contract solely, and does not result from the construction of man. I believe, on the contrary, that it is instinct, and innate, that the moral sense is as much a part of our constitution as that of feeling, seeing, or hearing."[45]

Although the state is founded on contract, Jefferson believes

[42]Francis Hutcheson, *Illustrations on the Moral Sense,* ed. Bernard Peach (Cambridge: Harvard University Press, 1971), pp. 118–19, 132.

[43]Thomas Reid, "Of the Rational Principles of Action," in *Inquiry and Essays,* ed. Keith Lehrer and Ronald Beanblossom (Indianapolis: Bobbs-Merrill, 1975), pp. 320, 322.

[44]Wills, *Inventing America,* pp. 200–201.

[45]*The Adams–Jefferson Letters,* ed. Lester J. Cappon (Chapel Hill: University of North Carolina Press, 1959), 2:492, quotes in Wills, *Inventing America,* p. 204. For a fuller discussion of the relation of moral atomism to democracy, see below, chap. 3, sec. IV in particular.

justice has its source in men's moral sense. But can these two views be made consistent? The social contract made voluntarily by all parties seems to have implicit justification; it was chosen freely. Rawls interprets justice this way, as "the virtue of practices where there are assumed to be competing interests and conflicting claims, . . . where it is supposed that persons will press their rights on each other . . . [being] mutually self-interested."[46] But if every individual has a moral sense, justice ought to relate to that sense. Both of these conceptions of justice cannot be right. Nonetheless both belong to our tradition, and the tension between social contract theory and a moral view of human nature is reflected in the history of our political theory. It is a conflict that cannot be resolved.

VIII

Viewed from a distance, the idea that government derives from a contract is intrinsically curious. A contract is a device that is useful under two conditions. First, a contract is useful when two parties wish to bind one another formally—that is, when they do not trust one another sufficiently to accept a promise or some other mere signal of intent: being legally binding is what you might call its primary feature. Second, and in consequence, a contract is useful when some authority exists to enforce it. It would make no sense for two people to draw up a contract on a desert island where no enforcing authority existed. They might agree to do some-thing—act cooperatively, say—but that wouldn't be a contract. The authority doesn't need to be a government in the fullest sense; a community might enforce contracts by informal means, by so-cial pressure, for example. But some authority must exist or there is no difference between a contract and a promise.

Now it is clear that the state of nature by any definition—Hobbes's, Locke's, or Rousseau's—lacks the second condition. The point of their social contracts was to *set up* an enforcing au-thority. But to set up such an authority *by contract* involves a *petitio principii*: Who will enforce *this* contract? Surely not the authority

---

[46]John Rawls, "Justice as Fairness," *Philosophical Review* 67 (April 1958): 175.

that the contract itself sets up. It cannot enforce what its existence depends on. So it follows that a civil government cannot be set up by a contract if that term is taken strictly. One has to conclude that the contract is at best a metaphor.

Did the framers of the Constitution really take the notion of contract seriously? Consider this passage in the Virginia Resolutions: "That this Assembly doth explicitly and peremptorily declare that it views the powers of the federal government as resulting from the compact to which the states are parties, as limited by the plain sense and intention of the instrument constituting that compact, as no further valid than they are authorized by the grants enumerated in that compact; and that, in case of a deliberate, palpable, and dangerous exercise of other powers, not granted by the said compact, the states, who are parties thereto, have the right . . . to interpose."[47]

Their use of the formal language of contracts reflects, I believe, a deep concern of the framers of the Constitution to propose that they were really signing a contract. They wanted not only (like Hobbes and Locke) to depart from traditional justifications of government but to set up a new *form* of government, a constitutional one that everyone concerned could be said to have agreed to. This form would be *chosen,* much as the terms of a contract are. And in the document they devised, the power of government, the rights of the citizens, and the general relation of citizen to government were all explicitly spelled out, just as the terms of a contract are. There were to be no assumptions about the role of authority. Limiting the power of government had an English precedent that the colonists were eager to follow, and a constitution subscribed to by the population was a logical instrument.

Now both a constitution and a contract are documents, both are drawn up and accepted. But their implications are very different. A constitution explicitly sets up a government but is subject to change. A contract, by contrast, is rigid; once made, it isn't subject to alteration except by consent of all parties. Did the framers think that all parties to the Constitution might agree to alter it?[48] Con-

[47]Virginia Resolutions, in *People Shall Judge,* 1:439.
[48]Alexander Hamilton, in *The Federalist Papers,* writes in support of the "funda-

tract theorists have therefore struggled with the question of how the original parties to a contract can bind succeeding generations; as the theory of contracts is usually construed, they cannot.[49] One free agent cannot bind another.

But in any case a constitution is not a contract: from the beginning the enterprises are different. For one thing, a contract is a deal, an exchange of one thing for another. This is how Hobbes saw the social contract: each person gave up some of his rights on the understanding that others would give up some of theirs. But writing a constitution is a creative enterprise whose distinctive feature is not exchange of goods or services but the exercise of judgment about how a good government can best be guaranteed and made to work. It's a work of imagination. One person could do it, or many; the number of people who participate in the writing doesn't determine the validity or bindingness of the Constitution. Anyone who fails to sign a contract, in contrast, is simply not bound by it.

To see this difference more clearly, compare the views of Rawls and Aristotle. It is crucial for Rawls's "original position" that each man see *himself* in the positions of the others. This requirement flows from the assumption that one can come to fair principles— that is, principles that will be fair to every self-interested party— only from one's own self-interested point of view. One could speak of Rawls's principles as the beginning of a constitution. Aristotle, however, looks at the state as something to be constructed wisely, judiciously, with an eye to the welfare of the whole civil body. Self-interest could never be counted on to yield the principles he is looking for, nor could the fairness of a game or bargain suffice as a translation of justice.

Constitutional government is compatible with a variety of assumptions about human nature. The fact that people agree on how

---

mental principle of republican government, which admits the right of the people to alter or abolish the established Constitution, whenever they find it inconsistent with their happiness" (no. 78).

[49]Edmund Burke defends the "conservation" of traditions as consistent with the ability to make changes and thinks the revolutionists forfeited such opportunities. "A state without the means of some change is without the means of its conservation," he writes (*Reflections on the Revolution in France* [Harmondsworth: Penguin, 1968], p. 106); conservation and change are both needed principles.

to form a government doesn't guarantee its justice: any group of men, some good, some bad, can be imagined to form a constitutional government—a band of thieves, for instance. A constitution is like a contract, for both involve some agreed-upon arrangement and neither need be just to be valid.

It was easy to confuse making a contract with setting up a new government when no government or traditional procedures existed. The point of drawing up a constitution was to signify a new beginning, a departure from the old conceptions of government held by Europe's monarchs. The framers were in harmony with Hobbes and Locke on one important point: they wanted and needed a government that represented their standards of political propriety. But for this purpose they did not need those authors' atomistic model. A constitutional government is perfectly consistent with the idea of an organic community and existing traditions regarding justice, as Aristotle thought. And the importance of general agreement to the constitution doesn't require the assumption that all actions are motivated by self-interest, an assumption that conflicted with the framers' moral views. Therefore it is not surprising that the confusion, however natural, should have left a legacy of difficulties.

IX

The atomistic model has important virtues. It founds the values of the community on private values; it encourages criticism of government and requires any government to answer to its original justification; it limits government's powers, as they may threaten to interfere with the needs of atomistic units. It gives us assumptions about the nature of man and the composition of society to start our reasoning, gives us a common ground in the values of freedom, autonomy, respect, equality, and the sanctity of desires. It thus frames a multitude of important political disputes, holds them together, shapes them, and sheds a clear, unequivocal theoretical light on them.

But it leaves a great deal out, as we have seen. In it one cannot picture human connections or responsibilities. We cannot locate friendliness or sympathy in it any more than we can imagine one molecule or atom moving aside for or assisting another; to do so would make a joke of the model. Michael Sandel is right, I believe, when he says that our political and economic theory is "a view about the way the world is, and the way we move within it, . . . [and] at the heart of this ethic lies a vision of the person that both inspires and undoes it."[50] The atomistic person is an unfortunate myth.

Complaints against the American version of atomism are plentiful. Tocqueville said that individualism "disposes each citizen to isolate himself from the mass of his fellows and withdraw into the circle of family and friends; with this little society formed to his taste, he gladly leaves the greater society to look after itself." Those of some economic means "form the habit of thinking themselves in isolation and imagine that their whole destiny is in their hands." As a result, "each man is forever thrown back on himself alone, and there is danger that he may be shut up in the solitude of his own heart."[51]

Emile Durkheim concurs with this view: individualism, he says, "detaches the individual from the rest of the world . . . confines him in himself and closes off every horizon," and eventually the emphasis on self-interest leads to pessimism, even suicide.[52] And Alasdair MacIntyre describes the preoccupation of the individualistic tradition in philosophy as "the condition of those who see in the social world nothing but a meeting place for individual wills . . . who understand that world solely as an arena for the achievement of their own satisfaction, who interpret reality as a series of opportunities for their enjoyment and for whom the last enemy is boredom."[53] The ground of these criticisms is not located

[50]Michael Sandel, "The Procedural Republic and the Unencumbered Self," *Political Theory* 12 (February 1984): 81–96.

[51]Alexis de Tocqueville, *Democracy in America*, trans. George Lawrence, ed. J. P. Mayer (Garden City, N.Y.: Doubleday, 1969), 2:105; 308; see also Bellah et al., *Habits of the Heart,* chap. 2, where these passages are quoted.

[52]Durkheim, "The Sciences of Morality," in *Emile Durkheim: Selected Writings,* trans. and ed. Anthony Giddens (Cambridge: Cambridge University Press, 1972), p. 94.

[53]MacIntyre, *After Virtue,* p. 24.

in any historical circumstance, but lies squarely in the atomistic model.

On a number of grounds the model needs challenging. A larger picture of human life needs to be considered, one that allows a firmer juncture between the moral and political realms, between the grammar of good and the grammar of justice. Or, what may amount to the same thing, we need to loosen the hold that the atomistic picture has on our thinking, and recognize the importance that theory has on our judgments and our moral condition.

2

Wrong Rights

If the basic units of society are discrete and autonomous individuals, that fact must determine the way they should be treated. Thus it is a natural step from atomism to the concept of individual rights, rights that will attach to each individual regardless of his or her characteristics. As persons are independent, so their rights will be defined in a framework of independence. And as the indistinguishable atoms are equal, so their rights need to be equal. The concept of individual rights is a natural adjunct to atomism.

The language of rights is also a way of looking at wrongs, a conceptual grid, a schema. It both gives us a sense of *how* wrongs are wrong and points to the way to address them, that is, by establishing a right. Although it is a powerful and useful tool, still the schema of rights is sometimes unfit for the uses we make of it. It can bind us to a senseless stance, stereotype our reasoning, and lead to remedies that are grotesque. Our commitment to this language is deep, however; even in the face of bizarre consequences we hold it fast and view the consequent problems as demands for further rights. Thus our reasoning often goes on in an enclosed framework of rights, a framework from which counterexamples are excluded a priori. What does this commitment to rights mean to us, and how can it be sensibly limited?

I

Rights are often spoken of in the language of possessions. They are, Richard Wasserstrom writes, "distinctive moral 'commodities.'"[1] H. L. A. Hart spells out the metaphor: "Rights are typically conceived of as *possessed* or *owned by* or *belonging to* individuals, and these expressions reflect the conception of moral rules as not only prescribing conduct but as forming a kind of moral property of individuals to which they are as individuals entitled; only when rules are conceived in this way can we speak of *rights* and *wrongs* as well as right and wrong actions."[2] The idea of rights as moral property, as belonging to individuals the way property does, is an important aspect of the concept of rights. It focuses attention on the person to whom something is due, just as property law focuses attention on the possessor of property. The individual person with his needs and desires is the central motif.

This perspective is in contrast with one that focuses on the misdeeds of the offender, that condemns the misdeeds and castigates the doer. Instead of condemning, our perspective asserts something positive, namely, that a certain kind of thing—a *right*—exists. But what kind of thing is this, and how can we prove its existence? The answers given in response to this question are often vague, and they commonly lead to talk of "natural" rights as necessary features of human existence.[3] In the end we have something that sounds like a moral metaphysics. What is it that the possessor of a right holds? David Lyons explains:

> When *A* in particular, holds a certain right *against B, A* is a *claimant* against *B*. A "claimant" is one empowered to press or waive a claim against someone with a corresponding duty or obligation. He can, if he wishes, release the other from his obligation and cancel it, or he can insist upon its performance. . . . A claimant is thus one to

[1]Richard Wasserstrom, "Rights, Human Rights, and Racial Discrimination," in *Rights,* ed. David Lyons (Belmont, Calif.: Wadsworth, 1979), p. 48.

[2]H. L. A. Hart, "Are There Any Natural Rights?" in *Rights,* ed. Lyons, p. 19.

[3]See Alasdair MacIntyre, *After Virtue* (Notre Dame: University of Notre Dame Press, 1981), pp. 68–70, for a good account of the relation between modern talk of rights and the ideas of the Enlightenment.

whom the performance of a duty or obligation is *owed*—he is the one who holds the claim against the other and who is entitled to administer the claim as he chooses.[4]

Lyons describes an important feature of the language of rights: the power it puts in the hands of the owner to press his right against someone or some agency. Rights are there to be *claimed*—asserted, demanded, pressed—or, on the other hand, waived.[5] What the claimant is entitled to press for is no doubt a benefit; rights are generally associated with benefits, if only the benefit of being able to do something one doesn't want to do. But a right can be distinguished from a benefit in that a beneficiary often need not do anything; the role can be described as passive, you might say, while a rightholder can choose to claim his right or not; his right enables him to act in a certain way or to decline to do so.

Thus a right puts its possessor in an assertive position in which he may claim something, and to claim something is to claim it against another. So a right to a free education may be claimed by any child *against* the state, the right to vote may be asserted by any citizen *against* anyone who would interfere, the right of habeas corpus may be demanded *against* the court by anyone charged with a crime, and so on. But these rights differ quite a bit from benefits, since a gift generally doesn't need to be claimed, and the giver doesn't owe it if it is.

II

Rights put the rightholder in the driver's seat; a rightholder may be seen as active while the recipient of a benefit is

---

[4]David Lyons, "Rights, Claimants, and Beneficiaries," in *Rights,* ed. Lyons, p. 60.

[5]Joel Feinberg also emphasizes these options: if Nip has a claim against Tuck, he argues, then "Nip not only *has* a right, but he can choose whether or not to exercise it, whether to claim it, . . . even whether to release Tuck from his duty" ("The Nature and Value of Rights," in *Rights,* ed. Lyons, p. 85). For an interesting examination of the relation of rights and claims, see Alan White, "Rights and Claims," in *Law, Morality, and Rights,* ed. M. A. Stewart (Dordrecht: Reidel, 1983), pp. 139–60.

passive. Joel Feinberg captures the difference by comparing a world with rights to a world without them. He imagines "Nowheresville," a world without rights, and asks "what precisely [such] a world is missing . . . and why that absence is morally important." The crucial thing absent, he argues, is the activity of claiming: "Nowheresvillians, even when they are discriminated against invidiously, or left without the things they need, or otherwise badly treated, do not think to leap to their feet and make righteous demands against one another. . . . They do not have a notion of what is their due." Claiming depends on a prior right to claim, and although a right may be waived, rights' "characteristic use, and that for which they are distinctively well suited, is to be claimed, demanded, affirmed, insisted upon."[6]

Why do rights have such crucial moral importance? Feinberg answers that it is precisely the feature of claiming that "gives rights their special moral significance." It is "connected . . . with the customary rhetoric about what it is to be a human being. Having rights enables us to 'stand up like men,' to look others in the eye, and to feel in some fundamental way the equal of anyone. To think of oneself as a holder of rights is not to be unduly but properly proud . . . and what is called 'human dignity' may simply be the recognizable capacity to assert claims." People need to think of themselves as equal to others and thus able to claim their rights against others: that is a large part of what it is to be in the fullest sense a person. Nothing is more appropriate to a person than the possession of individual rights, rights that by their nature are given equally to everyone. In Feinberg's view the claiming of these possessions has a moral value of its own: "the activity of claiming . . . as much as any other thing, makes for self-respect and respect for others [and] gives a sense to the notion of personal dignity."[7]

The language in which Feinberg praises rights is recognizably atomistic. He thinks of individuals as independent units whose self-respect is of prime important to them *as* separate entities. Further, their capacity to claim rights is an important part of their active pursuit of their own interests. In such ways the language of

[6]Feinberg, "Nature and Value of Rights," p. 84.
[7]Ibid., pp. 87, 91.

rights both confirms the main features of the atomistic model and relies on its implicit values.

My claim is that such a conception of individuals and their rights may not be an effective means of addressing some injustices.

III

Consider the issue of the maltreatment of patients by doctors and medical staff in hospitals. In a hospital a patient is entirely at the mercy of medical people, whose expertise and positions give them great power, and so they are vulnerable to abuses of that power. The patient who is weak and frightened is by definition dependent on the staff; and they, in virtue of their practical knowledge and ability, are in the position of his rescuers—can instruct him and help him to survive. Abuse of such power and authority is, in view of the patient's helplessness, a frightening possibility.

Michel Foucault argues that with the development of clinics and the opportunities they offer to study disease, a new doctor–patient relationship develops. In this impersonal, scientific context the doctor becomes an expert in diseases, and "if one wishes to know the illness from which he is suffering, one must abstract the individual, with his particular qualities."[8] The doctor must look through the patient at the disease.

On the one side of the patient is the family, whose "gentle, spontaneous care, expressive of love and a common desire for a cure, assists nature in its struggle against the illness"; on the other side is the hospital doctor, who "sees only distorted, altered diseases, a whole teratology of the pathological." The traditional family doctor, in contrast, cannot have the clinical detachment of the hospital doctor, but in his practice "must necessarily be respectful" of the patient.[9] Foucault's account provides a plausible explanation of how the problem of disrespectful treatment of patients in a modern hospital comes about; it is a natural, logical development. Inevitably, too, the search for knowledge and the

[8]Michel Foucault, *The Birth of the Clinic,* trans. A. M. Sheridan Smith (New York: Random House, 1975), p. 14.
[9]Ibid., p. 17.

holding of power go hand in hand, and as the doctor seeks knowledge of a scientific kind, his patient becomes increasingly an object under his control, and less and less someone to be dealt with in personal terms.

Here's the problem, then. The patient is weak, frightened, helpless, but needs to be treated in many ways as a normal person—needs to be respected, even in his wishes regarding treatment, and ultimately perhaps in his wish to die or to be sent home uncured. The issue may be addressed in various ways, but the most common way of dealing with it is to say that the patient has a *right* to respectful and considerate treatment, a right to have his wishes in regard to his treatment respected, a right to be informed about the character of his treatment, and so on. To force upon him decisions he might not accept if he weren't ill and dependent is then to subject him to a kind of domination. It is as if the patient could be mistreated *because he is ill,* and that thought recalls Samuel Butler's grotesque society Erewhon, where illness is a crime demanding punishment. There a judge trying a case of pulmonary congestion pronounces, "You may say that it is your misfortune to be criminal; I answer that it is your crime to be unfortunate."[10]

In the wake of protests over mistreatment of patients, the American Hospital Association instituted a code of patients' rights which has been widely adopted in this country. The first of these rights is "the right to considerate and respectful care," the fourth is the "right to refuse treatment to the extent permitted by law and to be informed of the medical consequences of his action," the eighth is the patient's "right to obtain information as to the existence of any professional relationships among individuals . . . who are treating him." Yet at the end we are told: "No catalog of rights can guarantee for the patient the kind of treatment he has a right to expect. . . . All [the hospital's various] activities must be conducted with an overriding concern for the patient, and above all, the recognition of his dignity as a human being."[11] Nonetheless, these

[10]Samuel Butler, *Erewhon* (New York: Random House, 1927), p. 110.

[11]American Hospital Association, "Statement on a Patient's Bill of Rights," *Hospitals* 4 (February 16, 1973). This statement, which was affirmed by the Board of Trustees of the Association on November 17, 1972, is reprinted in *Contemporary Issues in Bioethics,* ed. Tom L. Beauchamp and LeRoy Walters (Belmont, Calif.:

rights are posted prominently in the hospital so that both patients and staff will be reminded of them as they go about their routines.

Now what can be wrong with this way of dealing with patient care? First, these rights, like the right not to be beaten by your spouse, call to mind the abuses they were designed to mitigate. They imply that hospital personnel are commonly guilty of unethical or insensitive conduct; otherwise there would be no need to protect patients against abuse. Second, the institution of rights focuses on a patient as complainant. As we have seen, the language of rights gives the rightholder a license to protest under certain circumstances; that is part of the language and the reason it's connected with self-respect. But as we have also remarked, the patient is not in a good position to exercise such rights. In his weakened condition, under medication, who is he to complain? Giving him rights puts him in the role of an assertive and able individual, but this role is inconsistent with being ill.

Someone who presses a claim and demands respect for his rights does so from the stance of a peer vis-à-vis the one complained against, as Feinberg says; but the doctor–patient relationship is not one of peers.[12] As one writer observes, "strong statements of patient rights imply a parity between physician and patient not usually possible in the situations under which . . . physician–patient relationships are developed." The patient needs the doctor; the doctor doesn't in the same way need him. Moreover, the patient "often enters into the arms of medicine as one might enter passionately into the arms of a lover—with great haste and need, but little forethought"; thus by definition a cool consideration of his situation is excluded."[13] Once recovered and out of the hospital, *then* the patient can exercise his rights—take the doctor and hospital administrator to court and sue for damages. But this rem-

---

Wadsorth, 1982). See also *Patients' Rights Handbook,* printed and distributed by the State of California under the administration of Governor Edmund Brown, Jr., which also assures a patient of "the right to decent living conditions and uncensored mail" (p. 13).

[12]For a discussion of the relation of peers, see Elizabeth H. Wolgast, *Equality and the Rights of Woman* (Ithaca: Cornell University Press, 1980), chap. 3.

[13]H. Tristram Engelhardt, "Rights and Responsibilities of Patients and Physicians," in *Contemporary Issues in Bioethics,* ed. Beauchamp and Walters, p. 136.

edy is no remedy at all. What a sick and dependent person needs is responsible treatment from others *while he is unable to press claims against anyone.*

How then ought the problem to be addressed? The moral difficulty comes to roost in the doctor–patient or staff–patient relationship: something isn't right there. As the Patient's Bill of Rights asserts, a doctor has to treat his patients with respect and concern, for that is his responsibility and part of his professional role. If he fails to do so, he is not a good doctor, no matter how knowledgeable he is. Then why is a set of rights given to the patient? It's the doctor who needs to be reminded of his charge, and that's where the focus ought to be, logically—on the doctor and his or her responsibility.

The doctor who sees the disease as the object of his interest, and sees the patient's idiosyncrasies as distractions from the pure case he wants to understand, is surely dehumanizing the patient. Foucault speaks of this outlook as a botanical view of medicine, for it is similar to the view found in botany, as well as in mechanics and physics.[14] Moreover, if we regard medicine as a science, it is difficult to see why a doctor *should* take the patient seriously *as a person.* Such a view isn't *objective;* that isn't the way a physical scientist would view his subject. Humanity, sympathy, and sensitivity have no place in physical science. The problem of patient treatment, then, is connected with the way medicine is conceived, its claim to be a science, and its place in the community.

An obvious way to address the issue of disrespectful treatment of patients would be to approach the medical community with exactly this concern, a concern that pertains potentially to everyone. One can imagine penalties being imposed when an ethical code is violated. Medical practice might be monitored by people outside of the medical brotherhood. Various legal and institutional ways could be devised to deal with the problem; we don't need to decide here which ones would be the most practical.

There are barriers to this approach, however. In the atomistic model, connections of responsibility and dependency don't appear;

[14]Foucault, *Birth of the Clinic,* p. 17.

there aren't any. In the same way that molecular theory cannot allow that some molecules take care of others or defer to them, independent autonomous beings cannot be connected. The language of rights reflects this atomistic fact, that relations of individuals to one another are relations between entities who are peers. And as we saw, these peer relations give rise to contracts in which both parties pursue their self-interests. Looking at the doctor–patient relation in this light, we see that there's no room for—no representation of—the doctor's *responsibility for the patient*. There is similarly no room in the model for anyone's responsibility for another; everyone is responsible for himself and that's all. Thus we are blocked from dealing with the problem in terms of the medical professional's responsibility for patients. Atomism prefers to give the patient rights.

But it doesn't make sense to do what we do in this case, to put the burden of straightening out the problem of medical negligence and disrespect on the shoulders of those already unable to handle the practical details of life—to say to such people, "Here are your rights; now you may press a claim against the doctor in whose care you placed yourself or waive your right, just as you please." The relationship between doctor and patient is appropriately one of trust, while this remedy implies the absence of trust.

It is no solution to assume that a patient has a healthy person to speak for him and press his rights. For even when such a person exists, the patient's dependency may still prevent his taking action against those who are supposed to care for him. When he is well (if he recovers), he and his representative can then bring suit against the doctor or whoever. But here again the right he possesses is a right appropriate to a well person, not a sick one. I conclude that the conception of patients' rights is irrational and impractical.

IV

Another area where rights are spoken of commonly but, as I will claim, inappropriately is the matter of children. The idea that children have a set of rights that their parents ought to respect is prompted by the prevalence of child neglect and child abuse, wrongs that undeniably exist. It's not in doubt that something needs to be done about such wrongs; wrongs are no less wrong when the perpetrators are the victim's own parents. Nonetheless, parents who abuse children present a difficult problem for the community.

The difficulty is with the strategy of putting rights in the hands of dependent children, rights they must exercise if they can against *those on whom they depend.* As with patients' rights, the model applied here is that of two equal and independent peers in a voluntary relationship—like that of parties to a contract. But that model doesn't fit this case. The child doesn't enter into its relationship with its parents voluntarily and isn't independent or a peer in relation to its parents. The main features of atomism are absent in this relationship.

Atomistic writers characteristically struggle with the place of children. Are they individuals with all the rights of individuals or not? Locke answers: "We are born free as we are born rational; not that we have actually the exercise of either: age, that brings one, brings with it the other too. And thus we see how *natural freedom* and *subjection to parents* may consist together."[15] Locke maintains both that children are free and rational and that they need their parents until they become rational. That is nothing less than a contradiction. Milton Friedman's answer is also problematic. He writes: "Freedom is a tenable objective only for responsible individuals. We do not believe in freedom for madmen or children. . . . We believe, and with good reason, that parents . . . can be relied on to protect them and to assure their development. . . . However we do not believe in the right of the parents to do whatever they will with their children. . . . Children are responsible individuals in embryo. They have ultimate rights of their own."[16] Both writers equivocate. They recognize that saying either that a child is independent or that it is altogether dependent is wrong. For the child its parents hold a unique position of intimacy and protection. The parent who abuses

[15]John Locke, *Second Treatise on Civil Government,* in *Two Treatises on Government,* ed. Thomas I. Cook (New York: Hafner, 1966), p. 150.
[16]Milton Friedman, *Free to Choose* (New York: Harcourt Brace Jovanovich, 1979), pp. 32–33.

a child may also provide warmth and affection. The wrong, like the relationship, is complex.

The community's concern about the problem is commonly expressed by references to children's rights against their parents. But realistically, any pressing of such a claim against one's parents usually threatens the earliest and closest relationship a child has. The child is expected to court his or her own insecurity. The child's position, like the patient's, is dependent, that of someone in need of the care and concern of another. But like the doctor–patient relationship, the parent–child relationship cannot be seen in our model. We protect children's interests by giving them rights, but in doing so blindly we ignore both the facts of human development and the various needs of children. Are children, who courts agree need protection, "dignified" by the possession of such rights or by the legal ability to claim them? They lack most ordinary rights because they are unready to use them, and generally are not good judges of the way they themselves should be treated. If there is an important right here, it should be the right to be given good parental care, but it is the parents that are responsible for providing such care. The alternative of giving children a right that they may claim is no substitute.

How should the wrongs of child abuse be addressed? As in the case of patients, we should speak to the wrong*doers* here; we need to restrain and admonish them, teach or punish them, remind them of the value and seriousness of parental roles, of the trust put in them by children on the one side and by society on the other. The matter at issue here is not only the place of the parent-culprit before the law but the place of the law in the parent–child relationship. The community has a profound interest here, not least because of its connection with the stature of its future citizens. Making the child and parent adversaries, encouraging the one to claim its rights against the other, is hardly a good way to pursue this interest.

Here, as in the medical case, we should be addressing the person in a *responsible* role and working with that relationship of responsibility, rather than dealing with the parties as independent peers. But the terms of atomism give us no purchase on this fundamental and complex relationship.

V

Another class of wrong rights affects women and the connections between them and their children. Consider the "equal rights" guaranteed to women who have committed substantial parts of their lives to raising a family and managing a home, and who then need work. The theory says that they have equal rights to a job, an equal opportunity in a free, competitive labor market. The image operating here is that of similar units—men and women of all ages—similarly situated, and in that case fair treatment would be identical treatment of them all. A woman is discriminated against and pays a penalty for her sex only if she is denied a job *when other factors are equal*. But if we suppose her situation to be as I have described it, then other factors are not equal. The model and its assumptions beg the essential question, namely, how she should be treated given that her situation is not like a man's. Affirmative action programs and a ban on "age discrimination" are stopgap efforts that inherently conflict with the model and bow in apology for the offense. They rest on the factors that distinguish people from one another, while in the model any distinctions of treatment are discriminatory and thus unfair.[17] Thus there is no theoretical solution to the problem. Measures that make reasonable moral sense are theoretically excluded.

Consider another issue, the debate over the constitutionality of mandated maternity leaves. The model requires this benefit to be couched in the language of equality; otherwise it appears as discriminatory against men. In order to avoid making a distinction between men and women, we assimilate maternity leaves to a disability or sickness leave, comparable to a leave one takes for the flu. When the benefit is thus clothed in sex-neutral terms, the

---

[17]See Richard Wasserstrom, "Racism, Sexism, and Preferential Treatment: An Approach to the Topics," *UCLA Law Review*, July 1977, pp. 581–622, which argues for a model in which no sex differences are recognized, where both sexes are in detail treated alike. Wasserstrom's exercise shows how complex and deep the theoretical problem is; if we are determined to deal with it in terms of equal rights, we have to reconstruct our society so that equal rights *will be fair*. For a discussion of Wasserstrom's argument, see my *Equality and the Rights of Women*, chap. 1; also see my "Is Reverse Discrimination Fair?" in *Law, Morality, and Rights*, ed. Stewart, pp. 295–314.

question arises whether or not a right to maternity leave is an "equal right." The argument then turns on the importance of men's immunity to pregnancy. In such famous cases as *Miller-Wohl* and *California Federal Savings*,[18] the issue is exactly this: If a maternity leave is an equal right, it may be fair; otherwise it provides to women a benefit that is unavailable to men, and therefore it is unconstitutional under Title V of the Civil Rights Act. Thus the very document that was meant to ensure fairness in employment and education is used to frustrate a policy to accommodate the most fundamental process of human life, reproduction.

The reasoning that ensues from a concept of fairness defined as equality among autonomous agents is often strange. It is seriously asked, for instance, whether men have an equal maternity right because they could have such a leave *if they should become pregnant*. What a strange question—and how can a reasonable person answer? One legal writer discusses the Miller-Wohl case in these terms: "The equal treatment proponents . . . are thinking metaphysically. They approach the question [of the legality of maternity leave legislation] . . . by asking whether or not the statute conforms to a particular legal construct, i.e., the equal treatment principle. They focus the debate on legal theoretical levels, rather than starting with an analysis of the concrete material problems of women in the workforce."[19]

Realistically, maternity leaves are needed because childbirth is exhausting and because a newborn baby and its mother need care. In part it is the child's needs that dictate that its mother shouldn't work full time just after its birth. But if we introduce the mother-child complex into the argument, we lose the framework of individual rights. And how else can we deal with the issue?

[18]Miller-Wohl Co. v. Commissioner of Labor and Industry, State of Montana, 575 F. Supp. 1264 (D. Mont. 1981); California Federal Savings & Loan v. Guerra, 55 U.S. Law Week 4077 (1987).

[19]Linda Krieger and Patricia Cooney, "The Miller-Wohl Controversy: Equal Treatment, Positive Action, and the Meaning of Women's Equality," *Golden Gate University Law Review* 13 (Summer 1983): 566. This article contains a good account of the theoretical problems presented by the maternity issue; however, the authors, like their opponents, couch the issue in terms of a *woman's* right, as if the problem involved no one else. For some suggestions about a different approach, see my *Equality and the Rights of Women*, chap. 4.

If we consider the central position of a baby in birth, we may decide that the baby has the principal right. But the issue is obscure: first we need to know if the baby is an individual who can possess rights, and then we have the harder question of whether that individual can have a right to its mother's maternity leave. On the face of it. that notion makes no sense. A right, as we have seen, attaches directly to a person; one person can't have a right *for* another. Moreover, involving the child in the maternal right won't work because it isn't born during the last weeks of pregnancy, when, just because its birth is imminent, the mother needs extra rest and leave from work.

The language of individual rights makes this issue into a puzzle in which by ingenious distortion we force something into a form that's essentially alien to it. How many people are involved in childbirth and do they each have a right, or together have a joint right, to maternity leave? And how does this complex of mother-and-baby compare with the less complicated case of a man? If both sexes are equal, which sex sets the standard? And if we are talking of disabilities, what kind of "disability" is it that leads to the birth of a child and a subsequent commitment to its care? The model gives no answers. Common sense would say that pregnancy isn't an illness but a strenuous productive period culminating in new responsibilities for a creature whose existence is fragile and who requires care to survive. But the model can't admit this description. The dignity of a rightholder brings no dignity to the condition of pregnancy or the occasion of childbirth.

The argument that a right to a maternity leave is a special and unfair right of women unless it is extended and adapted to men is a consequence of individualism and the language of equal rights. In this case it puts men in the position of jealous siblings, watching for any sign of partiality shown to others. They are in the position of competing with pregnant women for favorable treatment, and in this stance they show a blind disregard for the realities of childbirth.

The debate about abortion also shows the inadequacies of a theory of rights in regard to reproduction. It is a subject of serious debate whether the fetus is an autonomous individual with equal rights. If so, then it has all the rights of any person and should be able to claim its rights against its mother-to-be. But how can we imagine such a thing?[20]

The fetus's need for its mother is more total and unqualified than that of an infant for its parents. But if a fetus isn't a person, what else can it be? Some people have proposed to deal with it as a kind of property, as belonging to the mother as part of her body. To be sure, we sometimes speak this way of a foot or a kidney, and even of self-respect and reputation. But a fetus *isn't* like a body part or reputation. It is a potential baby, which is to say a potential human being, and its birth is not like an amputation or organ removal but is the advent of a new member (albeit immature) into the community.

Either way of representing a fetus, as a person or as property, is fraught with difficulties. On the one hand we make too much of it, granting it rights that cannot apply to its case, and on the other we make too little of it, treating it as property whose owner can dispose of it any way she likes, for the point and virtue of ownership is one's right to do what one wants with one's property.

There are certainly two sides to the question of whether abortions should be restricted and what restrictions should be imposed; that's understandable. What is strange is the way we are forced to *present* the two sides, forced to caricature both the pregnant woman and the fetus. We are forced to caricature them by our commitment to fit the issue into a grid that has room only for individuals who are autonomous, have property, and make contracts. But the reasoning is bizarre.

Imagine a Martian who has come to study us and make sense of our society. He hears arguments about whether the fetus is a person (in the full and legal sense) or a bit of property (in the tort-law sense). Wouldn't he consider us morally undeveloped or mentally handicapped? A human fetus is not like anything except another fetus, conceptually more like a rabbit fetus or a racoon fetus or an elephant fetus than like a fully developed human. It is a stage in a

---

[20]There is a wealth of a literature debating the question whether a fetus is a person. Mary Anne Warren, "On the Moral and Legal Status of Abortion," in *Philosophy and Women,* ed. Sharon Bishop and Marjorie Weinzweig (Belmont, Calif.: Wadsworth, 1979), pp. 216–26, works out a defense of the proposition that the fetus, while potentially human, lacks some necessary features of a human being, and thus cannot be considered a peer of its potential parent.

process by which an infant comes into a community—a community of rabbits or racoons or elephants or humans. Apart from this framework it's indefinable. It would be best to say, then, that a fetus is sui generis, its own kind of thing, and so irreducible to something else.

What is wrong with us, the Martian wonders, that we don't see this and persist in arguing about fetal personhood and fetal rights? But basically what is wrong here is the grid we press upon the facts of reproduction.

VI

One major problem with the model, as we have seen, is that it cannot show the variety of relationships in which people take responsibility and care for one another, some relationships of family, some of profession, some of simple concern. Its tendency to assimilate all relationships to that of independent, free, and self-interested persons also becomes a limitation in economic theory, as James Coleman observes. "Classical economic theory always assumes that the individual will act in his interest; but it never examines carefully the entity to which 'his' refers. Often, as when households are taken as the unit for income and consumption, it is implicitly assumed that 'the family' or 'the household' is this entity whose interest is being maximized. Yet this is without theoretical foundation, merely a convenient but slipshod device."[21] The "household" is a convenient device for preserving the outlines of atomism. But treating a family—which consists of more than one person—as a single individual "acting in its own interest" is at the same time at odds with the assumptions of atomism. The term *household* preserves the surface of atomism by making it a fictional person.

Rawls makes a similar adjustment, explaining that "the term 'person' is to be construed variously. . . . On some occasions it

[21]James Coleman, *Papers on Non-Marketing Decision-Making*, quoted in Howard Margolis, *Selfishness, Altruism, and Rationality: A Theory of Social Choice* (Cambridge: Cambridge University Press, 1982), p. 1.

will mean human individuals, but in others it may refer to . . . business firms, churches, teams," and of course families. Each of these units is then regarded as a rational and self-interested entity.[22] How else can we conceive of families? As a voluntary association of autonomous persons? That notion doesn't square with the facts.

When autonomous persons enter into an agreement, each party agrees to make some concessions in return for advantages to himself: mutual self-interest is the explanatory factor in all bonds. Milton Friedman emphasizes its exclusive power: "If an exchange between two parties is voluntary, it will not take place unless both believe they will benefit from it." Thus it is that "economic order can emerge as the unintended consequence of the actions of many people, each seeking his own interest."[23]

Apply this picture to the sick person, who needs help, and to the doctor, who has what Friedman calls his "personal capacity" to sell. According to Friedman, the doctor's only motive in helping the patient is his own interest, although he concedes that this interest can be defined as more than "myopic selfishness." "It is whatever it is that interests the participants, whatever they value, whatever goals they pursue. The scientist . . . the missionary . . . the philanthropist . . . are all pursuing their interests, as they see them, as they judge them by their own values."[24] The doctor may or may not be acting selfishly; he may have a personal interest in the patient's health. There's no room for a distinction, in Friedman's theory, between the good doctor and the clever mercenary one. None has any *responsibility* to concern himself with anyone else's health.

---

[22]John Rawls, "Justice as Fairness," *Philosophical Review* 67 (April 1958): 166. One has to be careful here, as Rawls also thinks of the group interest as consolidating but not merging the interests of individuals. An excellent criticism of this aspect of Rawls's argument may be found in Michael Sandel, *Liberalism and the Limits of Justice* (Cambridge: Cambridge University Press, 1982), esp. chaps. 1 and 4.

[23]Friedman, *Free to Choose*, pp. 13–14.

[24]Ibid., p. 27. Rawls also supposes that the interests of a person are sometimes benevolent and social, but they needn't be, and the moral justification of state policies is neutral on the question of whether it is these interests or purely selfish ones that are represented.

Plato thought the distinction between good and bad doctors was clear enough. In the *Republic* he has Socrates ask Thrasymachus, "But tell me, your physician in the precise sense . . . is he a money-maker, an earner of fees, or a healer of the sick? And remember to speak of the physician who is really such." Later he asks: "Then medicine . . . does not consider the advantage of medicine but of the body?" He concludes: "Can we deny, then . . . that neither does any physician in so far as he is a physician seek or enjoin the advantage of the physician but that of the patient? For we have agreed that the physician, 'precisely' speaking, is a ruler and governor of bodies and not a money-maker."[25]

Now if the doctor–patient relationship is a contract, and a sick person must approach a doctor who is motivated by his own gain, the contract is grossly unfair and susceptible to a multitude of exploitations, and therefore probably invalid. H. Tristram Engelhardt describes the initial approach like this: "The physician-patient relationship is likely to be assumed under circumstances that compromise the integrity of the patient. . . . At the very moments when much must be decided by the ill or dying person, he is often least able to decide with full competence. Disease not only places the patient at a general disadvantage . . . it also makes the patient dependent upon the physician.[26]

Here there is a relation governed by dependency, not autonomy, one in which most of the power and the clear options are on the side of the doctor. The patient is a poor example of the rational consumer. Given the doctor's motive and ability to get the best of him, it might be most rational in all self-interest for a patient not to approach him.

The best attitude of a sick person toward his doctor is trust, it is often remarked. The attitude intended is not trust that the doctor will fulfill a contract whose terms are unspecified, but trust in the doctor's concern. Without that sort of trust a doctor becomes a hired physiological consultant.

---

[25]Plato, *Republic*, trans. Paul Shorey, in *The Collected Dialogues of Plato*, ed. Edith Hamilton and Huntington Cairns (Princeton: Princeton University Press, 1961), V, 341c–342d.

[26]Engelhardt, "Rights and Responsibilities of Patients and Physicians," p. 133.

VII

A deeper question about the language of rights needs to be raised: Why, whenever we deal with a wrongful act or practice, do we feel impelled to refer to some right or other? Besides the influence of atomism, we think of a right as a justification for condemning something as wrong. Feinberg, for instance, says that claim rights are prior to and thus more basic than the duties with which they are correlated.[27] Thus they give a foundation for the demand that someone do or refrain from doing something and justify condemnation by showing the action as a violation of a (prior) right.

In practice the reasoning works like this. Burglary is wrong, everyone agrees; but what justifies us in calling it wrong? Some answer must exist, and one reasonable possibility is that it's wrong because a person has a right not to be burglarized, not to have his property invaded, abused, or stolen. Similarly we say that mugging is wrong, and then defend this judgment by arguing that it is wrong because a person has a right to walk down the street safely. Along these lines, murder is wrong because a person has a right to life; slander is wrong because a person has a right to be treated with respect; and so on. Rights proliferate as we seek justifications for every variety of things condemnable as wrong.

If justifications are needed, then the invocation of rights may make sense, but are such justifications necessary? Isn't murder simply wrong, wrong in itself? A common-sense answer might be yes—why should one need to justify such an obvious judgment? And if we reflect on the logical path that brought us here, we see that it is our conviction that we are justified in calling murder wrong that makes us sure that something must *justify* our judgment.[28] We are of course justified; but does our justification imply that some separate justification lies behind it? What would happen if none did?

---

[27]Feinberg, "Nature and Value of Rights," p. 84. A. I. Melden also uses "rights" to mean moral rights, as ways to justify calling things morally wrong; see *Rights and Persons* (Berkeley: University of California Press, 1977), esp. chap. 4.

[28]For a discussion of the primacy of our recognition of wrong, see chap. 7, below.

Murder's wrongness can be contrasted with the wrongness of something stipulated by a rule, such as moving a castle diagonally in chess. There a justification for the wrongness of the move clearly exists, that is, the rule that governs the way castles can move. And the wrongness of nonperformance of a contract has a justification, namely, that the contract specifies that one will do such-and-such. But in the case of some serious moral offenses it is less clear that analogous justifications exist. As Wittgenstein said of justifications of beliefs, "the chain of reasons has an end" and "at some point one has to pass from explanation to mere description."[29] Calling murder wrong is here like calling a certain color red, that is, what justifies us in using these terms is that the word means what it does. We are justified, but being justified is not the same as having a justification.

We have no particular reason to think that we need to invoke a right before we can call murder wrong. The "right to life" is unnecessary, and by eschewing it we avoid the curious consequence that death, which negates life, is wrong. We also acquire an important general benefit. When we leave rights aside, our view of murder takes on a different appearance, just as the mistreatment of patients looks different when we stop focusing on patients' rights. Saying that Smith is wrong in murdering Jones because the murder violates Jones's right to life puts the focus on Jones and his rights, even makes it appear that there is something that Jones can do with this right after the fact, which is nonsense. What really concerns us in such a case is what Smith did; *his* action belongs in the center of our perspective, his culpability, not the violation of Jones's now-useless right. Seen this way, an emphasis on individual rights serves to obscure the focus of moral objection to killing rather than giving the objection a firm foundation.

Without doubt rights have an important place in our legal and political system and they often do give reasons for condemning actions that would be permissible without them. But since they are justifications in some instances—the right to vote, for example, justifies us in calling a poll tax wrong or unjust—we are led to think

---

[29]Ludwig Wittgenstein, *The Blue and Brown Books* (New York: Harper, 1958), p. 143, and *On Certainty*, ed. G. E. M. Anscombe and G. H. von Wright, trans. Denis Paul and Anscombe (New York: Harper & Row, 1969), 189.

that they are always valuable, that without them our censure of wrongs is weakened and the substance of condemnation is in jeopardy. This conclusion is mistaken. Rights sometimes supply a justification, but sometimes they supply only the appearance or form of one. We should recognize that sometimes they are superfluous.

The corrective to the tendency to invoke rights as justifications is the realization that we know some things to be wrong more securely and fundamentally than we know what rights people have or ought to have. In discussing our demands for justifications for beliefs, Wittgenstein observed that "it is so difficult to find the *beginning*. Or, better: it is difficult to begin at the beginning. And not try to go further back."[30] We may distort our subject if we try always to find something deeper, look for another and another reason. There has to be an end to justifications, and with murder and lying and cheating we have hit bedrock.

This tendency to seek justifications has another, more unfortunate side. The notion that one really needs a justification for the wrongness of murder implies that one isn't sure that murder is wrong, and that its wrongness depends on the adequacy of some further proof. But in that case, one's moral judgment in regard to murder is uncertain, and if it is uncertain about murder, then a great deal of moral understanding is missing. In that event, it's unclear how the demand could be satisfied. Uncertainty about something so basic may put the questioner beyond the framework in which moral justifications are meaningfully asked for and given, and beyond that framework is a no-man's-land often identified with skepticism. The demand for justification thus threatens to weaken rather than support the structure of moral thinking. The move cannot do any good here.

I conclude that rights and their invocation are often important and valuable. The right to performance of contract and the right to vote and the right to assemble are all embodied in protective legislation and certainly justify court action against anyone who would prevent exercise of them. But three kinds of problems can arise when rights are invoked too freely. The first concerns their application to people who are not in a position to exercise them.

[30]Wittgenstein, *On Certainty*, 471.

There the invocation of a right is often a means of avoiding placing responsibility on someone in a position of strength and control. In such a case our moral focus is wrong. The second problem has to do with people in situations and connections that vitiate assumptions in other ways, as the situations of women and fetuses do. The third has to do with justifying the condemnation of offenses whose moral wrongness is perfectly clear and unequivocal. The invocation of a right does not automatically fortify a conviction but may echo a doubt, and in some cases the doubt, once raised, cannot be put to rest, not by the invocation of a right or by any other means.[31]

Rights have their place, but their place is limited. They don't provide a moral panacea, a handy set of justifications to be called on when justification is desired. They need to be used with judgment and restraint, without a blanket commitment to the atomistic vision.

---

[31]For a parallel argument with regard to belief, see my *Paradoxes of Knowledge* (Ithaca: Cornell University Press, 1977), esp. chap. 4.

3

The Governing Self

How are atomism and democracy connected? On the one side the question has to do with majority rule and why we should think that such rule is universally the best. On the other side it treats the concept of self-government as involving a self that both governs and is governed, and asks what determines a good relationship between these roles. I will argue that in the most common interpretations, these two aspects of democracy are profoundly paradoxical.

I

Herodotus held democracy to be "rule of the many" instead of the one of a few; it is also, he said, a form that involves equality before the law.[1] These two conditions seem to be universally associated with democracy, though others are often added.[2]

The philosophers and other writers of ancient Greece did not take the superiority of democracy over other forms for granted.

---

[1] See Roland Pennock, *Democratic Political Theory* (Princeton: Princeton University Press, 1979), p. 3.

[2] Henry Mayo, for example, emphasizes popular control of policy makers and political freedom among other conditions, and includes majority decision making only as a method for representatives to use "when they are divided" (*An Introduction to Democratic Theory* [New York: Oxford University Press, 1977], p. 67).

Plato, Aristophanes, and Xenophon all subjected democracy to harsh criticism, and none proposed that its superiority was derivable from some commonly accepted view of human nature; for instance, it was not thought to derive from the natural independence, freedom, and equality of men.

Nevertheless, it is easy to see why later thinkers should think of democracy as deriving from an atomistic view of human nature, for the central place that atomism gives to the individual is reflected in a government in which all participate and which treats all the same. When that freedom-loving self which precedes society—that self which jealously guards its freedom and resists arbitrary restrictions on its choices—rationally decides to found a government, what could be more natural than that it should choose a democracy? Such a government will provide scope for every variety of individual, each with his own standard and interests, which government must respect. What better kind of government for atomism than one that provides in egalitarian fashion for the desires of everyone? Moreover, atomism's corollary, the social contract theory, proposes that sovereignty rests originally with individuals, that any power government has comes from them. It is logical, then, that the form chosen by such individuals should also witness to their sovereignty.

At first glance atomism makes democracy appear to be a clearly superior form. "If men rule themselves, if they are both law-givers and law-obeyers, then they can combine the benefits of government with the blessings of freedom," suggests Robert Wolff. Then a person's "obligation to submit to the laws stems . . . from the fact that he himself is the source of the laws which govern him."[3] However (as Wolff insists), translating the concept of the people's original sovereignty into a particular form of government is a large and important step, and one that has been sorely neglected by political theorists.[4]

---

[3]Robert Paul Wolff, *In Defense of Anarchism* (New York: Harper & Row, 1970), pp. 21–22. This positive view of democracy is to be contrasted with that of Emile Durkheim, who reasoned that "the state is nothing if it is not an agency distinct from society," and therefore "if everyone governs, it means in fact that there is no government" ("The Nature of Democratic Government," in *Emile Durkheim: Selected Writings,* trans. and ed. Anthony Giddens [Cambridge: Cambridge University Press, 1972], pp. 196–97).

[4]Willmoore Kendall calls the subject of majority rule the "dark continent" of

First of all, the doctrine that the people should rule is not the same as that the "many" or a majority should rule. The French Constitution of 1789 identified majority rule with expression of the "general will": "La loi est la volunté générale, exprimée par la majorité ou des citoyens ou de leurs représentants," as if the will of the majority and the general will were one.[5]

But the wary Puritans, as Richard Wollheim has pointed out, argued that if the basis of legitimate government is consent, then "everyone should consent to every single law that commands his obligation."[6] Government by the people should be by *all* the people. On the same lines, John Stuart Mill spoke of rule by consensus as the "pure" idea of democracy: "The pure idea of democracy . . . is the government of the whole people by the whole people, equally represented. Democracy as commonly conceived and hitherto practised is the government of the whole people by a mere majority of the people, exclusively represented." Majority rule is therefore "a government of privilege, in favour of the numerical majority."[7]

What is the logical connection between rule by the people and rule by a majority of them? A modern writer characterizes the "majority rule democrat" as one who espouses "techniques for discovering the [unanimous or divided] popular will [and] reception of majority-decisions as the equivalent of (though not necessarily equally desirable with) unanimous ones."[8] But as a technique for discovering the popular will, discovering the will of the

---

modern political theory and gives a litany of writers who assume that democracy means rule by majority (*John Locke and the Doctrine of Majority Rule* [Urbana: University of Illinois Press, 1965], pp. 16–17).

[5]"The law is the general will, expressed by the majority of citizens or of their representatives" ("Déclaration des droits et des devoirs de l'homme et du citoyen," art. 6, quoted in Kendall, *John Locke*, p. 15). It is something of a curiosity in the history of ideas that Hobbes treated atomism as quite consistent with monarchy; however, his reasons for preferring monarchy derived from considerations other than atomism.

[6]Richard Wollheim, "Democracy," *Journal of the History of Ideas*, 1958, p. 229.

[7]John Stuart Mill, "Considerations on Representative Government," in *Essays on Politics and Society* (Toronto: University of Toronto Press, 1977), 2:422. It should be noted that what Mill objected to was a system in which minority opinions were not represented at all, not simply a system in which minorities were outvoted; but the reasoning is the same in either case.

[8]Kendall, *John Locke*, p. 33.

majority falls short by definition. If consent of the governed is important, what is needed is consent by all of them.

This is not to concede that rule by consensus is impossible. Wolff suggests that consensus may be practical for a community of persons "inspired by some all-absorbing religious or secular ideal" and for a community "of rationally self-interested individuals [which discovers] that it can only reap the fruits of cooperation by maintaining unanimity."[9] But democracy in the former instance is hardly distinguishable from theocracy, and in the latter it is secondary to the goal of cooperation. In both cases the value of self-legislation is greatly diminished.

The problems of majority rule are nonetheless formidable, as Mill wrote, for the obvious reason that "the 'people' who exercise the power are not always the same people with those over whom it is exercised; and the 'self-government' spoken of is not the government of each by himself, but of each by all the rest. The will of the people . . . practically means the will of the most numerous or the most active *part* of the people; the majority, or those who succeed in making themselves accepted as the majority."[10] Therefore majority rule allows a "tyranny of the majority" over a minority, domination by "the most numerous or active *part* of the people," which is not self-evidently just.[11]

Not only is the "tyranny of the majority" a real danger, Mill thought, but worse, the majority is likely to be inferior to the minority in its judgment. For most men "conformity is the first thing thought of: they like in crowds; they exercise choice only among things commonly done: peculiarity of taste, eccentricity of conduct, are shunned . . . until by dint of not following their own nature, they have no nature to follow."[12] The dominant majority will be less thoughtful, less rational, and less courageous than the losing minority. Majority rule thus gives full expression to the mediocre at the expense of sophistication, reason, and originality. Its tendency, like that of representative government in general, "is

---

[9]Wolff, *In Defense of Anarchism,* p. 25.

[10]John Stuart Mill, "Introductory" in *On Liberty* (Bungay: Penguin, 1980), p. 61.

[11]Wollheim traces the origin of "tyranny of the majority" to Madison; see his "Democracy," p. 230.

[12]Mill, *On Liberty,* p. 61.

towards collective mediocrity."[13] This view of the average person echoes that of Plato and Aristophanes: not much can be expected of ordinary people—the mob or the masses—in the way of judgment.[14]

Locke, who viewed human nature more optimistically, had a looser interpretation of self-rule. When men join to form a society, he proposes, they "have thereby made that community one body, with a power to act as one body, which is only by the will and determination of the majority." The commitment to majority rule is implicit in the contract itself. Locke captures this reasoning in a metaphor: "For that which [activates] any community being only the consent of the individuals in it, and it being necessary to that which is one body to move one way, it is necessary the body should move that way whither the greater force carries it, which is the consent of the majority."[15] The state is one entity, a body with parts, which must act with unity. Since the majority at any time constitutes the greatest force, majority rule is justified simply as an expression of that force. Democratic rule is rule by direct expression of the direction of those who give a government political authority in the first place.

Locke's analogy invites the question: How does this interpretation of majority rule differ from the notion that might makes right? What should convince us that rule by the most numerous is just? Following his analogy, should we say that the back and legs of a human body determine the direction of movement because they are strongest? In the end this argument gives poor justification for domination by the majority.[16]

---

[13]Mill, "Representative Government," p. 357.

[14]A belief in the superiority of the few and mistrust of the masses is reflected in numerous German works, e.g., Georg Jellinek, *Das Recht der Minoritäten* (Vienna: Alfred Hoelder, 1898); such criticisms of majority rule are discussed in Kendall, *John Locke,* pp. 24–25.

[15]John Locke, *Second Treatise on Civil Government,* in *Two Treatises on Civil Government* (New York: Hafner, 1947), p. 169. Despite this passage, Locke's position on majority rule is a subject of controversy. See, e.g., Kendall, *John Locke,* chap. 7, and Pennock, *Democratic Political Theory,* p. 371.

[16]Kendall concedes that this argument would be inadequate, but interprets Locke differently. To the question of whether Locke believed that "it is the fact of majority support which *makes* right in politics" he answers, "Obviously not; Locke could never have committed himself to the moral relativism implied in the proposition

Taking individuals and their private interests as fundamental, Jeremy Bentham reasoned that government could not proceed better than by reflecting those interests, and those interests are best reflected when the people make the decisions themselves.[17] Since the good of the whole is the sum of individual goods, and since no one knows a person's interests better than himself, it follows that we can determine the good of the whole by asking the people what they want and counting the answers.[18] What a majority approves is shown by the numbers alone. But of course such an exercise doesn't answer the moral objection to a majority ruling the minority, wisely or not.

If there are problems with direct majority rule, they multiply where democracy operates by representation. For as Bentham saw, under atomistic assumptions, each representative has his own personal interests, which compete with the interests of those he represents; and how can he be expected then to speak for the interests of others? The danger that the representative will give priority to his private interests was inescapable for Bentham, since he generally held that self-regarding interest is predominant over social interest. Altruism in the making of choices is, he believed, about as common as insanity.[19]

Mill, too, thought that everyone prefers his "selfish interests to those which he shares with other people."[20] Thus anyone who doesn't share the majority opinion, he argued, will lose out, and that is precisely why majority rule is susceptible to injustice.

that majorities make right" (*John Locke,* p. 133). Kendall holds that Locke's crucial argument for majority rule is that since the justification for authority is consent, and the majority represents more "consents" than the minority, the majority commands the obedience of the minority. On this interpretation, the majority cannot do wrong. For this interpretation to work we need a theory of consent as a moral sanction to action, and one that escapes Mill's suggestion that consent cannot be justification enough, that the majority may well consent thoughtlessly, and consent to things that are unjust. Kendall doesn't give an account of the moral import of consent which might deal with this difficulty.

[17]Jeremy Bentham, "Plan of Parliamentary Reform," in *The Works of Jeremy Bentham,* ed. John Bowring (New York: Russell & Russell, 1962), 3:446–47.

[18]Bentham discusses this matter in both "An Introduction to the Principles of Morals and Legislation," in *Works,* 1:2, and "Plan of Parliamentary Reform," in ibid., 3:448.

[19]Jeremy Bentham, "Constitutional Code," in *Works,* 9:61.

[20]Mill, "Representative Government," p. 252.

In some of his writings, it should be said, Bentham posited another source of motivation: public interest. Though most men will follow their narrowly defined private interests, some will see that it is also in their interest to pursue the public good. And those few will make the essential difference in the effort to attain good government rather than bad. But this public-spiritedness isn't consistent with Bentham's basic account of motivation and the atomistic definition of interest.[21] If an appreciable number of people are disposed to pursue the public good rather than their more narrow interests, then his general account of human nature is wrong.

There will of course be good and wise people who choose a greater community good over their private interests, or take the community interests as their own; no utilitarian would deny that such people exist.[22] But it is a serious question whether such public concern must be assumed if majority rule is to be justified, for it is at odds with atomism. Such people are eccentric in atomistic theory, and it is ironic to depend on them to redeem a democracy of atomists. A tyranny of the majority—a majority of egoists—is therefore an imminent consequence of atomistic democratic theory.[23]

II

The themes of atomism reverberate in contemporary political philosophy. Both John Rawls and Robert Nozick, among others, see society as a collection of individuals with separate aims and interests, and both claim that a just society is one that respects

[21]See Hanna F. Pitkin, *The Concept of Representation* (Berkeley: University of California Press, 1967), p. 199.

[22]Bentham and Mill both seem unclear about how good government can result from majority rule, and both are ambivalent about the claim that men are motivated only by their own interests. Both sometimes say that the interest of the whole community *is* one interest of each individual, an idea that is certainly not atomistic. But on the whole both subscribe to an atomistic idea of interest. See ibid., pp. 203–5.

[23]See Mayo's discussion of justifications of majority rule in *Introduction to Democratic Theory*, pp. 180–81.

and protects the individual and his interests.[24] Without considering the commitment of either to majority rule, I want to ask what light their views shed on this conception and that of self-government.[25]

Rawls announces that justice in society derives from certain principles: "they are the principles that free and rational persons concerned to further their own interests would accept in an initial position of equality as defining the fundamental terms of their association." Like Bentham, he believes that each person "must decide by rational reflection what constitutes his good." All individuals are eager to further their interests, their own chosen life plans, while their basic needs are similar and their relations for the most part competitive. That is the "Archimedean point" from which the shape of society can be understood and its justice evaluated.[26]

Rawls takes the individual as his starting point partly to avoid reliance on an "undefined concept of community," to avoid the supposition "that society is an organic whole with a life of its own distinct from and superior to that of all its members."[27] His atomism is therefore a defensive device, taken up to oppose social thinkers for whom the whole is an organic, transcendent unity. In the tradition of Locke and the utilitarians, he sets out to reconcile atomism with a fair-minded state and show how the latter may be derived from a given natural condition. "Questions of justice arise when conflicting claims are made upon the design of a practice and where it is taken for granted that each person will insist on his

[24]On the similarities of Rawls and Nozick, see Michael Sandel, *Liberalism and the Limits of Justice* (Cambridge: Cambridge University Press, 1982), p. 67.

[25]Rawls, Pennock observes, "seems to go to the brink" of accepting representative government with majority rule, qualified by fundamental rights, but then retreats and leaves the form of pure procedural justice undetermined (*Democratic Political Theory*, pp. 47–48).

[26]John Rawls, *A Theory of Justice* (Cambridge: Cambridge University Press, 1971), pp. 11, 260–63. Rawls is denying that we need a prior standard of perfection or any assumption about people's particular desires in order to evaluate society. He also avoids one criticism of contract theory by not positing any actual or implied contract. See also Sandel, *Liberalism*, pp. 16–17.

[27]Rawls, *Theory of Justice*, pp. 264–65. Like Locke and Nozick, Rawls also wants to describe political power as an artifact, as derivable (whether derived or not) from the voluntary actions of individuals, who are therefore the ultimate sources of authority.

rights." In an established society, we feel confident that the practices are "normally founded on the prospect of self-advantage."[28] In that context justice will be "the virtue of practices where there are assumed to be competing interests and conflicting claims, and where it is supposed that persons will press their rights on each other. That persons are mutually self-interested . . . is what gives rise to the question of justice." Justice concerns "a pact between rational egoists."[29] In a situation of conflict, self-interests need to be compromised; but since justice derives from multiple self-interests, it cannot require that self-interest be fundamentally compromised. In Rawls's account the definition of fairness requires self-interest to be fundamental in the choice process.

How does agreement come about? The principles people mutually agree to are, first, that "each person participating in a practice or affected by it has an equal right to the most extensive liberty compatible with a like liberty for all; and second, inequalities are arbitrary unless it is reasonable to expect that they will work out for everyone's advantage and provided the positions and offices to which they attach . . . are open to all."[30] Conflicts, real and foreseen, are the background of justice, though they are not present in the original position when the principles are formulated.

In this way Rawls's two broad principles lead from the individual with his or her interests to fair policies for everyone. One must be attached to one's own interests before one can understand the attachment of others to theirs; and thus self-interest allows one to reach principles that are fair. What Rawls fails to explain is why, since individual interests are so central and necessary to all choices, a person should be persuaded to take the perspective of the original position, to judge from behind the veil of ignorance instead of viewing the situation from his or her actual position.

Like Bentham, Rawls would be quick to deny that he requires people to be interested only in themselves: "we need not suppose . . . that persons never make substantial sacrifices for one another, since moved by affection and ties of sentiment they often do."[31] Moreover, once a fair society is formed, people's nature

---

[28]Ibid., pp. 172, 170.
[29]John Rawls, "Justice as Fairness," *Philosophical Review* 67 (April 1958): 175, 174.
[30]Ibid., p. 165.
[31]Ibid., p. 42. Also see Sandel, *Liberalism,* pp. 134ff.

may be expected to improve: "there seems to be no reason offhand why the ends of people in a well-ordered society should be predominantly individualistic."[32] But the "mutually self-interested" individuals Rawls began with, who "press their claims" and "insist, as far as possible, on what [they] consider [their] rights," are the Archimedean point of his account; and it is such people and their conflicts that make the virtue of justice possible. People of another kind, those who have concern for and connections with others, might of course be inclined to view others from behind the veil of ignorance or, which is the same thing, to be fair without using the veil. But they will not need Rawls's principles, since the mutual pressing of claims and conflicts of interest that invoke justice are for them not preeminent considerations. For them Rawls's definition of justice won't apply. It is not these people but the others—who may well be a majority—that present the problem Rawls's account aims to solve.

The dilemma found in Bentham appears in Rawls: under atomism, the chasm between self-interest and justice seems unbridgeable except for those who are fair-minded to start with, but for them the psychology of atomism proves false. By Rawls's own procedure, justice seems to be beyond the reach of individuals whose interests do not lie in a social direction. His account illuminates majority rule in much the same way Bentham's does, making its fairness seem doubtful.

Nozick's theory of the best state similarly begins with self-interested individuals concerned to improve and secure their advantages. This starting point, he explains, "picks out basic, important inescapable features of the human situation." A state that derives from these features without other machinery "explains the political in terms of the non-political," an "invisible hand" explanation, which is the best kind.[33]

---

[32]John Rawls, "Fairness to Goodness," *Philosophical Review* 84 (1975): 544.

[33]Robert Nozick, *Anarchy, State, and Utopia* (Cambridge: Harvard University Press, 1977), pp. 7, 6. Like Rawls, Nozick doesn't mean that people ever lived in his "natural" condition. What is important is the simplicity and power of the explanation such a starting point offers. With an "invisible hand" explanation he can show how a result comes about without invoking an agent who aims at it. Such explanations are best, he says, because they "minimize the use of notions constituting the phenomena to be explained" (like Occam's razor). They "yield greater understanding than do explanations of [phenomena] as [having been] brought about by design

Like Rawls, Nozick finds the state's origins in conflicts and disputes among people. And how can disputes be resolved once they arise? Without a government it is difficult to resolve them: "men who judge in their own case will always give themselves the benefit of the doubt . . . [and] overestimate the amount of harm or damage they have suffered." Such actions will eventually lead to "feuds, to an endless series of acts of retaliation and exactions of compensation," which there is no way really to settle. Thus the state comes into being partly as an impersonal judge and protector of interests. But as self-interests take various forms, the very least amount of governmental restriction on individual choice is necessarily the best. In a just system, people are free to organize for any cause they want and to participate in political matters. And where there's scope for voluntary action, many things are possible: "any large, popular, revolutionary movement should be able to bring about its ends by such a voluntary process."[34] For Nozick's purposes, the form of government need not be specified, but one infers that the only legitimate government will be government by the people, the political corporate shareholders.

Other theorists, particularly economists, use similar assumptions in the same way, that is, to justify the maximum individual freedom and minimal governmental restraints. Milton Friedman, following Adam Smith, explains a free market as the idea "that economic order can emerge as the unintended consequence of the actions of many people, each seeking his own interest." Human desire and freedom to pursue it are crucial factors in this democratic world. "If what a person gets does not depend on the price he receives for the services of his resources, what incentive does he have to seek out information on prices or to act on [it]? . . . If your income will be the same whether you work hard or not, why should you work hard? . . . If there is no reward for maintaining capital, why should anyone postpone to a later date what he could enjoy now?"[35] But these assumptions don't give much support to

---

as the object of people's intentions . . . therefore . . . they are more satisfying" (p. 19).

[34]Ibid., pp. 11, 327.

[35]Milton Friedman, *Free to Choose* (New York: Harcourt Brace Jovanovich, 1979), pp. 14–15, 233. Also see Wollheim, "Democracy," on the connection between political democracy, laissez-faire economics, and egoism.

majority rule, Friedman recognizes, for the old problem remains that with majority rule goes minority subservience, which violates one's autonomy. Pragmatically "majority rule is a necessary and desirable expedient," but it is not a happy theoretical one. The freedom to choose a government is "very different from the kind of freedom you have when you shop at a supermarket. The ballot box produces conformity without unanimity; the marketplace, unanimity without conformity. That is why it is desirable to use the ballot box . . . only for those decisions where conformity is essential."[36] Like Nozick and Mill, Friedman prefers that conformity not be demanded, though he accepts it as an expedient where government is necessary.

Mill made the related point that "self-government" applies differently to governments than to individuals; thus he contests Locke's and Hobbes's metaphor of the state as an oversize individual.[37] While an individual who "governs himself" has conflicts, they are resolved internally when he decides; *he* has to deal with them as he makes his choice and subsequently. He may be unhappy at the need to choose, but the choice is nonetheless his. The self-governing community, in contrast, does not see its conflicts resolved when it reaches a decision. The conflicts that divide a community before an election continue to exist after policy has been decided, but one group has its desire while the other is frustrated, the one wins and the other loses. Where a permanent majority is in place, as with Protestants in Northern Ireland and Jews in Israel, tyranny of one part of the community over the other is a reality. With the possibility of such permanent divisions inherent in democratic decision making, no guarantee of any unified communal spirit can be given; the risk of division is permanent.[38]

---

[36]Friedman, *Free to Choose*, p. 57. In contrast to Friedman, Michael Walzer thinks that majority rule *is* like a free market: "Democratic decision-making . . . is a way of bringing the market home, connecting its opportunities and dangers to the actual effort, initiative and luck of individuals" (*Spheres of Justice* [New York: Harper & Row, 1983], p. 118).

[37]Joel Feinberg takes the opposite position, claiming that self-government of individuals and self-government of communities are analogous. See Feinberg, *The Moral Limits of the Criminal Law* (New York: Oxford University Press, 1986), 3:40–41.

[38]Mill and Mayo were both most concerned about majority rule in the light of *permanent* minorities rather than shifting ones. Morally the problems are the same,

III

Mill's answer to the problem of majority tyranny was protection of the rights of the minority—protection "against the tyranny of the prevailing opinion and feeling," not just against restrictive laws. The minority must be protected "against the tendency of society to impose, by means *other* than civil penalties, its own ideas and practices . . . on those who dissent from them"; thus even the effect that custom can have must be limited. There is a limit to "the legitimate interference of collective opinion with individual independence," Mill argued. "The only part of the conduct of any one, for which he is amenable to society, is that which concerns others."[39] When one's actions don't affect others, one should be left alone.

Some philosophers agree with Mill that democracy's justification involves the respect it shows for individual dignity and freedom, a respect most clearly expressed in the according of individual rights.[40] Let us look at the association of these two conceptions, democracy and individual rights.

Rights, as we saw in Chapter 2, protect an individual against someone. Dworkin writes:

Anyone who professes to take rights seriously . . . must accept . . . one or both of two important ideas. The first is the . . . idea of human dignity. This idea . . . supposes that there are ways of treating a man that are inconsistent with recognizing him as a full member of the human community, and holds that such treatment is profoundly unjust. The second is the more familiar idea of political equality [which] . . . supposes that the weaker members of a politi-

although politically a hardened division will yield an ongoing, warlike opposition between the groups.

[39]Mill, *On Liberty*, pp. 4–5, 10. For an exercise in the application of this policy, see chap. 5, below.

[40]E.g., Pennock, *Democratic Political Theory*, pp. 239–40. According to his account, "rights and duties theories" of democracy "suggest the maintenance of individual rights (and liberties) as one of the main tests for the acceptability of a democratic regime" (p. 196). Mayo also treats the protection of rights as a fundamental feature of democracy, and claims that "no democratic theory . . . advocates the majority principle without the other principles of democracy, in particular the political liberties" (*Introduction to Democratic Theory*, p. 185).

cal community are entitled to the same concern and respect of their government as the more powerful members have secured for themselves.[41]

Rights protect an individual's moral autonomy and deny the right of repression to a superior power. But from whom do rights protect the citizen? Some of them protect people from the government, Dworkin observes. "It makes sense to say that a man has a fundamental right against the Government . . . like free speech, if that right is necessary to protect his dignity, or his standing as equally entitled to concern and respect, or some other personal value of like consequence."[42] The moral importance of a citizen's autonomy and integrity is thus expressed in rights asserted against the government.

Dworkin sees that the accordance of such basic rights to individuals limits the power of government and implies that in general the government is not to be trusted. But this implication yields an interesting puzzle: in a democracy when we say "government" we are speaking of government by the people themselves. True enough, Dworkin concedes; still,

> a right against the Government must be a right to do something even when the majority thinks it would be wrong to do it, and even when the majority would be worse off for having it done. If we now say that society has a right to do whatever is in the general benefit, or the right to preserve whatever sort of environment the majority wishes to live in, and we mean that these are the sort of rights that provide justification for overruling any rights against the Government that may conflict, then we have annihilated the latter rights.[43]

The doctrine of basic rights expresses a deep distrust of, and is intended to protect us from, rule by the majority.[44] Thus there is

[41]Ronald Dworkin, "Taking Rights Seriously," in *Oxford Essays in Jurisprudence,* 2d ser., ed. A. W. B. Simpson (Oxford: Oxford University Press, 1973), pp. 219–20.

[42]Ibid., p. 220.

[43]Ibid., p. 214.

[44]Because majority rule is a form of government chosen by the citizenry, any rights of citizens against it must have existence prior to that choice or they could not limit that governmental form. This logic provides the reason for speaking of *natural* rights, which don't derive from government but precede it; they are more basic than government itself.

tension between the concepts of majority rule and individual rights, for each limits or threatens to limit the other. They are not, as rights-and-duties theorists claim, companion concepts joined together in a unified theory of democracy; they are antithetical and conflicting.[45]

A further problem is that the enforcement of citizens' rights is in the hands of the same government whose menace makes them necessary. Mayo makes the idea seem natural: "granted that the state can protect us against abuses of private power, can we not also ensure that the state will protect us against itself?"[46] But a government that has to enforce rights against itself, to protect citizens from the threat *it* poses, is certainly in conflicting roles. If it is more than merely a paradoxical idea, such a government in reality must be schizophrenic. Its roles are impossible to fulfill.

There is another paradoxical side to the problem. Where the citizens *are* the government, individual rights serve to protect them, taken individually, from themselves, taken collectively.[47] The picture is one of citizen mistrust of citizen government. Now as Pennock says, "any government, assuming it is to be legitimate, entails trust. That is part of what legitimacy means."[48] Therefore this mistrust casts a shadow on the virtue as well as the possibility of self-government.

Despite this tension, the two ideas—majority rule and protective individual rights—stem from one root: a commitment to the "inherent dignity" of individuals and their moral autonomy. How can they conflict, then? Because the government that is identifiable with the majority does not, as Mill said, need to represent the views, the moral values, or the interests of all citizens. Thus ma-

---

[45]This claim isn't new: Kendall relates misinterpretations of Locke to the "belief that the right of the majority cannot keep house, in a well-ordered mind, with individualism [and] natural rights" (*John Locke*, p. 53).

[46]Mayo, *Introduction to Democratic Theory*, p. 184.

[47]Pennock speaks of the tension between liberty and equality in democratic theory as being similar to the tension I mean here. He writes that "liberty . . . is especially congenial to the individualistic pole of democratic theory, while equality is assimilated more readily to the collectivistic pole" (*Democratic Political Theory*, p. 16).

[48]Ibid., p. 241.

jority rule comes to be linked to individual rights, which are as much its natural enemies as is the special status of a monarch.

If majority rule is guided by individual self-interests, then inevitably it presents the hazards of majority tyranny. Like the state of nature, it allows the strong to dominate and exploit the weak, politically and morally.[49] In the end, on the assumption that people are independent and self-interestedly motivated, we cannot support the claim that majority rule is inherently just. If it is to have even a probability of being just, the majority—indeed everyone—must have some concern for something other than their own interests and good.

IV

A promising means to reconcile majority rule with individual rights is suggested by Roland Pennock. Like Mill, he believes that because "human beings should be accorded a dignity . . . and permitted a moral autonomy and opportunities for self-development," individual freedom must be emphasized. But he claims there is also an internal connection between opportunities for self-development and democracy, for democracy provides opportunities to choose and appraise public policies, and such opportunities "are themselves vital elements in a satisfying life . . . and characteristic of what is most distinctively human about man."[50] The opportunity to participate in public life is important to a citizen's development, and therefore good.

This argument is interesting because of the kind of citizen it posits. It is not the "natural" egoist of Hobbes, Mill, or Nozick, and not Bentham's and Rawls's occasional person of goodwill. Rather it is a person who sees himself partly *through* a larger com-

---

[49]Mayo, for instance, believes that fear of majority rule springs primarily "from the well-grounded suspicion" that the majority might "seize the property of the well-to-do," though he acknowledges (with John Stuart Mill) that some people also fear that majority government will simply be poor government (*Introduction to Democratic Theory*, pp. 186–87).

[50]Pennock, *Democratic Political Theory*, pp. 132–33, 139.

munity, one who wants to participate in the community as part of his self-development. To call the objective of such opportunities "self-development," however, may be to mask the fact that a new and social conception of a person is involved here; it is a large step away from atomism. We need to ask what support can be found for such a conception.

Let us go back to the ideas of eighteenth-century America which influenced Jefferson and others of the framers. Following Hutcheson as well as Reid, Jefferson writes that "man was destined for society . . . [and] he was endowed with a sense of right and wrong, merely relative to this." It is because people are social that they have morality and a moral sense. Moreover, all of them are endowed with this sense: "State a moral case to a ploughman and a professor. The former will decide it as well and often better than the latter."[51] On such a view, though it may be possible for humans to live independently of one another, such a life would be pointless and uncomfortable. In this vein Diderot wrote: "Man is born for life in society; separate him, isolate him, and his ideas will go to pieces, his character will go sour."[52]

Now, without the self of atomism, some of the problems we noted for democratic theory are diminished or dissipated. Consider the tyrannical majority. If the voter no longer votes his own interest against the interests of others, then one aspect of the problem—the danger that the majority interests will dominate those of the minority—no longer looms, for self-defined interests are not the guide citizens use in their participation. A citizen can be understood to vote for the good of society as he or she sees it.

As for reconciling majority rule with rights, this new conception implies that a morally autonomous, social individual needs a setting in which the full scope of his or her understanding and moral perception can be expressed, a society in which one's participation is both broad and crucial. The protection of rights secures the citizen's position in this regard, secures the status of a free and independent agent vis-à-vis the political process. Rights prevent

---

[51] *The Papers of Thomas Jefferson,* ed. Julian Boyd et al., vol. 12 (Princeton: Princeton University Press, 1971), p. 15.

[52] Denis Diderot, *The Nun,* trans. Leonard Tancock (London: Folio Society, 1972), p. 121.

the majority—however well intentioned—from restricting the resources or participation of the minority. The two sides of democracy-with-rights are in this way brought together: the social person needs to be protected not as an individual with private interests but as an important participant in a process that allows that person a measure of fulfillment. And this fulfillment and the value of participation are not contingent on one's getting one's own way.

These ideas echo some of those in Athenian democracy, such as the emphasis on a citizen's role and on public participation as an important part of a citizen's life. Mayo describes this idea as the belief that "free participation in the political life is the proper mark of a citizen, the thing that makes him fully a person; that to be a participating citizen is . . . something of high value." In turn, a society in which such participation was valued tended to produce citizens of a certain responsible and social kind, of a kind that the Athenians thought a model for humans in general. In this picture "the citizens are assumed to have a [certain] . . . character: they will not sacrifice the public welfare for their private interests" and they will be rational in dealing with the problems of state. Moreover, for Greeks this conception and this standard are a matter of long-standing tradition, a tradition of avid interest in political affairs and active participation in them, the tradition of a "sociable, gregarious . . . people, living an all-pervasive common life, to which the meetings of the Assembly, . . . the large 'juries,' and the chance to hold other offices all contributed."[53]

Such a society was the background for Aristotle's cautious endorsement of majority rule:

> The many, of whom each individual is but an ordinary person, when they meet together may very likely be better than the few good, if regarded not individually but collectively, just as a feast to which many contribute is better than a dinner provided out of a single purse. For each individual among the many has a share of virtue and prudence, and when they meet together, they become in a manner one man. . . . Some understand one part, and some another, and among them they understand the whole.[54]

[53]Mayo, *Introduction to Democratic Theory*, pp. 50, 47, 48.
[54]Aristotle, *Politics*, trans. Benjamin Jowett, in *The Basic Works of Aristotle*, ed. Richard McKeon (New York: Random House, 1941), III, 3, 1281b.

Two heads are better than one, and in democracy every head contributes toward a well-governed state.

It should be remarked, however, that this justification does not favor democracy over other forms of participatory government, where citizen involvement is also broad and general.[55] It doesn't claim, as one interpreter would have Locke do, that rule by the majority is justified ethically, since "decisions made by the majority . . . are in some sense ethically right decisions," and that "an irrevocable obligation to obey the community of which [one] is a member . . . [is translated into] an irrevocable duty to obey the majority."[56] It does support the maximum possible participation as Mill recommended, but not for his reasons, that is, representation of privately framed interests. Any form that involves wide, frequent, crucial involvement by citizens will have a similar virtue, given an appropriate setting. The point is important: it reveals that this justification does not rest on unique features of democracy, but rather points to what makes democracy, *as well as other participatory forms,* valuable.[57]

But the price of such a justification is not modest. It involves the forfeiture of the goal of a "science" of society and politics from which the best form of government can be derived, given a sound theory of human nature. Atomism begins with factual premises about the nature of humans and shows how they account for the character of society: it possesses the power of the "Archimedean point" and the "invisible hand." The present view has no such unequivocal strength. In a just democracy, it says, individuals see themselves in a certain way; they have an attitude that cannot be

[55]Mill's characterization of representative government fits pretty well my concept of participatory government. In a representative government, he says, "the whole people, or some numerous portion of them, exercise through deputies periodically elected by themselves the ultimate controlling power. . . . This ultimate power they must possess in all its completeness. They must be masters, whenever they please, of all the operations of government" ("Representative Government," p. 422).

[56]Kendall, *John Locke,* pp. 112–13.

[57]Among other participatory forms we can imagine one in which political offices are rotated and each citizen is expected to serve a turn. In that case it wouldn't be necessary to think of an official *representing* the others, as having their endorsement for his or her policies. But it would be understood that sooner or later any who were offended would have their turn.

derived from anything else but is part of their traditional world view. Moreover, the just functioning of the society will depend in part on the actual institutions, practices, and traditions, which cannot be designed a priori. A theory of perfect generality is therefore beyond this account.

In the traditional Greek view, as we have seen, society and individuals were synergistically related, neither being ultimate nor derivable from the other. Individuals need the state for their fulfillment; the state depends on responsible individuals for its well-being. Even the distinction between public and private was drawn differently, "private" carrying the sense of privation of a social role, while "freedom" meant freedom to pursue public activity, not freedom from its demands.[58] Since local traditions were understood to be important and distinctive features of Athenian society, a science of society analogous to chemistry and physics was not envisaged. Moreover, the *polis* that demanded the citizen's time and attention also helped shape the young into the kind of citizens that would give their time and attention to it.[59] In short, the justification of Athenian democracy was not conceived in purely abstract, rational terms; it needed a particular context, and its force depended on accepted traditions.[60]

V

There is yet another hazard of democracy that even the Greek form of justification does not dispel. It is the danger not of

[58]See Hannah Arendt, *The Human Condition* (Chicago: University of Chicago Press, 1958), chap. 2, secs. 8–9, esp. pp. 58–59, 64–65. Cf. Mayo, *Introduction to Democratic Theory*, p. 48. Connected with this difference in the meaning of freedom is a difference in the meaning of "individualism." In the atomistic meaning, Greeks were not individualists, though one might say they were individualistic in a different sense.

[59]Werner Jaeger argues that in ancient Greece, stories and literature were designed essentially to teach the human virtues, including those of citizenship. He discusses the connection of the philosophies of Plato and Aristotle to Athenian traditions and the role of the *polis* as educator in *Paideia: The Ideals of Greek Culture* (New York: Oxford University Press, 1945), pp. 107 and 109.

[60]The same was true of the justification—and idealization—of Sparta's system; see ibid., pp. 82–83.

rule through self-interest but of a majority that acts with perfect self-righteousness, dogmatic and certain that it is doing what is best for the community as a whole. It is the danger that the majority may do what (it thinks) is absolutely right, not understanding a minority's moral objections, much less respecting them. Here is a tyrannical majority of a moral kind. And where it is present, how acceptable is majority rule under any interpretation?

This profound problem was addressed by Mill. If the electors are people of conscience and moral sense, concerned to do what's best for everyone, they will still not be justified in oppressing a minority, he argued. The assumption that voters are public-spirited and conscientious does not make the threat of a tyranny of the majority go away (as it did for Bentham). The threat remains; the tyranny now becomes a moral one, the tyranny of a moral majority.

The problem of moral repression has haunted democratic theory, often in connection with the puzzling duty to obey the law. Dworkin describes the positions of liberals and conservatives on the general duty to obey the law, observing that "both conservatives and liberals suppose that in a society which is generally decent everyone has a duty to obey the law, whatever it is. . . . But this general duty is almost incoherent in a society that recognizes rights. If a man believes he has a right to demonstrate, then he believes that it would be wrong for the Government to stop him, with or without benefit of a law."[61] Given a citizenry of decent, "law-abiding" people, the problem exists if different consciences dictate different things. Rights become the protectors of such differences.

Richard Wollheim cast the problem in the form of a formidable paradox that he believes plagues pluralistic modern democracies as it did not the more homogeneous democracy of Athens. Imagine a machine, he says—call it the democratic machine—into which "are fed at fixed intervals the choices of the individual citizens. The machine then aggregates them according to the pre-established rule or method, and so comes up with a 'choice' of its own." Now

---

[61]Ronald Dworkin, *Taking Rights Seriously* (Cambridge: Harvard University Press, 1977), p. 212.

Wollheim poses the question: "What is the authority of the choice expressed by the machine? More specifically, why should someone who has fed his choice into the machine and then is confronted by the machine with a choice non-identical with his own, feel any obligation to accept it?" We suppose a citizen judges conscientiously when he judges in an election that *A* rather than *B* ought to be the case, and consequently votes for *A*. But "if the believer in Democracy believes that what the democratic machine chooses ought to be enacted, then, whenever the machine actually chooses a policy, he must believe that that policy ought to be enacted." Given that a democrat has such a commitment to majority rule, a citizen may be committed to the view that *B* should be the case if the majority decides for it. But the citizen is then caught in a conflict between two oughts. Wollheim asks: "How can the citizen accept the machine's choice, which involves his thinking that *B* ought to be enacted when . . . he is of the opinion . . . that *A* ought to be enacted?"[62] The voter must then believe two contradictory things, an impossible task.

Wollheim avoids this consequence by making a distinction that allows the citizen to hold both beliefs without conflict. The proposition "*A* ought to be enacted" can be asserted by the citizen as a "direct principle," he argues, while the proposition "*B* ought to be enacted" is asserted only "as a derivation from . . . the principle of Democracy."[63] In the end he admits that the citizen's commitment to either policy cannot be total. That's all right as he sees it: one can be committed—in different ways—to both alternatives.[64]

But more serious than Wollheim's problem, democracy seems here to conflict with its own moral foundations in individual judgment. The place of conscience in the democratic state has been a perennial matter of concern. It led Thoreau to be skeptical not only

[62]Richard Wollheim, "A Paradox in the Theory of Democracy," in *Philosophy, Politics, and Society*, 2d ser., ed. Peter Laslett and W. G. Runciman (Oxford: Blackwell, 1962), pp. 76, 84, 78.

[63]Ibid., p. 86.

[64]Other answers to Wollheim's paradox are offered by D. Goldstick, "An Alleged Paradox in the Theory of Democracy," *Philosophy and Public Affairs* 1, no. 2 (1972): 181–89; Brian Barry, *Political Argument* (New York: Humanities Press, 1965), chap. 4; and Marvin Schiller, "On the Logic of Being a Democrat," *Philosophy* 44 (January 1969): 46–56.

about majority rule but about the justification of government itself. The majority manage to rule because they are physically
stronger, he argued; and what is just about the principle that the
most powerful should have their way? The main desideratum—
moral authority—has been left out of such a principle. "A government in which the majority rule in all cases cannot be based on
justice. . . . Can there not be a government in which majorities do
not virtually decide right and wrong, but conscience? . . . Must
the citizen ever . . . resign his conscience to the legislator? Why
has every man a conscience then?" Voting is like gaming, he says:
one cannot tell whether one will be part of the majority or the
minority. And, success aside, how is the majority opinion relevant
to what is right? "A wise man will not leave the right to the mercy
of chance, nor wish it to prevail through the power of the majority. There is but little virtue in the action of masses of men." How
can we leave important decisions about right and justice to the
counting of heads? If what is important is being in the right, then
any person constitutes "a majority of one," he argues: "it is
enough if they have God on their side, without waiting for the
other [majority]. . . . Any man more right than his neighbors,
constitutes a majority of one already."[65]

Some writers gloss over the moral problem. Pennock, for example, thinks that individual rights carry with them "an attitude
of healthy skepticism toward authority," and he concedes only
that a line is to be drawn between a citizen's right to defy the law
and his need to conform to it. Without trying to locate the line, he
concludes that "democracy needs citizens who respect the law and
resist its abuse. . . . It also needs citizens with clear ideas of the
proper limits of state authority . . . and readiness to do battle . . .
in support of these limits."[66] But wherever it's drawn, the line will
divide contesting opposites, both important features of American
political thought that so far lack a theoretical reconciliation.

Mayo's view is that our only protection against majority tyranny stems from "the conviction of virtually the whole of the American people that things are . . . not done that way," in short, a

[65]Henry David Thoreau, "Civil Disobedience," in *Walden and Reflections on Civil
Disobedience* (New York: Signet, 1960), pp. 223, 226, 230.
[66]Pennock, *Democratic Political Theory*, p. 241.

tradition of political good sportsmanship. Protection is not established theoretically but involves a background and institutional arrangements, which in turn rest "upon widespread beliefs and attitudes, upon usages and conscience, upon custom and 'traditions of civility.' "[67] Democracy has its proper context of institutions, traditions, and attitudes, and they are not traceable either to reason or to human nature. Democratic government is not, then, as Herodotus said, simply rule by the many, but majority rule *in the context of institutions that are characteristically participatory*.[68] But still a theoretical solution to the tension between majority rule and the authority of conscience is not in sight.

A second price is being paid for the justification of democracy suggested above: it doesn't imply that the resulting policies of majority rule—or any other participatory form—*will* be just; that conclusion doesn't follow from this justification, and everything suggests that democratic government cannot guarantee just policies. Some writers, however, including Rawls and Plato, would take this to be the first condition of any justification, any theory of government; for they suppose with Thoreau that the justice of a government has exclusive importance here. But under our account, a man of conscience, such as Thoreau, may need to face the dilemma of obeying either the law or his conscience, and to choose as best he can by himself.

VI

Plato described the democratic man as one so concerned to enjoy himself that he ignores participation in government. Freedom is of primary importance for such a person: "Is not the [democratic] city chock-full of liberty and freedom of speech? And has not every man license to do as he likes? . . . [Therefore] everyone would arrange a plan for leading his own life in the way that

[67]Mayo, *Introduction to Democratic Theory*, pp. 201, 202.
[68]Wollheim also regards democracy "as a form of government . . . rigorously connected with, if not identified by, certain specific political institutions" ("Democracy," p. 226).

pleases him."[69] So far Plato's belief is very like Rawls's, that the aim of each individual is to "insist on an advantage to himself" and "each person will insist as far as possible on his rights."[70] And it reminds us of Nozick's insistence that a just state "allows us . . . to choose our life and realize our ends and our conception of ourselves," limiting our freedom as little as possible.[71] However, on Plato's account the "free" democratic man is less rational. He is self-indulgent, undisciplined, and morally untrained, given to vacillations in his lifestyle, "day by day indulging the appetite of the day." He is spontaneous, thoughtless, saying "whatever rises to [his] lips." He will vote laws in and out whimsically, turn from one leader to another, and eventually destroy whatever is enduring in the state. The system governed in this way will gravitate toward an intolerable condition, that of anarchy. Thus when citizens neglect everything except their desires, there will arise the "necessity of a dictatorship"; and thus the "excess of freedom" will lead to its opposite, "too much slavery in the individual and in the state."[72]

Plato's democrat is not a good citizen. He is too busy with his personal desires, with freedom, with trying something new, with spontaneity; the state and its well-being have no lasting importance to him. But even if they did, a state could not survive the vacillations of fashions democracy encourages. Here Plato compares democratic citizens intent on governing with sailors who don't listen to their captain: "everyone is of the opinion that he ought to steer, though he has never learned and cannot tell who taught him or when he learned"; eventually they mutiny against the able captain and, "drinking and feasting, make such a voyage of it as is to be expected from such."[73] The state needs stability, constancy, harmony, and these qualities in turn require wisdom in government; its course cannot be dictated by individuals concerned only to express their private life plans or their changing, fanciful ideas about what is best.

[69]Plato, *Republic,* trans. Paul Shorey, in *The Collected Dialogues of Plato,* ed. Edith Hamilton and Huntington Cairns (Princeton: Princeton University Press, 1961), VIII, 557b.

[70]Rawls, "Justice as Fairness," pp. 174, 172.

[71]Nozick, *Anarchy, State, and Utopia,* p. 334.

[72]Plato, *Republic,* IX, 561d, 563c, 562c, 564a.

[73]Ibid., VI, 488c.

Our democratic citizen, however, unlike Plato's, takes public life as a serious ongoing responsibility. His conscience guides him, but so does his recognition that he is not the only one concerned. His vision includes the community, which deserves his attention and sacrifice. Such individuals participate in the institutions that require their service. And in participating, they need to have respect for the views and commitments of others even when those others are wrong, even when their mistakes may lead to pernicious consequences. The institutions themselves depend on such respect. Democratic participation is therefore a demanding condition, too demanding for the atomistic citizen. It doesn't tailor social life to the fundamental nature of the individual; instead, like the Greek ideal, it sets a challenge for him, often to act against his desires and impulses in the name of a higher purpose, to consider the welfare of others and the welfare of the community along with his own. It's a tall order.

Our democratic citizen does not dwell in an abstract state. On the one hand, the qualities demanded of him need to find their exercise in effective institutions of group decision making, where each person becomes a part of a complicated machine that can produce bad policies as well as good ones. On the other hand, this citizen needs to have respect for this kind of system and hold the values that will make the machinery work. Not every culture holds the values that support this form of political society. Justification of any participatory form of government arises within an existing tradition and framework of values.[74] The present argument must be seen, then, within the framework of our traditions and our way of viewing government. They help define its shape and validity; they are part of the grammar of our justification. We cannot pretend to have found an abstract conclusion, good for any context; our result, you might say, is not exportable.

The way of viewing the democratic man proposed here empha-

---

[74]Mill gives similar conditions for representative government: "1. That the people should be willing to receive it. 2. That they should be willing and able to do what is necessary for its preservation. 3. That they should be willing and able to fulfill the duties and discharge the functions which it imposes on them." Furthermore, when it is introduced in a new setting, "indifference to it, and inability to understand its processes and requirements, rather than positive opposition, are the obstacles to be expected" ("Representative Government," p. 413).

sizes his largeness of vision, his tolerance and self-restraint, both of which are a far cry from the image Plato draws. In challenging the citizen by giving him power, it also sets the stage for abuses, and we may agree with Mayo that only "restraint and forbearance" protect a democracy against majority tyranny. "To seek for more is to seek for the unattainable: a government legally powerful enough to do right but powerless to do wrong."[75] Restraint and forbearance and the tolerance associated with them have to characterize legislators and citizens alike.

This picture of the democratic society makes government an uneasy proposition. While such a society, as Pennock stresses, offers opportunities for fulfillment to the morally autonomous person, its justice and stability are uncertain. Justice cannot be built into the institutions but needs to be sought after continually, in specific and changing circumstances. Not only does the citizen face a challenge of tolerance and forbearance, then, but the society itself faces the risk of errors, of a majority deciding against a wiser minority and effecting a policy that's unjust. Mill's fear on this point is not unfounded. Yet in the total vision, participation is held valuable and desirable even when the wise are outvoted.

The state I have been describing is one involving tremendous risk. Unlike Plato's Republic, it has no means to ensure that its policies will be just. So the democratic citizen has to be ready both to take up the challenge and to assume the risk, something the atomist has no reason to do. But people raised in the democratic tradition have their reasons in their early training, in the expectation that their abilities are equal to the double challenge, and the assurance that a proud and capable person will accept it. The willingness to take on this risk and this challenge is part of their conception of a mature and responsible citizen, as it was of the Greeks'.

With such a conception of participatory government, in a community with such an ethos—where, that is, there is virtual certainty that no one will consistently be favored—the two sides of a person, the citizen self and the privately interested self, can finally be joined in a democratic vision.

[75]Mayo, *Introduction to Democratic Theory,* p. 187.

4

Sending Someone Else

Any kind of representative government, including democracy, presupposes that the government can represent the body politic and turn its decisions into actions, which are carried out by the public agent in the citizens' name. This presumption holds even where democracy is direct, as in some cantons of Switzerland and in early New England, where everyone comes to meetings to decide policy, and even where government is by consensus, as in Quaker meetings. In all cases some measure of representation is required. And the question here is how the moral quality of an individual's action attaches to actions taken by his agents, in particular those taken by his government. It is the question of how morality connects with agency.

I

In the Gospel according to Luke, the story of the Good Samaritan goes like this: "A certain man went down from Jerusalem to Jericho, and fell among thieves, who also stripped and wounded him. . . . And it happened that a priest went down the same way . . . [and] a Levite. . . . But a certain Samaritan . . . came near him; and seeing him, was moved with compassion."[1] This traveling Samaritan stopped and bound the stranger's wounds, set him on his own beast, and took him to an inn. The following morning he instructed the innkeeper to keep the wounded man and said he would pay for his further care when he came that way again.

The Samaritan's behavior is contrasted with that of other travelers who are countrymen of the unfortunate Levite; for he is an outsider and has no special reason to help one of them. The moral of the story is, then, that the Samaritan comes to the aid of the stranger as to a member of a wider community, the community of all mankind. The story thus explains what a good neighbor does and who one's neighbor is.

Now suppose we change the story in one way: instead of tending the stranger personally, the Samaritan sends his servant to bind up the man's wounds and take him to an inn (on the servant's beast, say), and tells his servant to convey the same instruction to the inkeeper as was given in the original version. And suppose the servant does as he is instructed.

Let us assume that the care the stranger receives is the same in both versions: his wounds are bound, he is fed and cared for the same way, the innkeeper's treatment is the same, and so on. Even with this proviso, the actions are morally quite different.[2] In the second, no one would say that the action is exemplary of what a good neighbor does. Why not? The answer has something to do with *who* performs actions that are unpleasant and ministrative, actions that might be accounted demeaning. The washing and binding of wounds, like Jesus' washing of people's feet, are actions of humility, of a person who doesn't respect rank. In many of the Gospel stories, Jesus' actions exemplify a capacity for tender care, which in turn shows humility in dealing with others. These are qualities that cannot be shown by the second Samaritan.

Can they be shown by the servant? Perhaps in the second exam-

[1]Luke 10:30–37; I have used the King James version here. Since the story was told to answer the question "Who is a good neighbor?" the device of a Samaritan who helps a Levite was especially pointed; the unfriendly relations between Samaritans and Jews is made clear in John 4:9.

[2]This version need not be substitutable in the biblical context to make my point. Even to a modern ear, the two actions have different moral significance.

ple the goodness of the original Samaritan is simply divided between master and servant. The former inconveniences himself by
the delay involved in having his servant perform this errand; the
latter does the necessary things for the stranger, though under
instructions from his master.

But from the contributions of both men and the equivalence of
the actions it is still not possible to reconstruct the goodness of the
Good Samaritan. The second Samaritan does not exemplify the
same qualities of respect and humility or show us a person of
similar virtue. But neither are respect and humility shown by the
servant, except as all of his responses to his master's orders show
them. But this "humility" is simply the posture of a good servant,
and being a good servant is not being a good man. Finally, the
second story provides us no example to follow. Even if we were to
take our cue from the not-so-good Samaritan, we would first have
to have a good and obedient servant, and then, coming upon a
person in need, give him the appropriate commands. But satisfying these complex conditions can't be what being a good neighbor
requires. The action of the second, not-so-good Samaritan is frac-
tured in its agency, and as a result the location of any goodness is
unclear. In fact, some of the original goodness seems to have been
lost.

I am aiming to show that even though the practical details—the
practical description—of the action is the same, the actions are
very different. From what does this difference stem? Not from the
intentions of the two Samaritans, since both intend to help the
stranger and to the same degree and in the same ways. You might
say that *practically speaking* the actions are the same, since they are
the same from the point of view of the stranger in the light of his
care. But in some important ways they are not alike; as reflections
on the agents they are quite different. The difference connects with
who did the things that were done, the instigator or the agent.

How can the distinction between the actions of the two cases be
drawn? It seems clear that both cases involve actions that are good.
Insofar as the actions are alike, each is a good thing to do. On the
other hand, only the action of the Good Samaritan is a virtuous
one—the action of an exemplary man. Some connection between
action and agent in the first example is missing in the second. One

way to describe what is missing is to say it's a connection that consists partly in the fact that what the Good Samaritan does in the first example expresses his character, and so reflects his goodness; while what happens in the second example cannot in the same way reflect the goodness of either the servant or the master. It is not that the second case is ambiguous as to whose virtue is being reflected—that is, that while one of them *is* really virtuous, we don't know which. Rather the division of the action and the roles that are involved in the division do not permit the same quality of virtuousness to be expressed. We can express the difference by saying that, while the actions performed or effected are the same, the virtue of the first action has been lost. The second case does not conserve it.

The difference between the actions of the two Samaritans might be said to show how difficult it is to give examples of really virtuous actions and how ambiguous moral instruction can be. For if the action of taking care of the stranger is a good one (one might think), it ought to be good regardless who does it—Samaritan or Levite, servant or master, man or child. The lesson is for *all* if it's a lesson for any. That is what we might suppose. Yet it makes a great deal of difference to the virtue of the action whether it is carried out under orders or performed with one's own hands. So it is more difficult to find an action that is someone's good deed than to find one that's a good thing to do.[3] While caring for the stranger was a good thing for the servant to do, it isn't a good deed.

The difference can be presented in even more striking form. Let us change the story again. While the Samaritan is visiting a large and modern urban community in one of the Scandinavian countries, say, he comes upon a stranger lying in the street, robbed and left for dead. He goes to the nearest phone booth and calls the police to report the incident. An ambulance arrives and takes the stranger to the hospital; there a nurse binds his wounds, and there he is fed and cared for until he recovers. When he leaves he is not

---

[3]One might think that this distinction is illustrated by the different moral recommendations of Kant and Bentham, the first of whom extols the good will that shines of its own light, while the second looks at the action taken by itself. But the distinction I am making is more primitive, I think, and may underlie the deontological–utilitarian opposition.

charged for anything. Except for substituting a hospital for the inn, we leave the details much the same as before—that is, the treatment is identical or comparable, and his recovery proceeds at the same pace as before.

Now is this the same action as in the last case? Yes, in the sense that someone put into motion a sequence of events in which the stranger was provided with similar assistance and care. The action "caring for the wounded stranger" is the same, and it is still a good thing to do. But no, insofar as it is even less than before anyone's *good deed*. Although it was good of the Samaritan to call the police, and a good thing to do, it was not he that rescued the stranger. The ambulance attendants and hospital staff understood some of the things that were good to do, such as caring for the stranger's wounds. But theirs were not good deeds either. Their deeds, like the servant's, are part of their jobs, their roles, their chosen professions; thus their actions don't exhibit any virtue other than that of doing what they are supposed to do, given their jobs.

One way to characterize the difference between this case and that of the Good Samaritan is to say that none of these people was personally involved or personally responsible for what was done overall. The modern Samaritan began the process by making the telephone call, but even his responsibility doesn't extend beyond this small effort. And no one pays the bill, since the service is provided publicly for everyone. You might of course say that the taxpayers pay for it, and that answer we will look at later.

A good thing to do, such as caring for an injured stranger, is quite different from a good deed because, for one thing, a good deed reflects substantial moral credit on the agent. Sometimes the description of an action will not allow us to say whether the action described is a good deed or only a good thing to do; the description may be ambiguous in some crucial respect—who exactly does the deed, the way it is done, the circumstances in which it is done. Helping an old person across an intersection may be a (small) good deed for a busy commuter, for example, but not for the policeman assigned to the post. The policeman does a good thing, but it doesn't reflect upon him as a good deed would; it only reflects a concern to do his job well. His position is like that of the servant of the not-so-good Samaritan, that is, his goodness consists in conscientiously doing what he is supposed to do, however inconvenient or unpleasant.

It is very tempting to distinguish between the Good Samaritan and the not-so-good ones by saying that the latter use others as *instruments* to accomplish a good thing, much as the original Samaritan used his beast to transport the stranger. On these lines one could then argue that the Samaritans in all three cases are really alike: each is the instigator of an action that requires the use of instruments, and thus the differences have to do with degree and with the kind of instruments that were used (which aren't serious ethical differences) rather than with the ethical reflection on the agent. Thus if the Good Samaritan is to be praised for his action, the not-so-good one should be praised for his, and the modern Samaritan praised in the same terms. Modern technology doesn't change the moral significance of the actions. But our ethical intuitions do not equate the cases in this way; there is a difference and it needs explaining.

One clear reason that virtue is not conserved through the series of actions described—actions that are in some sense alike—has to do with the role of an intermediary between the initiator of the action and the thing that is eventually done. Therefore, the non-conservation of virtue in these cases raises in turn the question how good deeds of individuals can translate into institutional actions. It comes to concern any organized society whose institutions are charged to perform morally commendable actions, and particularly to concern any community whose government is supposed to be a vehicle for expressing the citizens' moral concerns.

II

Jeremy Bentham proposed that actions, whether of a government or of an individual, can be treated in the same moral terms. If a thing is a good thing to do, then it's as good for government to do as for an individual and vice versa; it's good regardless of who does it.[4] Bentham thought it was first important

---

[4]"An Introduction to the Principles of Morals and Legislation," in *The Works of Jeremy Bentham,* ed. John Bowring (New York: Russell & Russell, 1962), 1:12.

to characterize *actions* as good or bad or in between, for it is from the goodness of actions that other ethical values flow, in particular reflections on the agent that does them. And while he specifically sets public actions on a par with private ones, many other philosophers would at least agree that it is actions that are first of all good or bad; the goodness or badness of individuals derives from the actions they do. It seems to follow that governments derive goodness in the same way.

Actions, which we thus may call the first possessors of goodness, may be performed by a variety of agents—servants, states, delegates, and so on. Therefore, the actions of all three Samaritans can be assimilated to one action, Bentham implies. I would like to characterize the issue raised in the second and third cases as that of moral representation. It concerns not only actions done publicly but those done by other agents, such as servants or employees of a person or corporation. It concerns the sending of a representative to do something one might have done oneself, where the description of the outcome is held constant. And the problem with moral representation, as I see it, is whether moral values can be conserved with respect to it, and if not, what the moral consequences of action by agents are.

Take a striking example of a good deed: a passerby jumps in the water upon hearing cries of distress and attempts to rescue the person who called. What makes this a good deed is not just that it is a good action, a good thing to do; for if a lifeguard on duty were to do the same thing, we would say only that he did his job. He is an analogue of the servant. The lifeguard is paid to perform actions of a kind that, were someone else to perform them, *might* be considered good deeds. Of course, one can say that it is precisely because such deeds are good things to do that this job exists, and to be sure, his actions in saving people from drowning are good things to do. But the goodness of the lifeguard's action doesn't make it morally like the action of a passerby, who acts on his own, because the lifeguard, like the servant, acts in the performance of a job.

This role or job, however, involves moral representation. That is, this person is hired to do what another person thinks sufficiently important to pay someone to do, and its importance has a moral ground. Someone's moral judgment is behind such actions. The expressions of this judgment and their implications, however, may vary widely: the owner of a swimming pool may hire a lifeguard on his own initiative; or he may be required to do so by a public authority; or again, the community may hire and pay for one. But although these cases of moral representation differ, all contrast with the case in which a private citizen jumps in himself, for that case does not depend on anyone else's concern any more than the action of the Good Samaritan did. What both the passerby and the Good Samaritan do reflects upon their characters, reflects credit on their goodness as people; what the lifeguard does shows that he is a conscientious lifeguard and employee.

We might distinguish between the goodness of a person and the goodness of a deed, so that we could say that the deeds of both the passerby and the lifeguard are good deeds, but only the first reflects credit on the man. Such a distinction would encourage a further discussion of how, in general, a person's deeds connect with his character.

III

A person's actions and character are surely connected. The connection was developed best perhaps by Aristotle, who proposed that men become just only by doing just acts, and temperate by doing temperate ones. But to this argument Aristotle himself raises the objection that "if men do just and temperate acts, they are already just and temperate, exactly as, if they do what is in accordance with the laws of grammar and of music, they are grammarians and musicians." Aristotle's answer is that a man will be a grammarian only by having done things grammatically, and so, mutatis mutandis, with the musician. That is, they learn to do these things as arts; as a result of developing their skills they *become* grammarian and musician. Similarly, the good man *becomes* good by practicing—by repeatedly doing—what is good; thus doing good things seems very like an art that characterizes the good man: "By doing just acts . . . the just man is produced, and by doing temperate acts the temperate man; without doing these no one would have even the prospect of becoming good."[5]

Having pressed this analogy, however, Aristotle proceeds to insist that there is still an important difference between doing good actions and *doing them as the good man does them,* and this difference separates virtue from the arts, where no such distinction exists. For performing music well cannot be distinguished from performing it well *as a musician does* in the same way that doing a good thing can be distinguished from doing it as the good man does. The good man does a good action in a particular way, Aristotle proposed: he does it with knowledge, choosing to do it for its own sake, and "from a firm and unchangeable charater."[6] His *manner* of doing it is therefore distinctive.

Aristotle acknowledges the tension between his account of the acts that a man needs to do to *become* good and his account of acting *as a good man does,* which is more than practicing good actions. When it comes to specifying the acts that are good, he asserts sensibly that they are the ones that a good or virtuous man does; thus he characterizes good men by their good actions and characterizes good actions in terms of the good men who do them, moving in a circle. One infers that the relation between being a good man and doing good deeds is at least not simple and direct.

What light does this argument shed on the difference between doing a good action and doing a good deed? Surely the lifeguard may or may not have knowledge—just as the passerby may or may not. And as to choosing to do what he does, there is a sense in which the lifeguard as well as the Good Samaritan may or may not choose from "a firm and unchangeable character." Nevertheless, there is an irreducible difference: the lifeguard doesn't choose at the moment to save someone for the sake of saving someone—that is, with only the worth of the action in his mind—since he is also committed to performing such actions as part of his job. Thus the feature "doing a thing for its own sake" does bring out one difference between his action and that of a passerby. Being charged to do a certain thing and having responsibility for doing it imply that

[5]Aristotle, *Nichomachean Ethics,* in *The Basic Works of Aristotle,* trans. Richard McKeon (New York: Random House, 1941), II, 3, 1105b, 1105a.
[6]Ibid., 1105a.

one is not doing it for its own sake, or not simply for its own sake, and therefore not doing it as the good man does. Aristotle comes closer than anyone else, I believe, to showing us how to make the distinction we want, though the job is not yet done.

Moral representation can now be connected with the notion of a role. The lifeguard's job gives him a role, the servant's job gives him one. But there is no role that is the role of a good man, and no role that is that of performing good deeds. These actions fall outside roles. So we might say at least that a good deed is *not* an action done in a role that involves doing such actions; it is *not* an action done out of a duty that comes from one's role.

Another example may help here. Imagine that there is a destitute family whose needs may be met in either of two ways: neighbors may come in to help and offer provisions as each is able, or a welfare worker may come and assist them in getting help from public programs—help them to fill out forms and give advice. In the former case there is merit in the actions and they reflect upon the good characters of the neighbors. The actions of the social worker, however, cannot in the same way reflect on her virtue. They are the actions of someone paid to perform a role, are part of her job. If she were to do the same deeds as neighbors do them, her actions would have the same merit as theirs, but her role precludes her acting in this way while she is working. One can say that she cannot act at the same time in a role and as an individual whose actions reflect on her character. The evaluation of her action as a good deed will depend on whether she acts within or outside of the role.

The same distinction can be applied to other professions, those of doctors, lawyers, nurses, counselors, policemen, and so on. When they act as professionals, their actions exhibit professional competence, seriousness, dedication to the roles they undertake. And these are very important and commendable qualities. But a surgeon who saves a life in the course of an operation is not comparable to someone who saves a life outside a professional role. The distinction between the action of the servant and that of the Good Samaritan seems to be morally fixed and unexceptionable.

Paul Ricoeur, in discussing the Good Samaritan, introduces a distinction between the *socius* and the neighbor. The perspective of the *socius,* he argues, excludes the relationship of neighbors, not least because "the neighbor is the personal way in which I encounter another *over and above all social mediation*." One must "choose between the neighbor and the *socius*," between these two exclusive relations with others; they are not compatible.[7] Ricoeur sees the *socius* view as pernicious to morality.

But surely we cannot distinguish the neighbor and the *socius* so sharply. Our neighbors are part of what we mean by society. And in the end Ricoeur himself concedes that they are connected: "It is the same charity which gives meaning to the social institution *and* to the event of the encounter. The brutal opposition between community and society, between personal and administrative or institutional relationships, can only be one stage of reflection."[8] The two *must* come together somehow, but the question is how.

The problem is particularly clear in the context of representative government. Using Bentham's assumption that if an action is good it does not matter whether it is done by an individual or a government, we must infer that it cannot matter much whether we do an action ourselves or send someone to do it or arrange for the government to do it. For from Bentham's assumption it seems to follow directly that a citizen should direct his government to do things that would be good to do himself. The actions are convertible. Thus the government can represent him, act for him, in a moral dimension; it might be called his servant or an extension of himself, reflecting his own moral choices.

But now, when the government performs the actions that the citizens see to be morally good, does its doing so reflect moral credit on the individual members the community? In fact, both anonymity and coercion count against the possibility that moral credit passes through and reflects back on the citizens. As the citizens who voted for the policy are anonymous, sponsorship and the merit of sponsorship are ambiguous.[9] And when all *must* sup-

<hr>

[7]Paul Ricoeur, "The *Socius* and the Neighbor," in *History and Truth* (Evanston, Ill.: Northwestern University Press, 1965), pp. 101, 102.

[8]Ibid., p. 102.

[9]The matter of who can claim the "community's money" is equally ambiguous. Milton Friedman is quick to say that welfare programs are arrangements whereby some of the people spend "someone else's" money, a kind of spending much less efficient and therefore less commendable than the spending of one's own money, Friedman argues (*Free to Choose* [New York: Harcourt Brace Jovanovich, 1979],

port these policies under threat of coercion, even those who did not choose them, acting under such a threat is hardly a mark of particular goodness. But there is a more serious block than either of these.

The case of a policy established to do a good thing is more complicated than the earlier cases because the good action has now become institutionalized. Instead of an action that is done by someone we now have a right belonging to people characterized in a certain way. So a family that is miserably poor may have a right to assistance and food, and even a right to the social worker's help to claim the first right. Such people have these rights simply by virtue of being citizens with a particular need living under laws that provide for that need. The matter is between them and the government—and it is *their* government—not between them and some other part of the community. With institutionalization we lose not only an identifiable agent but also the object of generosity. Given the right to receive help, generosity is superfluous. But without some such expression of benevolence, clearly nothing is left of the good deed.

Comparison with the not-so-good Samaritan shows the differences clearly. It is imaginable that after the Samaritan has sent his servant (with his donkey) and paid the bill, the stranger might send the Samaritan thanks for his help. And if the unfortunate stranger had been particularly surly in the first instance, the Samaritan might have gone by and left him instead of giving him care. Therefore there is a dimension of personal interaction between Samaritan and stranger of the sort Ricoeur emphasizes. And while the interaction is less personal than in the case of the Good Samaritan, it is personal in some degree. In the modern institutional case, however, this feature is entirely missing. A person might understandably be grateful to a social worker and thank her, but these thanks lack the moral weight of the thanks given to the Samaritan; they are more like the thanks given to the servant.[10]

---

pp. 115–17). This hazard in the translation of spending from individual to government is considered in sec. IV, below.

[10]People do thank the firemen who put out their fires, the ambulance drivers who take them to the hospital, and the policemen who give them directions, of course. But it is difficult for me to see these expressions in the same way as the thanks due someone who acts outside an institution.

There is no significant role for gratitude in the institutional case; not because no one was responsible for the policies—some were, of course—but because there is no room for a *relationship* of any human variety between the benefactors and the recipients of help. As Ricoeur expresses it, "the social realm tends to block access to the personal and to *hide* the mystery of interhuman relationships, to dissimulate the movement of charity."[11]

Besides this lack of relationship and interaction between the helpers and the helped, there is another curious feature of the institutional case. The recipient of benefits may himself have a role in the decision to provide them, a *self-interested* role in the action that led to his being benefited, which casts a further, ironical light on the lack of a role for gratitude.

Let us return to the most striking difference between the institutional case and the other cases, that, once a policy to benefit someone is instituted, the recipient has a *right* to the benefits. It is characteristic of rights (as we have seen) that they are possessed by individuals and only wait to be asserted or claimed. Now what a person already owns he doesn't need to thank anyone for; the right is possessed even before the benefits are received. Moreover, this kind of possession is related, as we saw in Chapter 2, to a person's self-respect. So it would be altogether out of line to expect the recipient of the benefits to thank someone for his benefits even though they are paid for by others.[12]

This feature puts a curious light on Bentham's principle that good actions are indifferent to the matter of who does them, government or individuals. For those individuals who view the government as a servant who morally represents them may surely look at the policy as a generous one, an expression of their compassion for those in need. They view their support of the policy in much the way they view their support of church programs or

---

[11]Ricoeur, "*Socius* and Neighbor," p. 108; the italics are Ricoeur's.

[12]Citizens sometimes reproach the needy for taking their benefits as a matter of right, without thanking the rest of the community who are their benefactors. But benefits provided institutionally *are* a matter of right, and we don't thank others for what is ours by right. It would be exceedingly curious to thank anyone for the right to vote or own property, for instance. Yet in view of the confusion about the translation of virtue through agency, the protest is understandable.

other charitable causes. But because the policy establishes rights and requires taxes to fund them, public policies cannot deserve thanks or reflect credit on the instigators and those who are taxed. Thus the public case is unlike that of a church, which might be thanked, and whose contributors may justifiably feel moral satisfaction; government is not even capable of arm's-length charity. Given this circumstance, the private citizen's moral contribution is necessarily blocked.

I don't mean to deny that there are such things as good or humane public policies. But I deny that these policies can be viewed as actions with the moral properties, the moral dimension, of good deeds. And this is a puzzle that a representative government has to face. It has to face the fact that policies intended to benefit people in need cannot be seen as variants of the actions of a good neighbor. The good neighbor is not a role that the government can have or that morally conscious citizens can give it.

A government, it might be said, simply cannot have the moral properties of individuals. It is never virtuous, and never petty or mean or vicious. So a priori it cannot be generous. If we were to attribute goodness (or wickedness) to a government, we would be making a kind of category mistake, anthropomorphizing the government as a Hobbesian giant with all the characteristic human properties. But it isn't clear (and has been disputed) that government cannot have these properties.[13] The case still needs to be proved.

One might argue that the government can never have motives, and that since motives are intimately connected with both character and virtue, they are also connected with the actions that reflect character and virtue. Therefore the government cannot be virtuous. Similarly a welfare agency cannot act charitably or deal generously even though it distributes food to the needy. In a sense, it cannot *give* food, but only distribute it. Therefore, the actions that a human can perform and that have moral significance cannot

---

[13]It has been disputed by Alan White, for one, who claims that governments may indeed by virtuous in the same sense as individuals. The occasion was a reading of an earlier version of this argument at the University of Hull in April 1982.

be performed by such an agency. Moral significance, on this objection, simply stops where government begins.

If such objections were all that were needed to settle the issue, we should have been on the wrong track all along. For we took it that there is a sense in which the government can do the same actions as a person, while this objection suggests that neither the government nor a servant *does* anything, strictly speaking, that it or he is sent to do. But however neat this solution may seem, there are powerful reasons for not accepting it.

IV

When Bentham proposed that government actions could be evaluated in the same moral terms as individual ones, he supposed that a citizen—or better, a group of citizens—could send the government to do things that seemed good to them. The government could represent the community and its moral values through public policies and programs. Indeed, for there to be a plausible conception of representative government, some such representation of moral values in policies seems absolutely necessary. Otherwise the idea that the government *is* the people and that the people are collectively responsible for their government would be empty. There would be no firm moral connection between government programs and the values of the people who supported them— which would be senseless. What, then, would be the meaning of voting for a program whose plainest recommendation is that it is a good thing to do? Surely welfare programs, aid to the sick and handicapped, and universal education are meant to express the concerns of the community, concerns that may be unequivocally moral.

So the assumption of a connection between personal morality and its representation in government policies *must* be justifiable. Consider Aristotle's fully developed man, whose life must include, besides the roles of husband, father, and master, an active role in politics. He must serve on juries, take his turn at public offices, and so on. He must go to war in the event of war, and if he is of ample means, he must support military efforts and public events. Most important, perhaps, he must vote in elections and thus indicate the course he thinks the government ought to take.

Now it is clear that in service on a jury a person cannot judge without consulting his or her conscience and moral convictions; these are a juror's indispensable guides. One's moral convictions also guide one in voting and in performing other official duties. In fact, the sum of one's responsibilities as a civic agent is, as Aristotle suggested, an extension of his responsibilities as a spouse, parent, and manager of affairs. One's responsibility for the government is more attenuated than one's responsibility for employees and children, but the two are continuous, forming one cloth. If the government does what it shouldn't, then the citizen's duty is to criticize and try to change it. That is one's moral duty in the context of a representative system. How does such a person go to the polls, then? What assumptions does one make? It seems that one *must* assume that the ballot is in part a means for expressing moral convictions.

The good man approaches the polls with a quick conscience: Aristotle, too, would expect that. If prisoners are mistreated, that wrongful practice should be stopped. Its continuation reflects upon the community much as a man's actions reflect upon him, and insofar as the community's actions derive from the views of its members, then, even though one citizen's voice is small, it is his duty to speak up. A citizen's duty as a private person and his or her duty as citizen are not sharply separable.

But under what conception of government is it possible for private and public roles to be joined? A representative government is often said to be the citizens' servant; if it is, the government reflects the masters' values as surely as the Samaritan's servant reflects his master's values. And in that case, this theory of government cannot get around the original problem, the nonconservation of virtue through moral representation.

The question is whether the government *can* be conceived in this way, as doing things in the place of a citizen who might—in some sense—do them himself, and as thus fulfilling the citizen's moral values. And can this be the right model of the way citizens choose when they go to the polls?

Our first step has been taken: a citizen's choice must be guided by his or her moral judgments and convictions. The next step is to determine how that choice is guided. So if a policy or practice is deemed wrong, and if citizens have an opportunity to vote on it, a conscientious citizen must square that vote with his or her moral values.

What, then, of the relation of the government to citizens? If we think of government as a servant, a servant constituted by institutions and laws, it is tempting to look at it as a sort of gigantic mechanical creature, an idiot Leviathan that forever needs to be told what to do.[14] It can be conceived as a machine built to do certain work according to commands, but insensitive to the results it produces.

The idea of the government as a machine raises in starker form the problem we began with—whether an action instigated by someone else is even roughly the same as an action a person performs on his own account.[15] For if one thinks of the intermediary or servant as a machine, then the answer to the question of what it *does* may be nothing at all. It runs, functions; it doesn't *do* things in the sense that humans do.[16] The government doesn't sacrifice in giving to the poor, it doesn't deprive itself of luxuries, it doesn't regret that it couldn't give more, doesn't sympathize with the destitute, and so on. In the same way it doesn't give anything or help, or even pay or borrow, nor does it earn the money it spends—though these terms are commonly applied to it. To look at it as a machine is to relinquish the tendency to think that a representative government is *responsible* for what happens. If it is a mechanical servant sent to do a job, then it isn't responsible for what it's sent to do—or for the success of the outcome or even for its own proper functioning. In this case, there is no moral quality to anything the government does, no question of its acting as a person does.

The bare possibility of a moral representative—that is, of an

---

[14]For a discussion of the mechanical analogy as it applies to one aspect of representation, see Hanna F. Pitkin, *The Concept of Representation* (Berkeley: University of California Press, 1967), chap. 7.

[15]Ibid., pp. 145–46.

[16]Wallace Matson makes this point about machines very neatly in chap. 4 of his *Sentience* (Berkeley: University of California Press, 1976).

agent through whom moral values can be expressed—is threatened here. For if a representative becomes in that role a part of the machine, then the moral coloring of the act of voting will be instantly lost as quickly as votes are counted and someone is chosen. Therefore, treating the government as a machine or a mechanical tool not only begs the question that concerns us—whether the government can represent the moral concerns of citizens—but prejudges the very possibility of representative government with any moral dimension. This consequence is so paradoxical as to make us suspect the mechanical analogy.

V

We would like to assume that the government serves the people in a surrogate role, acting for us as we would act ourselves, doing what we would do if we had the power, the time, and the resources, and for our reasons. This assumption connects with the picture of a servile Leviathan that walks with larger steps and works with larger hands to do the things smaller creatures would do themselves if they could. It is a servant perfectible to the degree that it can be trained to do precisely what is wanted and do it efficiently. But this conception and imagery led to theoretical problems, as we saw. No servant, neither a human nor an institutional one, can represent our choices in the moral dimension, and without moral representation the notion of representative government appears to lose its moral foundation.

The difficulty in our reasoning, I think, lies in supposing that representative government requires the servant conception and that therefore the moral qualities of private actions delegated to government carry through. But there are two errors here: first, in the supposition that representative government can have such a simple relation to the citizenry, and second, in the supposition that moral qualities of actions are communicated in representation. Aristotle's example is instructive; he explained the conception of democratic government without assuming that citizens needed a public servant to act for them. Unlike the contractarians Hobbes and Locke, he did not view government as a creature made by men to serve their presocial motives. On the contrary, for him the state is an expression of man's essentially social nature; it has and needs no other justification. The state grows out of small communities, which in turn grow from families, and the family itself is a miniature community.[17] A state is then as natural a thing for man as a particular fruit is for its vine.

So for Aristotle the supposition that the state must *serve* the citizens is unecessary. It is part of the virtuous man's role to be engaged in politics, and to be engaged in it for the good of the community. In this vision the distinction between an individual's actions and the state's actions takes on a new form: the state's actions are extensions of individual ones, the results of individual choices, but they are not surrogates—deeds to be compared with the deeds a person does. The government, in short, does not act *for* the individual, but acts *as a state,* with its own kind of action and its own appropriate ends.

Neither the myth of the government-servant nor its logical source, the myth of the presocial individual, is logically tied to democratic or representative government. We do not have to think of a representative as either a servant or a tool that must do our bidding. We do not have to think of government as the servant of a master who pays him and sends him on errands instead of going himself. On the contrary, to make moral sense, the idea of representaion needs to be detached from social contract assumptions.

We have seen that Aristotle's picture of the complete man is that of a many-sided creature with many responsibilities and roles. He cannot be a good husband and father, for instance, without respecting the interests and welfare of many other persons, and as a good manager, he is necessarily concerned about the welfare of his employees. And after his family and employees, he needs to be concerned about the welfare of his community.[18] He needs to be concerned about it in ways that affect him personally and in ways that don't: both kinds of matters are joined seamlessly when they are seen from the perspective of the welfare of the state as a whole. Thus a citizen may be justified in putting the state's interests ahead

[17]Aristotle, *Politics,* trans. T. A. Sinclair, rev. Trevor Saunders (New York: Penguin, 1981), I, 1–2.
[18]Ibid., chaps. 7 and 12 in particular; see also bk. III, chaps. 1–4.

of his own in a given case, but in the long run the two are bound together.

The setting Aristotle provides for the citizen does not allow one to introduce the master/servant, user/tool distinctions. The citizen votes, but not as a private individual with distinct interests that he bids the state to fulfill, for the state's concerns are ipso facto his own—part of a larger set of concerns but nonetheless his. And the kind of state that exists will reflect the kind of citizens who are in it. A good action performed by a person acting as a citizen is one kind of virtuous action; a good deed performed by a person acting as a private individual is another. Again, the problem of the servant representing the master is blocked.

In this picture of representative government the notion of representation is changed. The citizen and his state are aspects of one thing. They reflect morally upon one another, their actions concern one another's welfare. Insofar as the good state is good, it reflects on a good citizenry and in turn it will nourish virtue in its people. Then in what does representation consist? It might be said to consist in electing good and capable people to positions of public trust and in removing those who betray trust or lack competence. "Representation" in this sense has nothing to do with commanding specific things to be done and still less with representing interests, except for the interests of the community itself.

VI

The nonconservation of virtue, I have argued, raises a problem for a theory of representative government only under the assumptions made by social contract theory—namely, that society is a creation of men made to satisfy their individual interests and serve them as individuals. Under these assumptions government takes on the guise of servant, and criticism of it must concern how well it serves the citizen-master. In a servant role, however, the government cannot express the moral values of individuals; like the servant of the not-so-good-Samaritan, its actions are de-moralized. As with a machine, the predicates of morality fail to apply.

I argued that representative government doesn't require these assumptions. A representative conception of government is quite compatible with a theory such as Aristotle's, and like him we are free to espouse democracy without accepting atomism. Moreover, I argued that the Aristotelian framework allows for participation in government to be continuous with other aspects of a citizen's moral life, connected with his private actions but not analogous to them. His public decisions have their own moral context. Therefore the Good Samaritan story doesn't serve to illuminate the role of a morally sound citizen in a democracy. Insofar as it invokes the assumptions of social atomism, the framework is too pinched and lean. It shows us, at best, how *not* to conceive the relation of a citizen to his state.

The example of the not-so-good Samaritan and our exploration of it as a case of moral representation bring us to the interesting conclusion that representative government, which cannot be conceived as either a servant or a monster or a machine, and whose actions are also not surrogates for the actions of human individuals, has a nature and form of action that are sui generis. The aim of social contract philosophers was and is to reduce and explain government in terms of something else.[19] But this is precisely what we have found cannot be done.

[19]Robert Nozick is quite clear on this point; see his *Anarchy, State, and Utopia* (Cambridge: Harvard University Press, 1977), pp. 6–9.

5

Pornography and the
Tyranny of the Majority

The respect that atomism accords individuals justifies the maximum degree of freedom of expression, and that freedom protects pornography from public control. But many objectors to pornography, righteously indignant, also emphasize individual respect, particularly the respect due to women as sexual partners. Thus conflicting views, on both sides fervent and moralistic, draw their support from a single atomistic root. Where does such conflict lead us?

I

"If all mankind minus one were of one opinion," John Stuart Mill wrote, "mankind would be no more justified in silencing that one person than he, if he had the power, would be justified in silencing mankind." No matter how great the majority, the very power to control opinion and expression is illegitimate, he argued. Worse, such power "is robbing the human race" of the chance to hear different sides of a question whether right or wrong, and thus does injury to the whole community.[1]

Society has no right to demand conformity to a set of beliefs, to "maim by compression, like a Chinese lady's foot, every part of

[1] John Stuart Mill, *On Liberty* (Bungay: Penguin, 1980), p. 76.

98

human nature which stands out prominently, and tends to make the person markedly dissimilar in outline to commonplace humanity." A person needs opportunity to live as he chooses, to take up causes passionately, make mistakes, change his or her mind. Only in this way can anyone develop to the fullest potential. "Human nature is not a machine to be built after a model, and set to do exactly the work prescribed for it, but a tree, which requires to grow and develop itself on all sides, according to the tendency of the inward forces which make it a living thing."[2] Society will itself benefit when people have liberty to experiment in ideas and ways of living, Mill believed, for it is innovators, not conformists, who advance culture.

Truth also is advanced when people are allowed to express all opinions and to debate every question. And who is it argues against a popular view but a minority of dissenters? They are the ones, then, who need the most protection: "On any of the great open questions . . . if either of the two opinions has a better claim than the other, not merely to be tolerated but to be encouraged . . . it is the one which happens at the particular time and place to be in a minority. That is the one which for the time being represents the neglected interests, the side of human well-being which is in danger of obtaining less than its share."[3]

Even in the gentler form of custom, majority tyranny is as much to be feared as political tyranny, Mill believes, and maybe more. His criterion for interference is that only if harm or injury to someone results should people be restrained from acting and living as they please. There is a presumption that in the absence of proof of injury, individuals should be left alone.

I quote extensively from Mill because his language is echoed in modern discussions of free speech, particularly those related to control of pornography.[4] Control is seen as a simple case of the

[2]Ibid., p. 135.

[3]Ibid., p. 123.

[4]A presidential commission formed to consider pornography and obscenity remarked that Mill's "market-place remains a correct and profound idea," relevant presumably to the defense of pornography (*United States Commission on Obscenity and Pornography, Report* [1970]. p. 55). Other references to the "marketplace of ideas" can be found in Abrams v. United States, 250 U.S. 630 (1919) (Holmes

majority forcing others into conformity with their (puritanical) moral standard without argument. It appears a clear case of social compression, what Mill would call a "Calvinistic" demand for "Christian self-denial," aimed at stifling the virtue of "Pagan self-assertion." Similarly Joel Feinberg refers to control as "moralistic paternalism." Other writers echo Mill's attitude.[5]

For Americans this is a powerful and seductive argument against restrictions on any published material, including pornography.[6] All the libertarian or the nonconformist minority asks of the majority is tolerance of its curious ways. What problem is there in that? Others don't have to look or buy; one person should be free to enjoy pornography even though others prefer not to, just as they are free to accept or reject escargots or dandelion wine. Passionate tastes are not a bad thing, Mill argued; they are the very "raw material of human nature," capable of both more good and more evil than ordinary feelings. "Strong impulses are but another name for energy. A person whose desires and impulses are his own—are the expression of his own nature—. . . is said to have a

---

dissenting); the "competition of ideas" figures prominently in Gertz v. Robert Welch, Inc., 418 U.S. 339–40 (1974); Police Department v. Mosley, 408 U.S. 92, 96–97, refers to the importance of self-expression for personal development; and many other examples could be given.

[5]See, for example, Robert Haney, *Comstockery in America: Patterns of Censorship and Control* (New York: Da Capo, 1974); Fred Berger, "Pornography, Sex, and Censorship," in *Pornography and Censorship,* ed. David Copp and Susan Wendell (Buffalo: Prometheus, 1983), esp. pp. 99–100. Mill's reference to Calvinism is in *On Liberty,* pp. 126–27; Joel Feinberg's remark is in "Pornography and the Criminal Law," in *Pornography and Censorship,* ed. Copp and Wendell, p. 133. Fred Berger also sounds very much like Mill, attributing to the moralists a stultifying influence on sexual practices. He writes: "The fact is that most sex is routinized, dull, unfulfilling, a source of neurosis, precisely because its practice is governed by the restraints the conservatives insist on. . . . Moreover, the web of shame and guilt which is spun around sex tends to destroy its enjoyment, and thus to stunt our sexual natures—our capacity for joy and pleasure through sex. The result is a society which is highly neurotic in its attitudes toward and practice of sex—all of which interferes with honest communication and self-realization" (p. 89). Robert Haney also echoes Mill's view when he writes that "cultural creativity must always be ready to stand up and fight for its existence. Societies all too frequently equate the good with the familiar" (p. 12).

[6]I intentionally don't speak of "pornographic literature" in anticipation of a distinction to be made later between pornography and expressions of opinion.

character."⁷ And society needs people of strong character: that is the romantic message.

To understand the role of Mill's argument, it is important to recognize that he wrote long after the Bill of Rights became law, and that his view of freedom was not the one that prompted the First Amendment, or even one shared by the early Americans. The idea that truth depends on a "marketplace of ideas," that freedom of expression advances the universal search for truth, that self-expression is an essential part of a person's self-development, that—most important—the only restriction rightly placed on a person's freedom is the injunction not to injure others—such ideas are those of Mill's time, not of Jefferson's. They originated with romantic philosophers of the nineteenth century, not with the political and moral thinkers of seventeenth-century England and eighteenth-century America, who stressed individual responsibility, restraint, and self-governance.⁸ Such virtues Mill would probably find much too straitlaced. It is therefore a wild anachronism to use Mill's *On Liberty* as a gloss on the First Amendment. But my argument does not turn on this point. I will argue that one kind of moral issue raised by pornography overshadows and requires us to reevaluate the free-speech issue. Further, once the argument against protecting pornography is spelled out, I believe Mill can be rallied to its support instead of to the libertarian side.

Two points about "harm" should be made. First, the language of injury and harm are no part of the First Amendment. The framers of that amendment did not suggest that if someone's practice of religion, for example, were to cause injury in some vague

---

⁷Mill, *On Liberty*, pp. 124–25.

⁸Mill cites Wilhelm von Humboldt as his source on the ultimate value of self-development. Humboldt stated his laissez-faire political theory in *The Sphere and Duties of Government (Ideen zu einem Versuch die Grenzen der Wirksamkeit des Staats zu bestimmen)* in 1791–92. But other thinkers in Europe were working along this line in the early nineteenth century, including Alexis de Tocqueville, of whose *Democracy in America* Mill wrote a lengthy review. Later the American pragmatists William James and John Dewey gave these ideas an important place in American philosophy. But they were not ideas that Jefferson and Hamilton, Franklin and Adams connected with the need for free expression of opinion. My source here is Garry Wills, *Inventing America* (Garden City, N.Y.: Doubleday, 1978).

sense, the right of religious practice is restrictable. One might conclude from their terse statement that on the contrary, the right to practice religion should be very difficult to restrict. The "injury" proviso, which may originate with utilitarians, is therefore a gauntlet I do not propose to pick up. Second, Mill's single proviso that a person's exercise of freedom should not harm others places a heavy burden of proof on anyone defending pornography's restriction, and sets the presumption that freedom should prevail. How can injury be shown? How can it even be understood here?[9] Who is injured when pornography is aimed at adult customers, free to decide whether they are interested in it?

To answer these questions we appear to need both a specific conception of harm and persuasive evidence of a causal connection, both of which various critics have shown to be problematic.[10] I will argue, on the contrary, that to accept this burden of proof—that harm or injury to an individual has been caused—is an error of strategy. It is to accept a difficult or even impossible challenge when a more direct and powerful moral argument is available.

II

Freedom of speech and press are commonly connected with democratic government and seen as essential to it. Tocqueville, for instance, wrote: "In the countries in which the doc-

[9]Among those who use this strategy is Helen Longino, in "Pornography, Oppression, and Freedom: A Closer Look," in *Take Back the Night,* ed. Laura Lederer (New York: Bantam, 1980), esp. p. 48. Longino, however, uses "harm" and "injury" in very broad ways, as if such latitude makes the case easier to prove. I think that, on the contrary, it makes the whole "proof of injury" argument look vague and unpersuasive.

[10]The report of the presidential commission felt that the harm argument was in both respects defective. Among the many others who raise the same doubts are Haney (*Comstockery in America*) and Berger ("Pornography, Sex, and Censorship"). The question of whether the personality of an offender determines his use of pornography or vice versa is exceedingly ambiguous, and seems to need a sophisticated theory of psychological causation. If the burden of devising one can be pressed on its opponents, pornography's position appears secure.

trine of the sovereignty of the people ostensibly prevails, the censorship of the press is not only dangerous, but it is absurd."[11] It was a connection not lost on the framers of the Constitution, who were on their guard against the danger that government might seek to impose its will on reluctant citizens. We don't need to doubt the connection here. The question is: Does protection of free expression legitimately protect pornography?

A reasonable statement on this point is made by Ronald Dworkin, who argues that the right to have an equal voice in the political process is not denied when a person "is forbidden to circulate photographs of genitals to the public at large, or denied his right to listen to argument when he is forbidden to consider these photographs at his leisure."[12] Some other basis for protection is needed, according to him.

The Supreme Court argued along similar lines in *Roth v. United States*. What the amendment protects, it says, is the "unfettered interchange of ideas for the bringing about of political and social changes desired by the people." And pornography is "no essential part of any exposition of ideas."[13]

In my view the distinction set forth in *Roth* is important and should have been developed. But instead of developing it, the Court went on to give another reason not to protect pornography, namely, that a "social interest in order and morality" clearly "outweighed" pornography's right to protection. Such a move was plainly hazardous: if other "social interests" can "outweigh" the right to free expression, then the protection of the First Amendment has been greatly diluted. The better argument would follow along the original lines, saying that pornography isn't in the category of "expression" meant to be protected.

[11] Alexis de Tocqueville, *Democracy in America,* trans. George Lawrence, ed. J. P. Mayer (Garden City, N.Y.: Doubleday, 1969), 1:10, 118.

[12] Ronald Dworkin, "Do We have a Right to Pornography?" in *A Matter of Principle* (Cambridge: Harvard University Press, 1985), p. 336. Dworkin goes on to argue that we can value free expression and "accept a presumption against censorship" and still allow that presumption to be overcome, for example, "by some showing that the harm the activity threatens is grave, probable, and uncontroversial" (pp. 337–38). This is basically the strategy of the report of the Committee on Pornography and Obscenity.

[13] Roth v. United States, 354 U.S 481.

A knotty problem arises, however, when pornography is excluded from protection: the amendment speaks of freedom of the *press*. So from one angle it looks as if the amendment was meant to protect not citizens who want to read but publishers in the business of selling printed matter of whatever kind. And pornography certainly belongs in this large domain.[14]

Were the framers trying to protect one kind of business while refusing to protect others? We are helped here by remembering that the First Amendment also dealt with freedom of worship and the right to congregate. The rights to worship and congregate in public rest on the respect of one's need to commune with God on the one hand and with one's fellow citizens on the other. The latter right has something to do with the role citizens play in the whole process of government, their sense that the government is there to serve them and it is their job to monitor it. None of this suggests why publishers should be protected by a fundamental constitutional right, rather than cobblers or hotelkeepers. The more plausible connection is that between protecting the press and protecting citizens from oppression through censorship. The citizens have a need to know and hear printed opinions, just as they have a need to get together and talk, if they are to do their civic duty and live by their consciences. However, this ambiguity in the language of the First Amendment, this way of speaking of the press as if publishers per se are protected and not the free exchange of opinion, seems never to have been cogently dealt with by the courts, and it perennially causes problems, as it does in the present case.

The main point here is that if the amendment is understood to protect publishers as a special form of business protection, then it has no particular moral weight; business protections and trade restrictions may change with the times and do, and a business may seek protection for some political reason or other without invoking the First Amendment or any basic constitutional values.

Another problem with the *Roth* argument is that it invites the comparison of pornography with art, thereby suggesting that good art is more entitled to protection than bad. Good art presum-

---

[14]I include films in this argument, since they, like the press, deal with fiction and pornographic materials as well as with information.

ably should survive lack of social value; bad art shouldn't. But what validity is there in this idea? It invites the comment that the degree of badness is relative and may well be a matter of taste, that history has shown . . . and so on. A more important point is that bad literature—bad essays on politics, appealing to weak and unworthy motives of a reader—*are* surely protected by the First Amendment. And bad political art too. Then why not the poor-quality stuff called pornography? The case made in *Roth* for restricting pornography is worse than unconvincing: it provides ground for a kind of moral repression that both the Constitution's framers and Mill would abhor. We still have to explain what is bad about pornography that is not bad about bad literature and bad art in general.

III

Joel Feinberg's use of "pornography," he says, is "purely descriptive"; he uses the term to refer to "sexually explicit writing and pictures designed entirely and plausibly to induce sexual excitement in the reader or observer."[15] According to this definition, pornography is a genre of materials of an erotic sort, some of which may be objectionable while the rest is not. Some Japanese prints or Indian murals could be described as pornographic and still appreciated as art by this characterization, for "pornography" is used in a morally neutral way. But since we are not concerned at the moment with erotic materials that are not offensive, I propose to use "pornography" as a pejorative term, which is to say in the way Feinberg would speak of *offensive* pornography. In response to the objection that the word is (most) commonly used in a descriptive and neutral way, I suggest that many ordinary people, including many feminists, commonly use it in a pejorative way, and that in much ordinary speech to call something pornographic is to say

[15]Feinberg, "Pornography and the Criminal Law," p. 110. Ann Garry writes that couples might watch pornographic films as they watch "old romantic movies on TV" ("Pornography and Respect for Women," *Social Theory and Practice* 4 [Summer 1978]: 395–421; reprinted in *Applying Ethics,* ed. Vincent Barry [Belmont, Calif.: Wadsworth, 1985], p. 110).

that it is offensive.[16] That is sufficient justification for using the term in this way.

It needs to be pointed out that to say that pornography is objectionable is not to demonstrate that it should be controlled. Many things that people do and say are acknowledged to be bad, including being unfaithful to one's spouse, misusing and deceiving friends, neglecting elderly parents, and lying. But we don't have laws against these things. As Feinberg says, in many respects "the Court has interpreted [the Constitution] . . . to permit responsible adults to go to Hell morally in their own way provided only they don't drag others unwillingly along with them."[17] Such interpretations constitute a formidable defense against controls.

Though pornography may be objectionable in various dimensions (and I believe it is), I will focus on only one kind of objection that I claim to have moral weight. I will substantiate the claim that there *is* such an objection by citing expressions of it. Then I will defend the claim that this kind of objection should carry enough legal weight to justify the control of the objectionable materials. Last, I will argue that such control is quite compatible with the Constitution and the First Amendment and, finally, John Stuart Mill.

The objections I focus on are those expressed by women against certain representations of women in sexual situations:[18] objections against representations of women "being raped, beaten or killed for sexual stimulation," and women enjoying brutal sexual treat-

---

[16]There is a problem with using "obscenity" to do the work of "objectionable pornography." First, there is no more a generally accepted definition of obscenity than there is of pornography. But also an invocation of the broader category doesn't clarify anything and can be a positive hindrance, widening the discussion to matters that are not offensive in the same dimension and deflecting the effort to clarify the issue of why we should control pornography.

[17]Feinberg, "Pornography and the Criminal Law," p. 133.

[18]Certainly objections other than the demeaning of women can be raised against pornography: the exploitation of children is an important case. The argument for controlling child pornography, however, will not be patterned on the one I propose here. It is tempting to argue (as I did at first) that a symmetrical objection might be made by men against a kind of pornography that demeans them; but Christine Littleton has convinced me that against the current background, no really symmetrical situation in which men are similarly demeaned is imaginable. Their objection would therefore have to be different.

ment, usually at the hands of men. One pornography model demands censorship of "all pornography which portrays torture, murder, and bondage for erotic stimulation and pleasure."[19] What is objectionable is not just the representations but the lack of a context in which they are understood to be reprehensible and condemnable. Without some such context. the representations carry the message that such treatment of women is all right. This is one kind of objection.

Another model protests against the circulation of any representation "that reduces women to passive objects to be abused, degraded, and used in violence against women, because now every woman is for sale to the lowest bidder and to all men." She adds that a government that protects this kind of image making expresses "an ideology of women as sexual objects and nothing else."[20] A related criticism was made by Gloria Steinem: "[Pornography's] message is violence, dominance, and conquest. . . . If we are to feel anything, we must identify with conqueror or victim." It is a poor choice for women: "we can only experience pleasure through the adoption of some degree of sadism or masochism. . . . We may feel diminished by the role of conqueror, or enraged, humiliated, and vengeful by sharing identity with the victim."[21]

These quotations illustrate one general kind of objection made to pornography. That it is objectionable in these respects is an

---

[19]Diana Russell with Laura Lederer, "Questions We Get Asked Most Often," in *Take Back the Night*, ed. Lederer, p. 25. Russell adds that "pornography is detrimental to all women" (p. 29). A similar complaint from another pornography model includes this observation: "The misogyny I see today is so blatant and so accepted as a matter of fact that when we challenge it, we're seen as irrational or bad sports. . . . We're training little girls and boys to view sadomasochistic behavior as normal. . . . To me the acceptability of pornography is the clearest statement about the acceptability of women-hating and of women's real place in society" ("Then and Now: An Interview with a Former Pornography Model," in ibid., p. 70).

[20]"Testimony against Pornography: Witness from Denmark," ed. Diana E. H. Russell, in *Take Back the Night*, ed. Lederer, pp. 84–85.

[21]Gloria Steinem, "Erotica and Pornography: A Clear and Present Difference," in *Take Back the Night*, ed. Lederer, pp. 37–38. A similar voice is Andrea Dworkin's: in pornography, she says, "a woman's sex is appropriated, her body is possessed, she is used and she is despised: the pornography does it and the pornography proves it" (*Pornography: Men Possessing Women* [New York: Putnam, 1979], p. 223).

inference I make from the facts that (1) people do make vehement objections to it and (2) they see the offense as a moral one, concerning the respect due any individual.

I emphasize that although I take it for granted that pornography deals with human sexuality, I am not defining it, although many writers consider a definition crucial for a coherent argument.[22] There is a variety of erotic material that could be called pornographic, and whether we call something pornographic or not will depend in part on whether people find it seriously objectionable. But my argument isn't meant to fit all varieties of such material.[23] I am testing only one dimension of objectionability against the First Amendment defense with the claim that it has moral weight.

My partial characterization is this: some pornography is objectionable because it is perceived as seriously degrading and demeaning to women as a group. This characterization draws on the fact that the materials are perceived by women as representing them as inferior or less-than-human beings to be used by others in sexual and sadistic ways.[24]

Now, why should we take this complaint seriously, so seriously

[22]Helen Longino defines pornography as "*verbal or pictorial explicit representations of sexual behavior . . . that have as a distinguishing characteristic the degrading and demeaning portrayal of the role and status of the human female . . . as a mere sexual object to be exploited and manipulated sexually*" ("Pornography, Oppression, and Freedom," pp. 42, 43; italics are Longino's). But it turns out that Longino sees in pornography more than sexual manipulation and abuse of women; pornography, she says, contains also a recommendation that women be treated in this way. "What makes a work a work of pornography . . . is not simply its representation of degrading and abusive sexual encounters, but its implicit, if not explicit, approval and recommendation of sexual behavior that is immoral, i.e., that physically or psychologically violates the personhood of one of the participants." Andrea Dworkin traces the word's origins to "the graphic description of women as vile whores" and says that the word still has the same meaning (*Pornography*, p. 200).

[23]Michael Krausz, in correspondence with me, proposes that some materials are offensive in portraying human sexuality without being demeaning to any group in particular. It isn't clear to me that such materials are pornographic, but in any case their control would rest on a different moral objection. The general question whether a definition of pornography is needed is discussed further below.

[24]Edmund Cahn expresses a common response to such objections as I make here when he says that "the sense of injustice may be and frequently is applied mistakenly" (*The Sense of Injustice* [New York: New York University Press, 1949], p. 184). I would say that while our perceptions differ, people's moral objections are important moral data. For the importance of moral objection, see chap. 6, below.

as to control a class of printed and pictorial materials? I hold that such complaints are the stuff of a serious moral issue.

Let us see how the reasoning works. Where is the moral problem? Who is to blame that the speaker was a pornography model? Presumably she chose to be one and her choice—*volenti,* as Feinberg argues—applies to her as well as to the consumers. But this answer is not clearly adequate. The complaint is against the role in which women are portrayed, not against the working conditions, as it were.

The perception that one is being demeaned and that sanction is given to one's mistreatment—to mistreatment as a means to sexual satisfaction here—is a complaint that touches an important moral nerve. It offends basic moral ideas, in particular the Kantian one that everyone should be treated with dignity and respect and not used as a means to another's end. The complaint or objection needs therefore to be taken seriously. That is the first inference.

But several questions leap to mind. First, what determines that this complaint justifies—or lays the foundation for justifying—control of the objectionable materials? Does just any group have the license to insist that laws be changed to improve that group's image? How is the line to be drawn so as to prevent censuring of political caricatures, for instance?

The answer to this question is complicated but contains a general point. If respect for individuals is an important community value, then complaints by any group that their members are demeaned by some vehicle or other *must* have some weight. Such complaints must be addressed by the community seriously, for otherwise the value of respect is immediately and automatically undermined. The message conveyed that it doesn't matter if these people—members of this group—are demeaned suggests that some people are less important than others.

Therefore the answer to the question whose complaints count is that *any* complaint by *any* group that its members are not treated with respect deserves and needs to be treated seriously. To treat such complaints seriously isn't to concede automatically that the complainers *are* treated with disrespect, or that the changes they want should be made. But at issue is not which is the right and which the wrong side of the question; justice doesn't have to be conceived in this way. The issue is the need to deal seriously with the complaint, the need to discuss it in a serious way and then either answer it or act upon it. Ignoring it, laughing at it, and dismissing it are self-incriminating responses that tend to undermine the trust that the emphasis on respect helps to guard.

An underlying theme here is that *if* respect is valued and presumed to prevail in the society, then the respect given one group cannot be casually evaluated by the perception of other groups. What respect for all others amounts to cannot be defined by a single authoritative group, say the group of the majority; the relation of this point to the pornography issue is explored below. Therefore if a number of members of some group perceive their treatment as demeaning, that is prima facie evidence that there is a problem.[25] And given the seriousness of the matter, the rest of the community must take it seriously either by answering it or by making changes.

I conclude that although there may be different ways of responding to pornography and alternatives to control of such materials, this kind of complaint cannot be lightly dismissed. It needs to be handled in terms of the respect felt to be accorded the complainants by the rest of the community. One way the complaint against pornography by women is *not* addressed is by reference to the First Amendment and the possible "slippery slope" of censorship.

IV

Granted that there is a prima facie reason to think women are demeaned by pornographic materials, how does censorship become justified? Isn't some other means to deal with it available and wouldn't that be preferable? The answer is that of course it's possible and other means may be preferable, for there certainly are dangers in permitting one group to control what others may read

[25]Such perceptions by a large number of people—by most members of the group —would certainly suggest that there is a problem; but what about a small number, what about only one? Then one may have to make a tough moral compromise, but I concede that compromise may be necessary in any case.

or see. It is not my thesis that censorship of pornography is the only answer to the moral complaint or that it should be invoked lightly. In fact, it might be invoked as a last resort when such moral protests are raised. But censorship is one answer, and my aim is to show that the justification for using it is not rebutted by an appeal to the First Amendment. Whatever answer is given, that answer needs to address the moral objection to the way treatment of women is represented. The establishment of guidelines for sexual representations might be a solution. Must we decide in general which kind of response is best? I propose rather that there is no theoretical and final answer, but that an acceptable response will take serious account of the perceptions of the objecting group.

One has to ask, however, whether there isn't a danger in appealing to the moral standards of any one group when laws are formulated. As Mill suggests, shouldn't anyone have the right to live anyway he wishes? Isn't experimentation generally a good and not a bad thing?

One kind of answer to the libertarian would relate a society to a "moral community," showing that morals and laws must be joined together. Harry Clor and Patrick Devlin each defend such views, the former defending a restrained use of censorship, the latter a freer use.[26] The problem with such views is that they are too broad. What is the "moral community" and where is it to be found? Is it represented by the majority? If so, then surely moral

---

[26]Clor argues that in the libertarian view "there is no community. Society is made up of a variety of 'communities'—the masochistic, the sadistic, . . . [etc.], which are entitled to equal social status." Such a community has lost its value, Clor thinks; the government has a clear obligation to prevent the development of such a state. It "cannot afford to be neutral toward a perception . . . which undermines its efforts to make of man something more than a creature of elemental passions and sensations." Censorship, used with restraint, is quite justifiable "for the promotion of public standards of civility which our democracy needs" *Obscenity and Public Morality.* [Chicago: University of Chicago Press, 1969], pp. 200, 242, 204). Devlin holds that "the government of a state rests upon the moral virtue of its subjects. The law cannot make people good; it can only punish them for being bad or at least discourage them." The function of the criminal law, he argues, is "to protect the citizen from what is offensive or injurious . . . ." Society "is held by invisible bonds of common thought," part of which is a common morality. "This bondage is part of the price of society; and mankind, which needs society, must pay its price" (*The Enforcement of Morals* [Oxford: Oxford University Press, 1965], pp. 83, 10).

constraints are worse than paternalistic: they are downright tyrannical, as Mill said.

Even though the complaint of women against pornography cannot be dismissed by appeals to freedom of the press, why shouldn't Mill's argument for freedom apply here? Why shouldn't the objection still hold that if women don't want to look at pornographic pictures or film, they shouldn't look? So long as there is "reasonable avoidability" and people can avoid pornography if they want to, where, as Feinberg argues, is the offense? "When the 'obscene' book sits on a shelf, who is there to be offended?" If pornography lies between "decorous covers," no one need look at it who doesn't want to. It is only when pornography produces an offense on a par with "shame, or disgust, or noisome stenches" (however they would translate in this case) that the law may justifiably interfere. That is to say, pornography should be restricted only when it becomes a nuisance difficult to avoid.[27] To restrict it on other grounds would be to engage in moral paternalism. It would be to set standards for those who enjoy pornography in order to save them from themselves.

This protest, however, misses the point. The felt insult and indignity that women protest is not like a noise or bad odor, for these are group-neutral and may offend anyone, while pornography is felt to single women out as objects of insulting attention. There is a clear division in the community here, unlike the division between people who mind an odor very much and others who can ignore it. The question of how the rest of the community should respond to the perceived debasement that women feel is not analogous to the way the community should treat people particularly sensitive to and offended by certain smells. There is a democracy with respect to smells but with pornography there is a felt hostile discrimination.

V

One way to deal with objections to pornography has been to appeal to a typical member of the community, an "average

[27]Joel Feinberg, *Rights, Justice, and the Bounds of Liberty* (Princeton: Princeton University Press, 1980), pp. 87, 89.

man" who can judge as a representative of the rest whether some material is sufficiently objectionable to warrant restriction.[28]

But there is an internal logical difficulty in this appeal. The "average man" is understood not to be a woman, as is clear from the way the perceptions of the average man are viewed. *Roth,* for instance, speaks of the "appeal to prurient interests"; but such interests are surely interests predominantly of men, not of women. Feinberg, too, speaks to public nudity in terms of "the conflict between these attracting and repressing forces, between allure and disgust," and again leaves the impression that he is speaking of general human reactions while those he describes are characteristically male reactions.[29] Other writers refer carelessly to the "effects" of pornography—sexual arousal or even criminal behavior—in such a way as to suggest that *all* people are included when in fact the effects referred to are specifically effects that pornography has on men.[30]

The premise is essential to my argument that pornographic materials may be seen differently by one group than by another. They may be felt as insulting by one group but inoffensive to another, as seriously demeaning by one and silly by another. An analogy can be drawn with the different perceptions of blacks and whites, or of Jews and Gentiles, regarding certain materials: blacks may find demeaning an image that others think innocuous. It is crucial for my argument that such differences in perception be acknowledged as a social reality, and that our understanding of what it is to treat everyone with respect allow for such differences in the *perception* of respect. It is important, in short, that we do not assume that there is one Everyman view, with the only question being which view that is. Only by respecting different perceptions about what is demeaning will we see that there may be a reason to limit materials that some group—even the largest—finds unobjectionable.

There is a further curious twist in the idea that there is an "aver-

---

[28]This was basically the tack taken in Roth v. United States.

[29]Feinberg, *Rights,* p. 87.

[30]Haney, for instance, writes: "Like the [drug] addict, the man or woman who depends upon pornography has lost control of his or her life. Like the addict, such a person is sick" (*Comstockery in America,* pp. 66–67). The phrase "his or her" does not convince us that pornography's addicts are commonly women.

age man" who can judge whether some materials are offensive and obscene, a man such as the "rational man" of English law or the "man in the jury box," as Devlin calls him, someone who expresses "the view" of the society.[31] For presumably when such a person is called upon to judge the offending material, he is to judge it from his own character and conscience. And of course his character will influence what he finds: a man of very strong character may find pornography only mildly or not at all objectionable, a man of weaker character will find it has an influence on him but not in consequence call it objectionable, an "average man" will fall somewhere in between. So sound judgment is difficult to come by.

But not only does a man's character influence his perception; the perception he expresses—his judgment as to the offensiveness of lewd materials—reflects back upon his character. Suppose he says that some materials are very provocative and could lead a viewer to do wicked things. He is testifying not only against the materials but also about his own susceptibility, and thus indirectly incriminating himself. We are told something about his own weakness if he sees pornography as dangerous. He is testifying about his character.

The result is that a bias is built into the testimony of the "average man" and particularly of the "right-minded man" regarding the offensiveness of pornography. A man—even a right-minded one—cannot judge that materials are "corrupting" without revealing his own corruptibility. And so there is pressure both on men who are strong and on men who are not so strong to find pornography harmless. On the other side, a person who objects to it is likely to be characterized as "often . . . emotionally disturbed," "propelled by [his] own neurosis," or a "Comstock."[32]

Given that there is a connection between a man's testimony about pornography and his character, should men who are weak and susceptible be consulted? That would be paradoxical: such people can hardly be counted on to give any reliable testimony.

[31]Devlin, *Enforcement of Morals,* p. 15.

[32]The first characterization comes from William Lockhart and Robert McClure, "Literature, the Law of Obscenity, and the Constitution," *Minnesota Law Review* 38 (March 1954): 320; the second is from William O. Douglas's opinion in Ginzberg v. New York, 20 L. ed. 2d 195 (1968), at 213; both are cited in Clor, *Obscenity and Public Morality,* p. 116.

But a particularly upright and conscientious man (say a respected judge) is not qualified either, for he may be unable to see any problem. And the ordinarily upright but susceptible man may be reluctant to reveal his weakness. Then whose judgment should be given weight? Given the lack of any "objective" or authoritative spokesman for the whole society, there's only one sensible answer.

If blacks are in a position to say what is demeaning to them, why shouldn't women's voices be heard on the pornography issue? Not because they are truly "disinterested" parties and therefore qualified as authorities. On the contrary; I have been arguing that there are no disinterested authorities, no "objective" representatives of the moral community. And if one group were acknowledged to be completely disinterested in regard to sex or disinterested in regard to heterosexuality, *that* would be no qualification but the contrary. The objectionability of pornography cannot be assessed in this way; there is no analogue here to the "average consumer" who might represent the whole community in judging a retailing policy.

The reason that women should be viewed as particularly qualified is their charge that pornography is an offense against *them*. That charge puts them in a morally authoritative position, just as blacks are in such a position in regard to racial insults and Jews in regard to anti-Semitic humiliations. Then we need only to add that a complaint of this kind demands to be addressed somehow. It does not follow what we should do.

What lies behind our invocation of an "average man" in regard to such issues is a powerful tendency to treat pornography—and other ethically colored issues—in androgynous terms. But common sense tells us that where sexuality is central, an androgynous point of view, even if there were one, would be irrelevant. Without sexuality and sexual difference, sexual attraction and sexual polarity, no pornography issue would ever arise. Therefore to treat the issue in terms of universal principles that hold objectively—atomistically—for all beings alike is to perpetrate a kind of legal comedy.[33]

[33]Catherine MacKinnon writes of the bias of gender perspectives on pornography as if we should be able to accommodate the two views without difficulty: "Not a Moral Issue," *Yale Law and Policy Review* 2 (April 1984). 327–34. I argue differently in my discussion of androgyny and sex equality in *Equality and the Rights of Women* (Ithaca: Cornell University Press, 1980), chap. 1.

VI

Feinberg questions Justice William Brennan's argument in *Roth* by asking, "What is the alleged 'state interest' that makes the unobtrusive and willing enjoyment of pornographic materials the state's business to control and prevent?"[34] What is the positive ground for interference?

This demand is legitimate and it needs to be answered in full. Even if a moral argument such as I have outlined can be made for control of pornography, how can the moral argument be translated into constitutional terms? If controls are justified, their justification should answer Feinberg's question. The need to protect respect may be clear but the means for protecting it are not. Is there an analogy or a precedent to guide us.?

I will argue at a common-sense level, not meaning to interpret the notion of "state interest" in its technical legal sense. Given that respect for persons is an important constitutional value, I propose to show a strategy that connects respect with controls on pornography, to show that the means, the logical path, is there already and has no need to be newly cut. The connection between respect and constitutional action has been made already.

What we need here is reasoning somewhat like that in *Brown* v. *Board of Education*. There the Court decided that educational facilities—equal "with respect to buildings, curricula . . . and other 'tangible' factors"—might nevertheless be unequal in an important sense. And one of the reasons they might be counted unequal was (as one summary puts it) that "to separate [children] from others . . . solely because of their race generates a feeling of inferiority as to their status in the community that may affect their hearts and minds in a way unlikely ever to be undone."[35] Such an institution

---

[34]Feinberg, "Pornography and the Criminal Law," pp. 132–33.

[35]This paraphrase is Gerald Gunther's, in *Constitutional Law: Cases and Materials*, 9th ed. (Mineola, N.Y.: Foundation Press, 1975), p. 715. Gunther goes on to quote an earlier decision in the Brown case which referred to the effect of segregation on a child's motivation and its "tendency to [retard] the educational and mental development of negro children." In this connection also see Edmund Cahn, "Jurisprudence," 30 *N.Y.U. Law Review* 15 (1955); he justifies the Brown decision by speaking of the humiliating treatment of any group as "morally evil."

with the "sanction of law" which thus produces the sense of inferiority of one race is unconstitutional. Respect is not to be measured in the specifics of equipment or curriculum but in the felt implication of inferiority.

In rejecting the justice of "separate but equal" facilities, the Court specifically rejected the protest that any "badge of inferiority" supposed to be implied by segregation exists "not by reason of anything found in the act, but solely because the colored race chooses to put that construction upon it."[36] The insult perceived by blacks has priority over protests of innocence by those charged with offending. It is not crucial that *they* see the offense in the same way. Thus the Court answered by analogy the parallel argument in the pornography issue, that women shouldn't be so sensitive about pornography, for, since no one intends to demean them by it, there is nothing demeaning in it. The parallel answer is that whether there was intent to demean or not is irrelevant.

The argument in *Brown* exemplifies the general form of reasoning we need: an institution that perceptibly demeans some group and represents its members as inferior impugns the claim to equality of those members; in doing so it violates the Constitution's provisions; thus it shouldn't be protected by the federal government. There is no reference here to interpretations of other provisions of the Constitution. Of course the production of pornography isn't an institution; yet insofar as pornography is felt to demean women, its protection by the government under the First Amendment cannot be easily argued.

A caveat is needed here. This argument does not imply that if some group feels demeaned—say, by advertising or institutional arrangements—then censorship is automatically justified. Considerations other than the offense taken are often relevant, some of which may also be moral, and these considerations may overbalance the initial concern for respect. Nonetheless, if what is needed is a line of reasoning that can be used to support control of pornographic materials in the face of First Amendment protections, then such a line is clearly available.

In its general conception this approach accords with Ronald

---

[36]Plessy v. Ferguson, 163 U.S. 537 (1896); Gunther, *Constitutional Law*, p. 709.

Dworkin's view that absolute principles are not what is needed in much legal reasoning. Instead we often need to balance one kind of claim or principle against others. That's the case here. The First Amendment is terribly important to us as a democracy; there's no dispute about that. But it doesn't give the last word on the question "What may a printer print and what may a store sell?" While this approach shows a way to defeat the absolutist claim of the First Amendment and open the possibility of censorship, I have no desire to insist that this course be taken. Other solutions may be preferable.

A number of features of the pornography issue are illuminated by its analogy with race discrimination.[37] For one thing, it would be irrelevant to argue that the demeaning of blacks causes no "injury" and therefore is harmless. What it causes is not the issue: the harm and the offense lie in the practices themselves, and the felt implications for people's status, the light cast upon them as citizens, and the like. Second, just as it would be bizarre to appeal to a group of whites to determine whether racial inferiority is part of the message of segregation, it is curious to consult only men about the offense of pornography. Third, the protest that not all blacks were offended would be taken as specious. Even if many blacks denied that they felt offended, we might still acknowlegdge the vigorous complaints of others. The same holds for women; if some are not offended by pornography, it remains true that many are, and that they see the offense as one against women as a group.

But imagine that the Commission on Obscenity were to make the following argument: If we do nothing in the way of controls, we shall at least be doing nothing wrong.[38] And in such a doubtful matter, with something as important as First Amendment protec-

---

[37]Ronald Dworkin also finds the analogy between expressions of racial hatred and pornography instructive, and remarks that while British law supports the control of incitements to racial hatred, the First Amendment prevents such laws in America ("Do We Have a Right to Pornography?" p. 335).

[38]In a recent federal court decision (American Booksellers Association v. Hudnut) the court took the attitude that the "state interest [in protecting women from degrading depictions that may contribute to discrimination] . . . though important and valid . . . in other contexts, is not so fundamental an interest as to warrant a broad intrusion into otherwise free expression" (quoted in "Anti-Pornography Laws and First Amendment Values," *Harvard Law Review* 98 [December 1984]: 481).

tion at issue, it is better to do nothing. The answer to this argument contains a point often overlooked. When a powerful plea for respectful treatment is addressed by some group to the government, no "neutral" or safe response is possible. Inaction is a kind of action; it signifies toleration of the practice and thus condones it, and in condoning endorses it.[39] Thus to respond to discrimination by arguing that the rights of states and communities are sacred matters, and that one risks a slide down a "slippery slope" if one interferes with them, would be hollow and disingenuous and recognized as such. Similarly I propose that there is also no "neutral" and safe response against pornography's demeaning of women. The issue demands to be addressed by a government that wants *not* to give sanction to the message carried by the images. A state that wants to ensure an atmosphere of respect for all persons has to face the issue in more decisive terms than protection of the First Amendment.

The Constitution does not lead us to believe that our first duty is to protect the First Amendment, as if its application needed no justification, as if it stood above other values, including that of respect for all persons. On the contrary, the rights of free speech, religion, and assembly are protected *because* of the respect due to citizens and their consequent need to be free of government control in certain ways. Freedom of speech is not a fundamental right of a certain kind of enterprise—namely, the press—but stems from a view of humans as morally autonomous.

Therefore it is curious that the Court and libertarian writers show such dedication to freedom of the press as an abstraction, as a principle taken by itself. They deal with it, so it seems to me, as with an ikon of a faith whose main tenets they have forgotten. In this respect theirs is less than a high moral stand. Remarking the irony of this liberal position, one writer comments that "women may rightly ask why the Constitution must be read to value the pornographer's first amendment claim to individual dignity and choice over women's equal rights claim to their own dignity and choice."[40] It is a curious turn of thinking that asks citizens to lay down their claim to respect at the feet of this idol.

---

[39]Chap. 6 below explores this point in a more general way.
[40]"Anti-Pornography Laws and First Amendment Values," p. 46.

Mill warned us about the threat presented by people who think they have the "right" moral perspective and therefore the only "right" answers to serious questions. I agree; we need to beware of all sorts of tyranny, however righteous, well-meaning, and scholarly. For on its side the protection of pornography also may represent a kind of tyranny of opinion, a libertarian tyranny that treats would-be censors as neurotic, misguided zealots and dismisses the moral complaint altogether.

Looked at from the perspective of women, the tolerance of pornography is hard to understand. Equally hard to understand is a point of view that sees the offense of pornography only in terms of its impact on and significance to men, as if the women of the society were irrelevant or invisible.[41] And a more political point can be added. In the light of women's increasing protests against pornography and the proliferation of defenses of it, the issue carries the hazard of generating conflict between two definable groups, roughly between libertarian men on the one hand and outraged women on the other. Given these dimensions, it seems imperative to straighten the arguments and the issue out.

VII

I wish to say something more about the claim that a definition of pornography is needed for the present argument. My argument has followed the tactic of considering certain objections to pornography without a definition of pornography or a criterion as to what objections are valid. While it focuses on objections of a

---

[41]The invisibility of women in much of our thinking and its connection with atomism are discussed in my *Equality and the Rights of Women*, chap. 6. Anthony Woozley argues that a law that made "publishers liable for prosecution for the publication of material which intentionally exploits sex by insulting it, and by degrading the parties to it," would have his support ("The Tendency to Deprave and Corrupt," in *Law, Morality, and Rights*, ed. M. A. Stewart [Dordrecht: Reidel, 1983], p. 221). By talking of "insulting sex" and of the genderless "parties to it," however, he defuses the impact of the feminists' complaint, namely, that it is demeaning of *them* in particular. That is to say, someone who argued, as Fred Berger does in "Pornography, Sex, and Censorship," that it isn't demeaning of sex or of the male participants would still not have dealt with the main objection.

certain kind, those imputing a demeaning character to pornography, it doesn't specify what kinds of things are legitimately objected to or what is really objectionable.

Where could we get a definition of pornography suitable to the role I give it, the role of materials to which a certain vague kind of objection is made? Who should define it authoritatively? Common sense does not endorse the view that legal authorities should set standards for the rest of the community, should decide about the inherent rightness or wrongness of certain pictures, for example; for there might be no strong moral objection to pictures the community calls pornographic, and in the absence of such objection the pictures are not, on my view, pornographic at all. My argument says only that the law *might* justifiably restrict materials that are found insulting in a sexual way, as some materials are by women.

Because the argument is so vague, however, it arouses concern. How will pornographic pictures be distinguished from sexy art, and pornography distinguished from sexy literature—Lawrence's portrayal of Constance Chatterly, for instance? The answer is that the lack of a sharp line is precisely what I allow for, as I allow for changing attitudes. If a public work of art is found insulting by some part of the community that has to look at it, then that is a reason—though only one—for restricting it in some way. If no one objects, then a definition that makes it objectionable would be superfluous and really beside the point.

The terms of the issue as I frame it require only the value of individual respect, which is part of our moral heritage, and the perceptions by members of the community about how they are respected. They therefore allow for changes in customs and tastes, allow that what is demeaning in one time may not be found so in another. When pornography is defined in terms of what is *perceptibly* demeaning, not what is permanently and abstractly so, there is no force to the protest that since "Grandpa was excited even by bare ankles, dad by flesh above the knee, grandson only by flimsy bikinis," no standards can be set.[42] As fashions change, their moral implications change too. So if what was found demeaning once is

---

[42]Feinberg, "Pornography and the Criminal Law," p. 122.

not found so any longer, any problem regarding it has vanished. It is better not to define pornography for all time, or to define it at all.

VIII

One important problem involving the First Amendment still needs to be considered. Suppose we are considering a work that asserts and argues that women are inferior to men, more animal than men, and that they enjoy brutal and sadistic treatment. Imagine such a work: it *asserts* that there is evidence to show that women enjoy a subservient, animal, victimized role, and that this is a correct and proper way to treat women, particularly with regard to sex. Some evidence or other is cited, and it is argued that "equality" is simply inappropriate for beings of this kind, belonging to an inferior level of sensibility or whatever.[43] To be sure, these ideas run directly against the moral idea that an individual, qua individual, has worth; nonetheless, we believe in free pursuit of all manner of debate, moral, scientific, and political, without government interference. So would such a work, purporting to be a scientific study, come under the protections of the First Amendment, or may it be treated like pornography and restricted on the same grounds? Does it differ from the case of hard pornographic pictures and films, and if so how?

On this question I side with the libertarians, for the difference between pornographic pictures and such a report is a signal one for us and for the First Amendment. Mill also would recognize the difference, for he based the freedom of circulation of opinion on the possibility of refuting an opinion that is false and criticizing one that's poorly founded. In his vision an opinion or argument is at continual risk of being refuted, and so it cannot endanger a community where reason and truth are valued. We can draw the distinction by saying that the materials that say nothing are beyond this risk of refutation, and therefore by protecting them we give

[43]Works that assert women's genetic inferiority include Aristotle's *Politics,* Schopenhauer's essay "On Women," and Otto Weininger's *Sex and Character (Geschlecht und Charakter);* none, however, goes so far as my fictional author.

them an immunity to criticism that expressions of opinion do not enjoy.[44] The argument of a work may be objectionable but, like all arguments, it is vulnerable to criticism, while pornography lacks such vulnerability.

This distinction is one I believe the framers of the Constitution would also have recognized. The need for opinions to be circulated freely is part of the respect for citizens which prompted the Bill of Rights. But protection of opinion could be distinguished then as well as now from protection of the press to print what it likes, including offensive pictures.

Defenses of pornography have often turned on leaving this distinction obscure, arguing, for example, "that pornography is intended not as a statement of fact, but as an opinion or fantasy about male and female sexuality." Taken this way, it cannot be prohibited on the ground of being false. At the same time, however, one hears that "correction of opinion depends . . . 'on the competition of other ideas.'" It is a catch-22. Critics of pornography who are told that they should "compete in the marketplace of ideas with their own views of sexuality" while pornography doesn't *present* ideas are placed in an impossible situation.[45] The pictures don't argue for a demeaning attitude toward women in regard to sex or present a view of sexuality; at the same time they *are* demeaning. They don't argue that women enjoy being brutally handled; they show brutality and insinuate the victims' pleasure. While an author would be correct in saying that pornography carries an *implied* message that brutal treatment of women is acceptable, the fact that it is implied rather than explicit is important.[46]

---

[44]Others have made suggestions along this line. See, for example, Frederick Schauer, "Speech and 'Speech'—Obscenity and 'Obscenity': An Exercise in the Interpretation of Constitutional Language," *Georgetown Law Journal* 67 (April 1979): 899–933. So far as I know, however, none have used this distinction together with the value of respect as an argument for control while leaving the First Amendment protection intact.

[45]"Anti-Pornography Laws and First Amendment Values," p. 471.

[46]Longino argues that pornography is a particular kind of speech, but that "speech has functions other than the expression of ideas" ("Pornography, Oppression, and Freedom," p. 52). In treating pornography as a form of defamation or libel, I think, she uses a mistaken paradigm and makes the case against pornography less persuasive.

With this argument I believe Mill would concur, for he consistently maintained the need for respect of differences, including different points of view, and here the difference is one relating to the two sex groups. Respect for persons in all their variety was at the heart of both his libertarianism and his ethical philosophy. However difficult they may be to understand in terms of one's own principles, people are worthy of respect: that was his repeated theme. "Man is not a machine," he wrote, and he surely did not think women are machines for sex.[47] To demean women in the way pornography is felt to do is to treat them as possessions or as servants. So in the end I think that Mill, who argued passionately for women's rights and equal worth and dignity, would find it intolerable to have his views invoked to protect pornography, as they have been.

Although the libertarian case against controls seemed clear-cut and irrefutable, appeal to atomistic ideas cannot solve such a powerfully felt moral issue. If respect for people really exists, it will appear in the way complaints of insult are handled and not only in the propositions used to rebut them. What is needed is not a vision of justice, a simple doctrinaire solution, but a carefully plotted middle way between broad and oppressive controls and reckless liberty. Such an approach will go beyond atomism and deal with injustice in a different and less theoretical way.

---

[47]One needs only to read Mill's essay *The Subjection of Women* (Cambridge: Harvard University Press, 1970) to see a heavy irony in using his arguments to defend pornography from controls. See particularly pp. 42–44, 59.

6

Why Justice Isn't an Ideal

We imagine that justice is an ideal or standard from which injustice departs. That we have such a standard seems necessary, for how else will we recognize a case of injustice when we come upon it? We need justice the way we need a pattern or standard that something can fail to fit. Though the idea is natural, I argue that it's mistaken. And from this mistake others flow, such as antinomies that have no rational solution in the face of morality's demand for one. My approach here involves looking not at the concept by itself but more broadly at its grammar, at the ways and the contexts in which justice is invoked.

I

It seems at first glance reasonable that injustice should be a violation of just rules or a just system, that injustice is a departure and goes contrary to justice, whatever it is. Justice is the prior notion, and it connects with some positive vision.[1] Thus we have

[1]John Rawls, in *A Theory of Justice* (Cambridge: Harvard University Press, 1971), proposes to "derive a conception of a just basic structure, and an ideal of the person compatible with it, that can serve as a standard for appraising institutions and for guiding the overall direction of social change" (pp. 26–27). And in "Justice as Fairness," *Philosophical Review* 67 (April 1958): 178, he speaks of justice as a

the image of the scales that are originally in balance, and imbalance comes as a departure from the original equilibrium. Therefore to redress injustice we must tip the scales back into symmetry.

How do we get the tipping done? By punishing criminals, fining civil offenders, granting claims to damages, and exiling traitors. Public justice, Kant writes, "is just the principle of equality, by which the pointer of the scale of justice is made to incline no more to the one side than the other."[2] The language of debt and repayment goes along naturally with the image of the scales, for both images suggest returning things to some prior condition of rest, or, as Plato would say, of harmony. When that point is reached, nothing further needs to be done. The condition of justice is one of stasis: the account books are in balance and can be closed. Injustice is an upsetting of the balance, which restlessly demands adjustment, while payment restores things to the state of satisfaction and rest.

Yet notoriously the metaphor fails at just this point, that is, the return of things to their original equitable state. For when a criminal is punished—having committed rape or burglary or murder, say—things are *not* returned to their original state.[3] Even though a theft is recompensed, the injury and wrong done cannot be undone; they become a permanent pat of the universe, never to be erased. Thus the condition of stasis, defined as the condition in which the wrong is essentially corrected, is unattainable. The debt cannot be repaid.

"primitive moral notion." But it should be remarked that he also supports the Humean idea that justice depends on circumstances of scarcity, which suggests that it isn't so primitive after all. In the same essay Rawls also writes that justice "is not to be confused with the all-inclusive vision of a good society," and that he will focus on the usual sense of "justice in which it is essentially the elimination of arbitrary distinctions and the establishment . . . of a proper balance between competing claims" (p. 165). This definition is more negative and so closer to mine than Rawls's usual formulations. For an excellent discussion of Rawls's ambivalence on this point, see Michael Sandel, *Liberalism and the Limits of Justice* (Cambridge: Cambridge University Press, 1982), pp. 169–75. The question "What is justice?" invites this way of conceiving the subject, since it points toward an answer cast in a description of some thing or state. In my view, that is to misconceive the grammar of the term.

[2]Immanuel Kant, *The Philosophy of Law*, trans. W. Hastie (Edinburgh: T. T. Clark, 1887), pt. 2, p. 196.

[3]The ineradicability of wrongs and its connection with my view of a just universe are considered in more detail in chap. 7, below.

If there were a debt it could be repaid; and scales out of balance can be brought into balance again. The problem with our reasoning here is a problem with the images we use. The images of debt and scales are unreliable guides to show us the grammar of justice, to show how that concept works. The point at which both fail is the identification of justice with a logically prior, harmonious state of affairs, a state to which theoretically we could return by redressing injustices in an appropriate way.

The view that wrong is inexpungible is defended eloquently by Fyodor Dostoyevsky in *The Brothers Karamazov*. Ivan asks young Alyosha, who plans to enter the priesthood, how there can be so much cruelty in the universe if a good God created it. Take the mistreatment of very young children; you cannot argue that they deserve what they are made to suffer, since they have had no opportunity to sin: they are innocent. Yet children are mistreated in terrible ways in every culture. How do you atone for such acts? If you suppose justice to be a state of harmony, the sufferings of these children "must be atoned for, or there can be no harmony. But how? How are you going to atone for them? Is it possible? By their being avenged? But what do I care for avenging them? What do I care for a hell for oppressors? What good can hell do, since those children have already been tortured? . . . I don't want more suffering."[4] A state of harmony looks like a state unspoiled by wrong or perhaps one where wrong has been atoned for. But atonement may be impossible; wrong cannot be undone. Therefore, once a wrong is committed, harmony or stasis must be forever unattainable. But in that case, what can we say of achieving justice? If justice *were* the state of wrong expunged, its attainment appears to be logically impossible.

This is the puzzle we are driven to by supposing that justice is a state of harmony, an "original state," morally speaking, from which injustice digresses. That idea is what leads us to think in terms of scales and debts.

From a psychological or a social point of view, one can find support for the argument that justice is an original state in the fact that wrongdoing takes place against a background of decency.

---

[4]Fyodor Dostoyevsky, *The Brothers Karamazov*, trans. Constance Garnett (New York: Random House, 1950), p. 254.

Only in a setting where people normally treat one another in respectful ways do hurtful and unjust actions stand out and shock us.[5] Injustice is then seen as diverging from these norms. I don't want to quarrel with this claim. What I contest is the idea that injustice is defined and made recognizable by some positive vision of justice, that the conception of justice is primary.

If wrong is ineradicable, then justice is a poor virtue. What might be preferable would be a state where the need for justice was absent; then the scales would be in balance, for they would be undisturbed. However, we need to look more carefully at the assumptions behind this picture.

II

Instead of fastening our attention on justice the substantive, let us examine some of the contexts where justice is invoked, that is, complaints against injustice. In the face of wrong, justice is demanded and cried out for, and with passion and intensity. "We must have justice!" and "Justice must be done!" are its expressions, and they characteristically have imperative force as well as urgency.

A demand for justice is generally a demand for action in the face of wrongdoing. It is a demand for counteraction, some kind of "corrective." The implication is plain: something must be done because to do nothing would be to accept the wrong and thus to sanction it. To tolerate the wrong is to associate oneself with it. This much is part of our everyday moral understanding.

The need to dissociate oneself from wrong pervades retributive theories of punishment, and is reflected in Kant's remark that a community that doesn't punish its offenders bears some of the guilt on its own head.[6] But what does the demand for justice tell one to *do*? Kant and other retributivists held that what is demanded is punishment of offenders, for only in this way can the innocent

[5]Colin M. Turnbull, *The Mountain People* (New York: Simon & Schuster, 1972), portrays a tribe that has apparently lost all moral values. Among the Ik, no action in particular seems to be wrong; in a sense the whole picture seems both wrong and ungraspable.

[6]In his *Philosophy of Law*, Kant asserts that a community at the point of dissolving itself must punish any remaining offenders or take some of their guilt on itself (pt. 2, pp. 197–99).

dissociate themselves from the wrong and bring about moral restitution. But how can this account be squared with the consequence that nothing can restore the harmony? And what kind of punitive action would restore it in their eyes? We are left in the dark.

If there *were* an ideal of justice which stood as the original standard for denouncing injustice, then the demand might be understood as a demand to move as close as possible back toward the ideal. Even though only small and partial steps could be taken, the route itself would lie clear, for the ideal of justice would define both the wrong and the degree of wrong, would show whether the departure from it was greater or lesser. But, as I argue, we have reason to doubt that there is such a state or ideal. And then how are we to understand the concept of a just response to wrong?

Let us go back one step. The demand for justice appears to be a demand for action, and the necessity of acting lies somehow in the fact that inaction signifies an acceptance of the wrong, which is to say toleration of it. So part of what is demanded is that one go on record as opposing a wrong and expressing abhorrence of it.

Such expression may take a variety of forms, none of them dictated by the wrong itself. In some cultures it may involve ritual cleansing and repentance, with a public ceremony; or the wrongdoer may be publicly condemned; in others the rule will be physical incarceration and punishment. So in its form the requirement seems exceedingly loose. The commission of a wrong, by its description, does not imply that any action of a particular description will be *the* appropriate response to it.

I think that this fact has sometimes been taken to mean that justice and injustice are entirely relative, even conventional, changing from culture to culture and impossible to pin down. This inference stems, however, from an attempt to see justice either as an ideal or as mere convention, while I suggest that neither of these options is right, that in setting these alternatives we misread the way the concept works. Justice is essentially and grammatically "unwilling," as Edmond Cahn put it, "to be captured in a formula" while it remains "a word of magic evocations."[7]

[7]Edmond Cahn, *The Sense of Injustice* (New York: New York University Press, 1949), p. 12.

The inference I draw from the fact that the character of a wrong doesn't dictate the just response is that we are mistaken in expecting it to do so. We are mistaken if we understand a demand for justice as a demand to do something in particular, analogous to a demand to fix the plumbing or replace the car battery. On the contrary, I argue, expressing a demand for justice *is one appropriate response to wrong.*

If this account contains some truth, we should leave behind the idea of justice as scales being tipped into balance and think of the concept in a different way. What I propose to do now is to make this account plausible.

III

The state of things as they were before a given wrongdoing must be preferable to the state afterward. We acknowledge as much when we say that a wrong was regrettable and should never have happened. Thus by simple extension of this move to return to the state before the one when this wrong happened, we can project back to the state before that state, one in which other wrongs had not come about, and see that *that* was preferable to its successor. And so we can follow Dostoyevsky's path, and project a time when our own wrongs had not been committed or even thought of, and envision that state as preferable to the one we find ourselves in now, with many of our actions to be regretted.

Now, I think it is tempting to suppose that we can imagine a time when no wrongs at all had been committed and call that the state of justice: justice is a state in which no wrongdoing exists. Then that state, standing to the present as an infant to a corrupt old man, would function as the ideal of justice we desire and ought to strive for.

But there is something very curious about this procedure. No one would speak of young children as exemplifying *just* behavior, or of childhood as a state that is essentially just.[8] On the contrary,

---

[8]This point emerges clearly from Jean Piaget's work with children, documented in *The Moral Judgment of the Child,* trans. Marjorie Gabain (New York: Macmillan, 1965), though it should be obvious anyway.

childhood is a state of innocence; considerations of justice and injustice have not entered the picture. This state of innocence is clearly preferable, to a moral accountant, to the condition of any real adult world. As Michael Sandel argues, "if the virtue of justice is measured by the morally diminished conditions that are its prerequisite, then the *absence* of these conditions . . . must embody a rival virtue of at least commensurate priority, the one that is engaged in so far as justice is not engaged."[9] On such a view justice can't be a primitive moral notion or have a supreme priority. It is also not merely a "privative" or negative idea, signifying the lack of injustice: that role belongs to the concept of innocence.

But further, innocence cannot be used to show how we should respond to wrong. It can show wrongs in sharp outlines, like figures drawn against a clean, uncluttered background. It can lead us to assess offenders and ourselves through reflection, to regret and perhaps to reform, to shape programs to avoid wrongdoing in the future. But the state of innocence can't show us how to deal with wrongs in general because, being irrecoverable, it doesn't define anything that we can demand. Its information, you might say, is merely negative; it shows what ought not to exist and what ought not to be done, but not how to deal with what does exist and what has been done.

The image of the Fall gives such a picture of innocence: we regret its loss, but our regret doesn't show or lead us to any kind of corrective. It doesn't lead us at all, which is to say that it cannot function as a guide to action or as an ideal.

Therefore a demand for justice is not directly and internally related to a state in which injustice is absent. The concepts of justice and innocence don't grammatically mesh, not directly. But while the two concepts don't engage directly, each stands as a kind of opposite to wrongdoing. On the one hand, wrongdoing signifies the loss of some measure of innocence, as Adam's indulgence in the fruit of the tree of knowledge signifies his loss of purity. Innocence gives an idea of the degree to which our actions depart from what is morally preferable, though it doesn't even hint what to do about it. On the other hand, injustice or wrong contrasts

---

[9]Sandel, *Liberalism,* p. 32.

with justice, in that the latter is conceived as an antidote or corrective to wrongdoing; injustice provokes and demands that correction. Therefore one can order the concepts in a sort of logical chronology, with innocence first, followed by wrongdoing, which in turn provokes the need for a justice.[10] On this view, justice comes into our vocabulary last. And this is my thesis, that justice is not an original notion from which injustice is derived but vice versa, and this fact is what makes it so difficult to say what justice *is*. J. R. Lucas puts the matter neatly: "It is only when somebody's rights and interests are in jeopardy . . . that issues of justice arise. . . . Injustice wears the trousers. And therefore we should . . . adopt a negative approach, discovering what justice is by considering on what occasions we protest at injustice or unfairness." As a positive virtue, he continues, justice appears "flat, without depth or dynamic vigour"; it is a "cold virtue." "But injustice is something we soon get steamed up about."[11]

The ambiguity in the demand for justice helps to explain why efforts to correct wrong may lead to further puzzles and even further injustice. The equation is tenuous.[12] Even under the impetus of acting against injustice, are we sure there is necessarily a net gain when an effort is made to redress it, or might there even be a

[10]A different, nonchronological ordering is given by Schopenhauer, who holds that between good and bad there is an intermediate stage that is the "mere negation of the bad," and "this is *justice*" (*The World as Will and Representation*, trans. E. F. J. Payne [New York: Dover, 1966], vol. 1, par. 66). He may be thinking here that justice is not the creation of some positive good or the recapturing of the good that was destroyed or lost through wrongdoing, but is less than that, something more neutral.

[11]J. R. Lucas, *On Justice* (London: Oxford University Press. 1980), pp. 4–5. Lucas's view differs from mine, for he thinks that by seeing how we respond to such complaints we can discover justice as a positive concept. Edmond Cahn also thinks of injustice in terms of its role as a spur to action. He writes: "Where justice is thought of in the customary manner as an ideal mode or condition, the human response will be merely contemplative, and contemplation bakes no loaves. But the response to a real or imagined instance of injustice is something quite different; it is alive with movement and warmth in the human organism" (*Sense of Injustice*, p. 13). But like Lucas, he doesn't take this response as a serious lead to the grammar of the term.

[12]Sandel observes of this peculiar "equation" that "when fraternity fades, more justice may be done, but even more may be required to restore the moral status quo" (*Liberalism*, pp. 32–33). It may be a long process.

net loss? Only when the conceptual order of justice and injustice is set straight can we understand why we find it so difficult to know how to address wrongdoing.

IV

Various kinds of evidence can be summoned to support this thesis. First, there is the fact that the word "injustice" derives from the Latin word *injuria,* meaning injury. Now it seems clear to me that an injury is not merely something negative, that the term does not signify only a lack or privation. It is not definable, that is, as a lack, with reference to a prior state of wholeness; it has its own positive characteristics.[13] Moreover, it is very difficult to define a prior state of uninjuredness or well-being, so if the identification of an injury were dependent on such a definition, the idea of an injury would be fairly obscure. But common sense suggests that suffering an injury, such as having a broken arm, is not simply the lack of a well-defined prior condition. On the contrary, the injury stands by itself. It can be described as a positive condition and its contrary as negative. as health might be defined as the absence of sickness; and this is something like the grammatical arrangement I argue exists in the case of justice and injustice.[14]

Second, if we look at the mythology of ancient Greece, we discover Dikē, or Justice, in an interesting role. She is daughter to Zeus and "comes to her father when she is offended, sits down beside him, and tells him of the unjust mind of men so that they

---

[13]Acknowledgment needs to be made nonetheless that etymologically the prefix in- in "injustice" does signify the negation of justice, as the same prefix in "injury" signifies the negation of some state in which injury is lacking. But it is clear that that prior state in either case is extremely nebulous and hard to specify, while the "negative" states of injury and injustice are quite specifiable.

[14]A parallel problem arises in the relationship of illness to health—that is, it is more problematic to define health than to characterize a given state of illness. See, for instance, Leon Kass, "Regarding the End of Medicine and the Pursuit of Health," *Public Interest* 40 (Summer 1975): 11–42, and Christopher Boorse, "On the Distinction between Disease and Illness," *Philosophy and Public Affairs* 5 (1975): 49–68; both of these papers are reprinted in *Contemporary Issues in Bioethics,* ed. Tom L. Beauchamp and LeRoy Walters (Belmont, Calif.: Wadsworth, 1982).

pay the penalty."[15] At her report Zeus plans his response.[16] Nothing in this imagery suggests a prior pattern of justice, a positive image, which either one uses. Justice works quite differently here from the idea of a balance, for here injustices precede any divine concern, while the balance conception requires a well-defined equilibrium before one can say that a given situation departs from it. Thus in the absence of such a touchstone or standard, the claim that any situation departed from a just one would be utterly unprovable.

Again, if we think of justice as the restoration of a prior state, then that state must be definable or somehow describable and the remedy specifiable. But nothing suggests that Zeus is restoring any prior state when he acts. " 'Whoever offends and contrives outrages, on them the son of Kronos brings from heaven great bane, hunger and plague', an army is destroyed, the city wall collapses, or ships are lost at sea: such is the punishment of the god."[17] What determines exactly what Zeus will choose to do? Nothing. In sum, the pattern of the mythological account suggests the truth of my claim, that injustice is not conceptually dependent on or defined by a prior idea of justice.

Third, in common life and speech we generally look backward at wrong when we speak about justice. We require just trials, just verdicts, just remedies, just sentences—all things that relate to wrongs already done. Moreover, we demand these things often without any agreement on what we seek or clear idea of what a just remedy would be. Thus the demand for justice may be loud and unanimous while the appropriate response is disputed. And this pattern, too, suggests that our idea of injustice may be sharp while that of its remedy remains fuzzy.

It may be reasonably protested that we do mean something by a just trial, a just verdict, and so on, in a particular case. We are not

---

[15]Walter Burkert, *Greek Religion,* trans. John Raffan (Oxford: Blackwell, 1985), p. 249.

[16]See the account by Hugh Lloyd-Jones in *The Justice of Zeus* (Berkeley: University of California Press, 1971). According to Aeschylus, Zeus is the champion of Dikē, following up her indications of wrongs with a plan of punishment (p. 87). This account is in agreement with Burkert's.

[17]Burkert, *Greek Religion,* p. 249. The inner quotation is from Hesiod's *Works and Days.*

134

simply railing against wrong with vague expressions of moral revulsion. It is true that we want fair trials, and that we have some criteria for such trials, and we want verdicts that are neither too harsh nor too lenient.[18] We want governments to take actions that really address the issues and don't introduce new wrongs. But though we can all agree on these generalities, in particular cases we notoriously disagree about exactly what should be done. We have a need for some morally satisfying response; that is what we demand when we demand justice. But the need isn't the need to see some action under a specific description. It isn't specific, such as a craving for pineapple or artichoke, but ambiguous, such as an appetite for something new and exotic. What satisfies it—or whether anything will—may be unknown. And the demand carries with it no definition or standard to guide us.

There are just and unjust ways of dealing with wrong, and the difference is of enormous moral concern to us. I argue only that the difference doesn't have its source in an abstract ideal or absolute, that nothing dictates in concrete cases how we should go.[19]

Consider Plato, who is often cited as giving an ideal of justice in his *Republic,* a model of a harmonious state that is a reflection of the just soul. Harmony there is a condition of stasis; and therefore it would seem that Plato's theory is just the kind that I have argued cannot be developed. Is there a conflict here? Only if one overlooks the fact that for Plato, the natural condition of both the soul and the state is *dis*harmony, which arises from within the soul and state themselves. Thus Plato tells us that the soul is like a charioteer with two horses, one manageable, the other impetuous and wild, and it is the charioteer's lifelong job to try to keep them together, driving them in coordination to the highest rational plane and

---

[18]It is interesting that Piaget, in seeking to identify children's ideas of justice, proceeds by asking them whether each of various responses to some offense is fair or unfair. It is clear that *an offense* sets the stage for exploring the child's idea of justice and also that the children identify unfair treatment without reference to any positive standard; see particularly *Moral Judgment of the Child,* pp. 298–99.

[19]A. I. Melden seems to me right in saying that just policies are frequently compromises, made when people's demands conflict; see his *Rights and Persons* (Berkeley: University of California Press, 1977), pp. 111–13. It *is* important to respect various concerns and not insist on absolute standards; this argument concurs with my own. If justice were an ideal, it would not be subject to compromise.

harmony. Imbalance and stress and conflict are built into this image of justice, which is anything but stable. In the state, too, Plato doesn't dictate exactly what laws the philosopher-king should lay down; he appears to be willing to leave the shape of just government to a wise man to work out, piecemeal perhaps. So although Plato speaks of justice as a form, and of the philosopher-king as someone who knows that form, his image of the government and its policies is much less tidy and less suggestive of an absolute than we sometimes think.[20]

In Greek tragedy, to cite a last group of sources, it's evident that injustice begins talk about justice and provides the background for it. The gods don't sit and debate the abstract nature of justice. But given a real situation—the misbehavior of a guest to his host in the saga of Oedipus, the killing of a sacred deer in *Iphigenia in Aulis*— *then* the question of response becomes pressing. Think of Antigone, who finds it necessary to do something in response to Creon's order that Polynices not be buried, who takes an action destined to be futile, takes it despite the counsel of the chorus to "be reasonable." However wrong Creon's order was, the chorus insists, no good can come of resisting it. But neither this advice nor the inevitable futility of her action diminishes Antigone's need to oppose Creon. She consults no ideal but only her sense of injustice.[21]

Or consider the fate of Iphigenia, determined by Artemis' indignation together with Agamemnon's intractable ambition. No one

[20]In bk. VII of the *Republic* Socrates reminds Glaucon that "the law . . . is trying to produce [happiness] in the city as a whole, harmonizing and adapting the citizens to one another by persuasion and compulsion, and requiring them to impart to one another any benefit which they are severally able to bestow upon the community, and that it itself creates such men in the state . . . with a view to using them for the binding together of the commonwealth" (Plato, *Republic,* trans. Paul Shorey, in *The Collected Dialogues of Plato,* ed. Edith Hamilton and Hamilton Cairns [Princeton: Princeton University Press, 1961], 519e–520a). Here he leaves the ruler plenty of latitude to decide how he will actually govern. He doesn't specify what laws should be laid down, or how the ruler should be guided in day-to-day problems—except that he should be guided by whatever disharmony exists. I owe to Caitlin Croughan the original and interesting suggestion that in the end Plato's theory does *not* depend on an ideal of justice, despite its connection with the theory of forms.

[21]She is of course guided by the religious demands regarding preparation of the dead for the afterlife and her duty to her brother; but it is clear that she has no general idea of the perfectly just state or a citizen's role in it.

would suggest that the oracle's demand is formed after an ideal of justice. Who would argue that forcing Agamemnon to sacrifice his youngest and favorite daughter is the right and just response for Artemis to make? Or who would argue that once Iphigenia is sacrificed, some recognizable state of justice is restored? The goddess's action isn't derivable from a pattern, the pattern of a just state of things. Even in the shadow of a demand for justice, then, the just response is undetermined, and not only for humans, who notoriously disagree, but for the gods as well.

V

We have the clear conviction that some actions are just and others unjust. It is generally thought unjust, for example, to turn a violent criminal back to mingle with other citizens. How do we arrive at such conclusions if we have no standard? The question is treacherous, for it leads back toward the assumption that justice must be some kind of ideal. What measure, what method *do* we use to determine what is just? Whatever it is, one wants to argue, let us call *it* our idea of justice. But the question is wrong because it implies that we do consult some measure or standard. It is true that we talk as if we did, talk about an eye for an eye sometimes as if it were a usable rule, and of just deserts as if we had an unequivocal standard to measure the justice of deserts. That's the reasoning behind the *jus talionis*—the right to give back an injury similar to one inflicted.

But when we come to decide what to do in particular cases, matters aren't this simple. We disagree about what is deserved and decline to give equal injury for injury done.[22] Then how do we decide on a just and fair response to wrongdoing? The same way we decide on other courses of public action and moral response; that is, by taking many factors into account and forging a response that tries to balance them. Which is to say, the question has no theoretical answer.

The temptation persists all the same to say that justice must be

[22]Chap. 7, below, discusses the dialectic of wrongdoing and punishment.

some kind of thing, even if it isn't an ideal or abstract form. Thus Edmond Cahn, after acknowledging the primacy of injustice, holds that justice is "the *active process* of remedying or preventing what would arouse the sense of injustice."[23] But this characterization is inadequate: if one said that some euphoriant or sedative would take care of the feelings of injustice, this solution would be thought spurious. What is wanted is a "process of remedying or preventing" *that relates to the wrong*. But now the original question has been displaced by another: What active process, if any, will appropriately prevent the sense of injustice from being aroused? The remedy needs to address the injustice and not only the sense or feelings aroused in us. Therefore while it rightly leaves behind an ideal of justice, this characterization makes justice into a different substantive, which in turn needs to be characterized.

I propose then that a demand for justice is not a demand for anything specific, not even for a process. It is unlike a demand for price controls or for higher educational quality, which specify definite and definable results. A demand for justice implies no such goal.[24]

But although it isn't a demand for action under a particular description, it also isn't trivial or expendable; it ranks high among our moral concerns. Dworkin says that "the single most important social practice we have [is] the practice of worrying about what justice really is." But such a statement is ambiguous: does it imply that the question has an answer that can eventually be found, or does it mean that the importance of the practice lies in the search rather than in any specific end? For it is true that the search for justice forces us to raise deep questions about our institutions and customs and values. And the search is never finished; to quote

---

[23]Cahn, *Sense of Injustice*, pp. 14–15.

[24]A rough parallel to this situation seems to exist in the concept of peace. Muriel Rukeyser remarks perceptively that "if we look for the definitions of peace, we will find, in history, that they are very few. The treaties never define the peace they bargain for: their premise is only the lack of war" (*The Life of Poetry* [New York: A. A. Wyn, 1949], p. 222). Thus she seems to be saying that peace is often treated as a "privative" concept, as the absence of its opposite. However, she does not concede that this is the logic of the concept, but challenges us to give it a positive content: "not the lack of war, but a drive toward unity," a creative effort, "fierce and positive," toward "completeness" (pp. 229, 227).

Dworkin again, "justice is our critic, not our mirror."[25] Justice's relations to our demands and questions and unending dissatisfaction are among its grammatical features.

Although injustice cannot be defined by a form of justice, one positive fact about it is prominent. In the face of wrongdoing it is mandatory to express moral objection. Outrage is required of any person of moral dimension, anyone expecting respect as a member of the moral community, for silence and complacency in the face of wrongdoing are themselves a kind of moral offense. Thus the capacity for righteous indignation is intimately related to a person's moral substance.[26] This is to say that there is no room for moral neutrality in the presence of wrong, for neutrality signifies a toleration of wrong. It is for this reason that Kant concludes that even a society on the point of dissolution must punish its last offender; otherwise the members risk condoning and thus "participating" in the offense.[27]

People must dissociate themselves from an offense. But if their response is not guided by the offense itself and if we have no model of justice to guide us, then in some cases all options may be flawed; there the demand may lead to nothing. Where no action is satisfactory, the protest lies useless, ineffectual, in the air. And then what is the point of demanding? It's easy to complain, to demand, one may say; *doing* is what is essential. That is why injustice wears the trousers, as Lucas put it. Thus my argument, in attaching moral value to the demand itself, may be seen as handmaiden to inaction, and inaction may be seen as toleration of injustice in the end.

When an appropriate course of action is clear and is not taken, an expression of abhorrence at the wrong and a demand for justice do

---

[25]Ronald Dworkin, "What Justice Isn't," in *A Matter of Principle* (Cambridge: Harvard University Press, 1985), p. 219.

[26]Werner Jaeger reports that Greek thinkers and the peripatetics in particular held the capacity for moral indignation to be essential to morality; Aristotle proves the connection in Fragment 80, according to Jaeger; see his *Paideia: The Ideals of Greek Culture* (New York: Oxford University Press, 1945), 1:124. The role of moral indignation in punishment is discussed in chaps. 7 and 8, below.

[27]Kant, *Philosophy of Law*, pt. 2. p. 198. The case of Kitty Genovese, who was repeatedly attacked and eventually killed while more than thirty neighbors watched from their windows and did nothing, is a good example of a situation that calls for action; we even want laws to *make* such bystanders do something. Their passivity itself signifies a kind of misdeed.

not absolve one of the charge of tolerating wrong. But in the case of many social and individual wrongs, no such course of action may be open. The injustice may be of such a complex kind, or the means of redressing it so meager, that we can do no more than protest. The assumption that every wrong must have some appropriate just response is made of the same stuff as the assumption that justice must be an ideal. We think it must be so; we are unwilling to see that it isn't. In the case of many awful injustices—child abuse, for instance—it is notoriously difficult to see what we can do practically and morally without creating another wrong. My conclusion is that we are inclined to think that a sense of justice can inform our actions in a way that moral experience shows it cannot.

When we look at justice through the demand for justice, we get a picture of how the concept works. We see it in action, as it were, performing its function. This approach is like Wittgenstein's when he tells us that it is part of the grammar of the word "chair" that *this* is what it means to sit on a chair.[28] How (one wants to protest) can sitting on a chair—a certain kind of performance—be part of the grammar of the substantive "chair"? Surely the grammar of "chair" needs to represent it as a thing; and a thing can be used in one way or in others, or not used at all, and remain unaffected throughout. But Wittgenstein admonishes us not only to look at a noun as if it showed us the metaphysical status of what it means. Rather we need to think of the way the word is woven into grammatical patterns—orders, questions, protests, expressions of our states—and these patterns integrated into our lives. When we have seen how it works, understood its grammar, we will have grasped its meaning.

The lives into which the language is woven are, furthermore, the lives of creatures with certain tendencies, feelings, affinities, capabilities, physical requirements, and so on. In terms of the lives of such creatures patterns of grammar have their place, and in terms of these patterns the elements (nouns, verbs, etc.) take on their sense. So when we consider the kind of meaning "pain" has, for example (is it private? do we really know about the pains of

---

[28]Ludwig Wittgenstein, *The Blue and Brown Books* (New York: Harper & Row, 1958), p. 24.

others?), we need to look at the grammatical patterns of pain's expression. These expressions include some that are merely cries or moans, sounds such as humans naturally make. Then we need to see how these expressions and verbal patterns fit into the lives of creatures like us—creatures who can both speak and cry, ask for help, express gratitude and relief, and so on. Following this route, we will begin to see the large and complex grammatical picture of which this noun forms a part, and then we can stop focusing on the pain, as if it were an elusive object that we need only put our finger on.

In a similar way, a focus on justice as a substantive gets us deeper and deeper in trouble. What is it if *not* an ideal? We try to keep our gaze fixed on it while we try to understand it. But to ask the question in this way is to overlook the fact that a demand for justice *is* a response to wrong, and is of a piece with expressing abhorrence at wrong. Such forms of expression are primary facts of morality. They express a person's ethical stance, one's standards and awareness of commitments. But more, they often express these things in a way that shows them to be passionately held and profoundly important.

VI

Think of the matter in this way. Imagine a person who uttered judgments of moral condemnation and praise in the same tone of voice as one says such things as "It's half past two" and "Today's Wednesday." This person says, for instance, "That was a frightful thing to do" or "He's a vicious man" or "What an unjust law" in the same unexpressive voice as one says that the dog has been fed. Surely we would find this difficult to understand; and if someone always spoke of such things unemphatically, we would wonder if he or she really understood them. How can one *not* feel offended at this misdeed, how can one speak so calmly? Is the speaker without any moral sensibilities, calloused? But then why use these sentences at all?

Consider this hypothesis: Perhaps the speaker does feel strongly but in general doesn't give expression to personal feelings. Thus the powerful feelings felt regarding this injustice are hidden.[29] The problem with this hypothesis is that it has no support in the circumstances. There is nothing for imagination to get a grip on. Thus the more reasonable alternative is to say that the speaker simply has no feeling about the wrong. But then, what do the utterances mean? Are they hypocritical? What would such a person do, where is the motivation to act? The whole picture of protestations without the feelings that go with them is incoherent.

This example helps to show that the language of condemnation and of praise is an emphatic language, a language of feeling; and powerful expressions of feelings of abhorrence and contempt, admiration and awe, belong to its grammar. If the feelings are subtracted, the authentic meaning is gone. Thus moral condemnation belongs with something besides an objective set of circumstances and requires the involvement of the speaker: a person must *feel* the wrong and be motivated by it to take action if something can be done.[30]

Consider the same issue from another side. Imagine a child brought up by parents who never showed moral shock or revulsion at the actions of others, no matter how awful the wrong. What notion of morality would that child acquire? He never sees repugnance conjoined with the statements "That's terrible," "It was a frightful thing to do," and the like. In this situation it is hard to think that the child would have any idea of morality at all, for

[29]This assumption reminds one of Wittgenstein's challenge to imagine that all the people one sees before one are in terrible pain.

[30]Cahn describes the sense of injustice as denoting "that sympathetic reaction of outrage, horror, shock, resentment, and anger, those affections of the viscera and abnormal secretions of the adrenals that prepare the human animal to resist attack." It involves a fundamental response of our species, he says: "the human animal is predisposed to fight injustice." He relates the sense of injustice to atomism: "The individual man stands at the center of all things, bound by the perspective predicament to his own brief time and narrow place. The sense of injustice gives him a lengthening tether so that he may wander away from self and its setting" (*Sense of Injustice*, pp. 24–25). The sense of injustice broadens a person's horizons by showing the wrongs done to others as attacks on himself; this perspective in turn readies the organism for action. Whether this sociobiological account is right is not important for my argument; however, a sense of injustice does seem to involve people with one another's situations and thus violates the conditions of atomism. But which comes first, the feeling or the larger framework, is also not my concern here. See chap. 9, below.

what has been left out—the involvement of the parents—is what conveys the force of condemnations. Even though the child had learned the sentences and knew when to use them in the sense of knowing the objective situations to which they were appropriate, something crucial is missing from his understanding.

The element of passion is an important aspect of the picture of most moral concepts, I believe, of concepts of praise and admiration as well as of the concept of wrongdoing. Others have proposed this idea, prominently Hume, who held that only some felt response could give moral praise or condemnation its force. And force here means motivation to act; how without feeling something could we be moved to do anything about someone else's wrong?

But the place of justice in Hume's theory is limited. It is a secondary virtue, he argues. "Let us suppose that nature has bestowed on the human race such profuse *abundance* of all *external* conveniencies, that, without any care or industry on our part, every individual finds himself fully provided with whatever his most voracious appetites can want." If we make this supposition, we will see that "every other social virtue would flourish . . . but the cautious, jealous virtue of justice would never once have been dreamed of. For what purpose make a partition of goods, where everyone has more than enough? Why give rise to property, where there cannot possibly be any injury? . . . Justice, in that case, being totally useless, would be an idle ceremonial, and could never possibly have place in the catalogue of virtues." Hume's point is that justice is grounded in social utility and would not otherwise exist, neither the virtue nor the moral sentiment that relates to it. The sense of justice isn't a "simple original instinct" but is derived from injustice and disorder. The role of justice depends on our natures and our problems. "What need of positive law where natural justice is, of itself, a sufficient restraint? Why create magistrates, where there never arises any disorder or iniquity?"[31] It is Hume's view that human nature—those of our tendencies that threaten the

---

[31]David Hume, *Enquiry Concerning the Principles of Morals,* ed. L. A. Selby-Bigge (London: Oxford University Press, 1951), pp. 183–84, 202–3, 205. Rawls also speaks as if without scarcity justice would not arise or be the important value that it is (*Theory of Justice,* p. 128).

interests of the community and of our fellow citizens—establishes the need for justice.

Justice for Hume is not an original passion like benevolence, which needs no ground. It can be imagined not to exist, that is, in a society *in which there is no wrongdoing or injustice*. Despite its derivativeness, however, justice remains a passion of some kind. Hume's account comes very close to mine, in which justice is also associated with a passion, one whose role is to point to a corrective response to wrong. So if there were no injustice to worry us, we would have no reason to speak of justice.[32] Unlike Hume, however, I don't view this qualification as a serious challenge to the final importance of justice.

VII

Taking abhorrence of wrong—of injustice and wrongdoing—as a basic moral phenomenon helps us to understand other facts of moral theory. For one thing, it helps explain why so much of morality deals with what one *ought not* to do, proscriptions, rather than recommendations what to *do*. If it is abhorrent to do wrong, no wonder that as children we are first of all told to avoid doing certain things. We learn "You shall not do this abhorrent, objectionable thing, whatever else you do."

Second, this account explains why guilt is so central to moral life. If a wrong thing is abhorrent, then when *we* do wrong we find our own actions abhorrent. We may even abhor ourselves for doing them.[33] A good thing that we have failed to do has no power over us to compare with that of a wrong thing that we have

---

[32]Hume's view diverges from mine in his idea that social utility must be the "sole origin" of justice. My argument stops with the conclusion that the concept of justice is understandable against a background of injustice. Whether something socially useful can be done in its name is for me a separate matter, while for Hume a call for justice would seem to be a demand for something that *is* in fact socially useful. Despite this difference, it seems to me that his view, seen in the light of the primacy of injustice and wrong, is both attractive and nearly right.

[33]John Rawls remarks that while feelings of guilt are essential to our humanity, "the moral feelings are admittedly unpleasant" ("The Sense of Justice," *Philosophical Review* 72 [1963]: 299).

done. Without this powerful feeling and its threat, what would our moral existence be like? It is unimaginable.

If the central concepts of our moral language—wrong, injustice, ought not—are negative rather than positive, then the philosophical treatment of morality ought to represent the importance of these negative ideas to us and show us how they function in our lives and what their connection is to action, not focus so much on the positive terms—right, good, virtue, justice—as writers generally do. Such an account would show us the importance of avoiding certain actions, and would show as a consequence that the "moral person" is often not a person notable for heroic or outstanding actions, but one who satisfies his responsibilities conscientiously, perhaps without imagination. We might not call such a person admirable; being moral and being admirable are not the same. We may find such a one dull and straitlaced, tiresome to be around, but his avoidance of wrongdoing is nonetheless an important moral qualification.

The man of virtue, in contrast, often acts in nonstandard, nonprescribable ways. He takes chances in regard to the way things will turn out and the way they will look to others; he is driven by something more than the avoidance of wrong. The virtue of such a man may indeed not be appreciated by observers until much later; that, too, is a chance he takes. His path is not marked out in advance, nor are the reactions of others to his direction. The distinctiveness of such a man and the distinctiveness of his actions may sometimes make him a tragic hero; the risk is a grave one.

In a similar way, I suggest, justice is not prescribable or something with a given form, but a creature of our effort, imagination, and demand. We craft responses to wrong, our purpose being not to satisfy some preconceived picture of justice but to address the snares of injustice.

VIII

In summary, the argument has been that we are mistaken in looking for a positive conception of justice that gives meaning to our talk about it—a pattern or model, an ideal from which injustice is a departure. Justice comes into our speech on the occasion of some injustice or wrong, which brings us to demand it. Justice appears then as an indefinite corrective to injustice rather than something definable in its own right. But how do we know what the corrective to an injustice is, or whether there always is one? We don't know and there may not be. In that case we cannot do any particularly just thing, but we are left with our expressions of abhorrence, moral objection, indignation.

I propose that the abhorrence of wrong is a primary and central notion for morals, but it does not imply that there is any correlative just response. The expression itself is part of what is required; it is a crucial aspect of morality, not an ineffectual show of feeling.

What remains for us to consider is how this "subjective" center of morality is consistent with a nonsubjectivist account of right and justice.

7

Intolerable Wrong and Necessary Punishment

Despite the unspecifiability of justice as a positive concept, we have a deep conviction that punishment of the guilty is mandatory, that justice can exist only if the guilty are appropriately punished. What is the impelling power of this idea? In what sense can there be repayment for wrong?

I

Punishment is said to be justified by the fact that injustice is intolerable and therefore must be answered. It is the wrongdoing itself that justifies punishment, the misdeed that calls for it; no particular view of justice or ethics needs to be invoked. Thus failure to punish on this view *is* failure to oppose wrong. F. H. Bradley writes: "Why . . . do I merit punishment? It is because I have been guilty. I have done 'wrong'. . . . Now the plain man may not know what he means by 'wrong', but he is sure that, whatever it is, it 'ought' not to exist, that it calls and cries for obliteration; that, if he can remove it, it rests also upon him, and that the destruction of guilt, whatever be the consequences at all, is still a good in itself; and this, not because a mere negation is a good, but because the denial of wrong is the assertion of right."[1] A

[1]F. H. Bradley, *Ethical Studies* (London: Oxford University Press, 1952), p. 27.

wrong is something that ought not to exist. It calls to be obliterated. If anyone is able to remove it and fails to do so, the wrong is also partly his.

Bradley believes that to deny or obliterate a wrong is to assert right, that the two are counterpoised, one able to cancel the other, as heat cancels cold and giving cancels taking. This concept reminds us of the balance held by the personification of justice, and of debts and credits in accounts, because paying a debt really does erase it; the debt no longer exists. In a similar way punishment is supposed to nullify and erase wrong. Because wrong is intolerable, leaving it unpaid for is also intolerable. It follows that punishment is both justified and necessary; it is mandatory.

That wrong is intolerable need not imply retributivism. Dostoyevsky, as we saw, thought that while wrong is intolerable, it's also irremediable, and punishment simply brings about more suffering without erasing the wrong. We desire harmony in our world, moral harmony, Ivan argues, but we will not produce it by punishing the wicked. Neither can it be brought about by forgiveness: indeed, the mother of a tortured infant has no right to forgive the torturer of her child: she *dare not,* Ivan argues. "And if that is so, if they dare not forgive, what becomes of the harmony?" Transferring the problem to a higher moral order that squares the books in a heavenly afterlife isn't a credible answer: "too high a price is asked for harmony; it's beyond our means to pay so much to enter" into the paradise promised by Christian theology.[2] There is no way back. Like utilitarian thinkers, he sees punishment as only adding to human suffering. Punishment is not the same as atonement, and neither is forgiveness; so punishment is morally pointless and atonement is impossible. J. L. Mackie expresses the problem as a paradox: "on the one hand, a retributive principle of punishment cannot be explained or developed within a reasonable system of moral thought, while, on the other hand, such a principle cannot be eliminated from our moral thinking."[3]

Utilitarians, like Dostoyevsky, have difficulty with the idea that

[2] Fyodor Dostoyevsky, *The Brothers Karamazov,* trans. Constance Garnett (New York: Random House, 1950), p. 254.

[3] J. L. Mackie, "Morality and the Retributive Emotions," *Criminal Justice Ethics* (Winter/Spring 1982): 3.

wrongdoing by itself justifies punishment. William Godwin, for example, denies that punishment can be measured against wrong: "Delinquency and punishment are, in all cases, incommensurable. No standard of delinquency has ever been, or ever can be, discovered. No two crimes were ever alike. . . . [Therefore it is] absurd, to attempt to proportion the degree of suffering to the degree of delinquency, when the latter can never be discovered." If people recognized that punishment and justice are "in their own nature incompatible," they would abolish punishment altogether, he thought.[4]

If evil is both intolerable and irremediable, then it is curious that we have a deep-seated sense that punishment answers it at all. If atonement is impossible, why do we think punishment is atonement?[5] And how does punishment finally differ from revenge? That is the issue we need to address.

II

Some philosophers emphasize that punishment is a reaction deeply natural to humans, and that its naturalness provides its foundation.[6] Our conviction that punishment is right is evidence

[4]William Godwin, *Enquiry Concerning Political Justice* (Clarendon: Oxford University Press, 1971), pp. 253, 255.

[5]Piaget describes the conception of just punishment possessed by small children as "expiatory"; but he seems to mean that they believe in the "absolute necessity of punishment," which is broader than expiation, and doesn't imply that wrong can be erased or expiated. See Jean Piaget, *The Moral Judgment of the Child*, trans. Marjorie Gabain (New York: Macmillan, 1965), p. 249.

[6]Durkheim, for instance, says that punishment is, "first and foremost, an emotional reaction," so that primitive people "punish for the sake of punishing, making [the guilty party] suffer . . . without seeking any advantage for themselves," simply to satisfy "the passion for vengeance" ("Forms of Social Solidarity," in *Emile Durkheim: Selected Writings,* trans. and ed. Anthony Giddens [Cambridge: Cambridge University Press, 1972], p. 124). Similar arguments are offered by Susan Jacoby, *Wild Justice: The Evolution of Revenge* (New York: Harper & Row, 1983), and Marvin Henberg, "Taming the Beast: Moral Views of the Criminal Law," *Duke Law Review,* June–September 1985, pp. 843–48. Edmond Cahn also proposes that the sense of injustice is a part of our nature and has evolutionary importance to our security and survival; see *The Sense of Injustice* (New York: New York University Press, 1949), esp. pp. 181–82. All seem to think such facts about our natural emotions tend to justify the phenomenon.

that it is; the retributivist principle has "immediate, underived moral appeal," J. L. Mackie argues. "If we did not feel that there was . . . a positive retributivist reason for imposing a penalty, we should not feel that even sound arguments in terms of deterrence or reformation or any similar future benefit would make it morally right to inflict suffering or deprivation on the criminal." Although he concedes that "the past wrong act, just because it is past, cannot be annulled," he thinks punishment is justified, on evolutionary grounds.[7] Punishment has its source not in reason but in a sentiment that evolution over time has favored. Durkheim takes a similar line. In primitive societies, he argues, punishment "often extends further than the guilty party and reaches the innocent, his wife, his children, his neighbors, etc. That is because the passion which is the spirit of punishment ceases only when it is exhausted. . . . It makes its presence felt by the tendency to surpass in severity the action against which it is reacting. . . . Is not the very common punishment of the *lex talionis* a mode of satisfying the passion for vengeance?" Mackie, Durkheim, and other retributivists view punishment as having its roots in revenge. In itself, Durkheim says, punishment sometimes "consists of a mechanical and aimless reaction, an emotional and unthinking action, an irrational need to destroy." Such a reaction "is a defensive weapon" that serves the purpose of self-preservation.[8] Generally, however, we mean by punishment something imposed by an authority, not a private expression of grievance between peers; and while it *may* have its origin in powerful anger, it need not do so. Revenge is conceptually different: it is personal and may be vicious. Punishment, in contrast, is supposed to be identified with justice.

In any case, a theory of punishment that justifies it on the grounds of deep-seated feelings, as Godwin observes, would "have been totally different, if [men] had divested themselves of the emotions of anger and resentment; if they had considered the man who torments another for what he has done, as upon a par with the child who beats the table."[9] Retributivism would not have had such influence if people had looked to the future when

---

[7] J. L. Mackie, "Morality and the Retributive Emotions," pp. 4–5.
[8] Durkheim, "Forms of Social Solidarity," pp. 124, 125.
[9] Godwin, *Enquiry Concerning Political Justice*, p. 246.

they dealt with wrongdoers instead of to the past. No matter if a desire for revenge is "natural"; so are all expressions of anger, many of which are nonetheless condemnable.

III

Retributive punishment is often associated with the *lex talionis,* the law of retaliation in kind, which requires equality between punishment and offense, but so far we have only metaphors of equality. If we think in terms of debt and repayment, we should conclude that a wrongdoer incurs a debt that must be paid—if he steals someone's sheep, for example, he must pay what it's worth or give it back; if he dents someone's car, he must pay to have it repaired. Under this model, wrongdoing is the incurring of a debt that demands repayment in some understood coin.

This model is reflected in phrases concerned with making a criminal "pay for his crime," his "owing a debt to society," and society's demand for "payment" from him. Yet there are problems with this explanation. First, there is nothing morally wrong with incurring debt. So if the person whose sheep was stolen should come and demand payment, the thief might calmly accept the obligation and give the sheep back or pay for it, in which case he would be released altogether from the charge of wrongdoing. In making restitution he has really "restored" the situation to what it was before. Similarly, the person whose nose is broken by another would have to consider himself fully compensated when the doctor's fees were paid and the nose was fully healed, just as a car owner has to count himself compensated when his car has been repaired.

Even if we suppose that something in the way of interest is added in these cases, the analogy still doesn't work, for the repayment of a debt releases the debtor absolutely. Once restitution is made, then, there is no reason to think there was anything wrong in the wrongdoing, any more than in borrowing money and repaying it, or borrowing a wheelbarrow and returning it. In fact, theft becomes a kind of borrowing. Although sometimes restitution is treated as a form of punishment, its grammatical character doesn't conform to that model.[10] Restoration of what has been stolen doesn't erase the theft, even though it erases the material consequences, and stealing is not incurring a debt.

Someone might respond: "But the debt that is incurred in the case of wrongdoing is not a debt for restitution in the material sense; it's a moral debt and must be repaid in moral terms." But now we must ask what the repayment of a moral debt requires. The imagery of debt and repayment, which at first glance seemed to fit the cases of compensation for the sheep and the car, lacks even superficial fitness in cases of personal injury, libel and slander, anxiety and misery. Furthermore, the idea of *moral* compensation is altogether obscure. Taking the law of torts as the model for punishment, as the *lex talionis* suggests, also leads us to a puzzling ambivalence toward ex-prisoners; for if a criminal can "pay his debt to society," then after he has "paid" we have nothing to hold against him.[11] We have no reason to be angry with him or to remember the offense; but for good or ill, this is not the way we treat wrongdoing.

The fact is that there's a problem with the notion that wrongdoing can be repaid in any currency, as we have seen. How much is owed when someone murders another, and how is the debt calculated? How much is owed when a child is mutilated or left handicapped? Is the currency monetary? Does a rich person pay more, a sensitive and contrite person less?[12] However "natural" the impulse to punish may be, one senses with Dostoyevsky that a radical mistake is at work here.

Then there is the problem that punishment of an offender generally does not mean any kind of compensation for the victim. In

[10]Piaget is among those who treat it this way; he says that "restitutive punishment may be taken as the limiting case of punishment by reciprocity. For here censure no longer plays any part and justice is satisfied with a simple putting right of the material damage" (*Moral Judgment of the Child*, pp. 208–9). On the other side Páll Árdal argues, rightly I think, that restitution is not punishment at all: "Does Anyone Deserve to Suffer?" *Queen's Quarterly* 91 (Summer 1984): 245–46.

[11]The interpretation of punishment as payment for wrongdoing is explored further in chap. 8.

[12]Michael Davis, "How to Make the Punishment Fit the Crime," *Ethics* 93 (July 1983): 74, considers punishment in terms of the advantage or profit sought by the wrongdoer. Looked at this way, the man who murders without profit should receive a lighter punishment than one who is guilty of grand theft.

what way does a term in prison or another form of suffering imposed on an offender compensate the victim? The murdered man, the victim of a hit-and-run driver who goes to prison, and the rape victim have nothing to gain from the "repayment."[13] Then to whom was the debt owed? If one answers "society," again the tort model of payment for damages seems forfeit, since "damage" here is metaphorical. It is not society that was murdered, struck down, or raped. Society doesn't suffer as the victim does, and society can't be benefited by the "payment" of a term in prison any more than a victim can.

When someone commits a wrong, one certainly can say that the community suffers as well as the victim. The moral atmosphere deteriorates as members lose their sense of security. An instance of theft or rape induces people to lock their doors and watch others anxiously. The offense could thus be called an injury to the well-being of the community. But this way of speaking makes it even clearer that the harm done is *not* like a debt that an offender owes to the others and therefore should pay. Removal of the offender may give reassurance and restore trust, but it doesn't constitute repayment.

IV

Despite the difficulties, the connection between wrongdoing and suffering, as in punishment, retains its powerful grip on our thinking.[14] It is further encouraged and given substance when it is connected with the notion of deserts, and this may even be the original source of the metaphor.

Consider some examples. If a person does injury to another and

[13]Richard Wasserstrom argues that despite our intuitions about punishment being "repayment," some important cases can't be seen in this way, including that of rape ("Punishment," in *Philosophy and Social Issues: Five Studies* [Notre Dame: University of Notre Dame Press, 1980], esp. pp. 144–46).

[14]Edmund Pincoffs claims that despite its difficulties, "traditional retributivism cannot be dismissed as unintelligible, or absurd, or implausible" (*The Justification of Legal Punishment* [New York: Humanities Press, 1966], p. 15). I prefer to say that despite its unintelligibility, it cannot be dismissed.

in the process brings about his own downfall, we are very inclined to say, "That's justice!" Or if a thief in the process of stealing is therefore absent when his own house is robbed, again we are prone to say, "He got what he deserved!" Or if someone who is insulting is himself wounded by someone's slight, again we will say it served him right. All of these cases strike us as showing what it is that justice demands. The offender in each case suffers an appropriate misfortune; he gets what is coming to him.[15]

One might hold up these cases to show what is meant by the model of repayment. But in contrast to the debt repayment model, here the injured party doesn't receive anything, nor does society. "Payment," if it applies at all, must be very loosely understood as signifying the state of *receiving* a misfortune that corresponds in some way to the misfortune one has inflicted: the fate of the offender and the wrong he has done show a satisfying symmetry. It is not that the offender acts, does something, as a debtor pays what he owes. And it is not that someone does something to him according to a rule or policy. Rather what makes us speak of repayment is that we see a pattern in what happens to the wrongdoer, *as if he were being paid back* by having to suffer for his wrongdoing. Again we ask, where does the debt come in, and how is it paid? But now the parties to the debt and repayment must be construed very differently. If the offense is the incurring of a debt of injury to himself, who holds the lien on him? Who is the collector of that debt? The answer is curious but illuminating.

Consider the fate of Agamemnon, who killed a doe in the sacred grove of Artemis. When he had his troops at Aulis and lacked winds to set sail for Troy—his men impatient and time running short—he sent back to know what he must do to have winds blow. The answer came from Delphi that he must sacrifice his

---

[15]Godwin claims that "there is no such thing as desert," but he means that "it cannot be just that we should inflict suffering on any man, except so far as it tends to good" (*Enquiry Concerning Political Justice*, p. 245). Also see Thomas Nagel, "Equal Treatment and Compensatory Discrimination," *Philosophy and Public Affairs* 2 (Summer 1973): 348–63. Nagel makes the same claim about the positive, nonpunitive side of the issue. There surely is such a thing as desert, even if no deserved treatment can be specified for anyone.

daughter Iphigenia, his favorite child; when he made this personal sacrifice, the winds arose and he could set sail.

It was Artemis who demanded payment for Agamemnon's offense, but the "payment" did nothing to restore her loss. Rather than talk of repayment here, we would more aptly speak of symmetry, a symmetry between what was done *by* Agamemnon and what was done *to* him. It is a theme of many Greek plays: undue pride or presumption leads—perhaps indirectly—to a downfall. A person's fate and character are so connected that his fate reflects his character. Ultimately Agamemnon's fate showed such connections, for his willingness to sacrifice Iphigenia and his triumphant manner on returning from Troy justified, in a roundabout way, his murder.[16]

Taken this way, justice might be said to characterize the pattern that reveals itself in time, a pattern that brings suffering to those who have caused it, and as an indirect consequence of their deeds and their characters. In a just universe no one gets away with anything: that is the universe of the Greek playwrights. All wickedness comes to an accounting in a man's destiny, and no one can be called happy until he is dead, when the opportunities for suffering for his sins are past.[17]

It is this idea, I believe, that lies behind the retributive justifications of punishment. The commission of a wrong demands a symmetrical misfortune to come to the wrongdoer, for only in that way will the moral universe find balance. It is the balance not of repayment, however, but of suffering, and it comes about as a natural or divine consequence of wrongdoing. Being intolerable, wrong creates a demand for such a response. If the universe were just, not only would wrongdoers suffer as a result of their wrongdoing, but their suffering would be evident to us in the course of time.

[16]Notice that it is unclear that the fate suffered by Agamemnon was the "right" one, the one he really deserved. It's fortunate, therefore, that the responsibility for devising it falls to Artemis, since our judgments about such things don't seem very secure.

[17]See Alasdair MacIntyre, *After Virtue* (Notre Dame: University of Notre Dame Press, 1981), p. 34, on the Greek idea of a self, which takes the whole of a person's life into account.

If we express the demand for justice in this way and in these terms, we can say that the demand for justice is a cosmic one.[18] For it is directed to superhuman or natural forces or deities; the working out of a person's fate requires a long view, and however impatient we may be, the justice we want belongs in this framework. Within it what seems accidental from a short view takes on the aspect of a purposeful scheme contrived by the fates, by the universe, or by God. The demand for justice can then be given this formulation: it is an unspecific demand that injustice be answered in the framework of a moral universe and be visible to us in the long run.

The justice demanded is a morally satisfying universe. "*Dikē* means not simply justice," Hugh Lloyd-Jones writes, "but the order of the universe." In Greek religion "the gods maintain a cosmic order."[19] Thus though we may demand this kind of justice, we cannot administer it; it belongs to a nonhuman frame of reference.

It now becomes clear why our natural expressions of objection and abhorrence of wrong take such forms as "This should not happen . . . should not be *allowed* to happen," as if there were or should be a divine means of preventing it. The protest is in turn connected with the satisfaction we take when "events" turn against a wrongdoer and bring him down, when the just universe in which the wicked are inexorably and appropriately punished takes care of this offender. We have no part in this scheme; the punishing is done by the universe itself. Of course the kind of

[18]Piaget describes children as having such a sense of "immanent" or cosmic justice. "Situations frequently occur in which the child quite spontaneously considers an accident of which he is the victim as a punishment, and we believe that this happens without anything analogous having been suggested by the parents in similar situations. According to [our] hypothesis, the child, having acquired, thanks to adult constraint, the habit of punishment, attributes spontaneously to nature the power of applying the same punishments" (*Moral Judgment of the Child,* pp. 259–60). That is to say, Piaget takes parental punishment as the basis for this cosmic sense. It seems to me, however, that the cosmic sense may be directly tied to feelings of guilt, that a child who does something wrong expects to be punished by *some power*; and conversely, misfortunes are interpreted as punishments for misdeeds.

[19]Hugh Lloyd-Jones, *The Justice of Zeus* (Berkeley: University of California Press, 1971), pp. 153, 162.

causation involved is not that impersonal, value-neutral causation of science, but causation mixed with moral justification, for the reason that disaster befalls someone will refer to his past wrongdoing. It is causation by a thoughtful and morally orderly universe. The idea is involved in our thinking when we view a mortal illness as if it were punishment for something in one's past, or good luck as a reward for patience and suffering.

One might suppose that this vision of a just universe is a positive ideal of justice. That claim would be defensible in a way, for humans don't think of justice only in terms of what they can do; sometimes they take the imagined perspective of a god or eternity, take an imaginary stance outside themselves and imagine a universe under some wise control. That is part of the ethical point of view, part of Dostoyevsky's demand for harmony. It is a view *sub specie aeternitatis*. Some philosophers might argue, now, that this view provides us with precisely the ideal of justice we want, a perfect state of things as far as justice is concerned. But as I argued in Chapter 6, this vision is unhelpful because its characterization is indeterminate; we cannot say what a perfectly just response to wrong would be, even though we claim to recognize it in the working out of events. Moreover, even in a perfectly just universe, justice is palpable only when wrong has been done, for wrongdoing is what brings justice into play. Justice characterizes a universe in which offenses are answered appropriately, not a positive model of a condition in which no injustice exists. Therefore visions of a perfectly just world will, necessarily and unparadoxically, still contain wrong.

V

From the statement "This is not how things should be—they ought to be different" it follows that some changes would have made this a better world. If there were a governor of the universe or some other cosmic agency, the remark implies, that agent should have made them. But what does the remark imply for human actions and human institutions?

Consider a familiar example. It was at one time commonly

agreed that, in view of Hitler's wickedness and the harm he did, the world would be a better place if he were dead. It was also commonly said, as if it followed from this statement, that it would be good if someone killed him, or even stronger, that someone *ought to* kill him. It was agreed in any case that the disposal of Hitler was something that cosmic forces or beneficent deities, if they existed, should concern themselves with. So if Hitler were struck by lightning, one might say that God had managed to do what was just. Does it follow that it would also have been just for a human to kill him?

Let us assume that Hitler's demise would have been a good thing and that the result of his death, however achieved, would have been an improvement. Does it follow that if someone had killed Hitler, he would have done a good thing? The first answer one has to make is no. Killing is not this easy to condone. Moreover, a person might kill Hitler with the worst motives, and then the goodness of the result would be quite clearly irrelevant to his guilt. To excuse the deed (not to mention praise it) on the ground that Hitler was wicked would be to commit the fallacy of supposing that two wrongs make a right, the one canceling the other. So we cannot infer from the proposition that some result is good the proposition that an action aimed at producing it would be good.

That we cannot make such an inference is a problem for practical reason. It seems to work for deities and cosmic forces and, logic being impersonal, might be expected to work for us. But it isn't antimortal discrimination that prevents the inference. Consider this example. Suppose that three men, *A, B,* and *C,* agree that one of their number should go and confront a common threat. At the same time each rejects the proposition that he should go. So that while the proposition that *one of them* should go entails that either *A* or *B* or *C* should go, it doesn't entail that *A* should, that *B* should, or that *C* should. There is no inconsistency in each of the three accepting the general proposition while rejecting the inferences that *he* should do what it recommends.

Now there is no person to whom the statement "Someone ought to kill Hitler" applies in such a way as to imply thal *he* should kill Hitler. But more significantly, we don't even make the inference that one of us would be *justified* in killing Hitler, even while we assert that "someone" should. Unlike the hypothetical case, the present one not only doesn't require the action but seems consistent with condemning it. Thus we may agree that Hitler should be killed and yet recoil from the implication that anyone should really kill him.

Much of our moral reasoning goes from a general rule, such as "No one should steal," to the particular proposition that I should-n't steal. What is curious is that in the case we are considering an analogous inference doesn't seem to work. There what we say *a person* or *someone* should do fails to entail what we should do, even though we are clearly in the class referred to. In the case of "Some-one ought to kill Hitler," not even a disjunctive inference follows, that is, "Either you ought to, or you, or you, or . . ." And the question of why the inference doesn't work needs to be met.[20]

The reason I propose is that when we speak of how things should be and what ought to be done, we are sometimes using "ought" in a cosmic way. It ought to happen, it would be a good thing to do, it is wrong for things to be so. But not "*We* ought to do something specific." The way things ought to be if the world is to be just doesn't tell us what any particular person should do. Indeed, if a person inferred from the general statement what he should do, he might be severely censured or even punished, even by just those people who most vehemently endorsed the behavior in its general form. We say that people ought to get what they deserve, the guilty ought to be punished, wrongdoers shouldn't profit from their deeds, and the punishment should fit the crime. But what do these propositions say about what *we should do*? They say nothing.

It is commonly said that a person deserves to be treated as he treated others—that is, a criminal will get what he deserves if he is treated just as he treated others. But are we then entitled to administer such treatment as punishment? No; for if the original treatment was cruel and inhumane, our treatment of him will be so as well. We would have two wrongs now, not one that has been righted.

To see this more clearly, imagine a world in which people regu-

---

[20]The present example shows a connection between this issue and the problem of "dirty hands" in politics, a theme explored in Jean-Paul Sartre's play *Dirty Hands* as well as by Michael Walzer in "Political Action: The Problem of Dirty Hands," *Philosophy and Public Affairs* 1 (1972): 161–80.

larly get what we can recognize as their deserts. (I don't mean imagine it in detail; indeed, I doubt that that's possible.) I mean imagine that in general we were confident that every wrongdoer would come to some misfortune, greater misfortune for greater wrongs, lesser for lesser. And this state of affairs would come about without any human efforts to arrange for it, such as the establishment of penal institutions. Those who were guilty would suffer and those who were innocent victims would be compensated by good fortune. Eventually. In such a universe we might feel much less indignation at wrongdoing, being secure in the expectation that the wrongdoer would come to a bad end and would "pay for" his offense.

Now if such a universe could exist, it would be better than the one we inhabit; that seems self-evident. This being so, then, why isn't it perfectly justifiable for us to do whatever we can, in our mortal and finite way, to bring our universe closer to that better one? Allowing that we won't reach perfection, surely we can do *something*, impose some punishment on wrongdoers. This seems no more or less than taking seriously the truth that the wicked should be punished and applying it in our actions. Since they deserve to suffer and not to profit from their misdeeds, we ought to arrange things in this way.

But this is the inference that I maintain doesn't work.

VI

It is only just and right, Bradley and Kant would argue, that the guilty should suffer. Yes, I agree; their punishment is morally right and just. But that proposition doesn't imply whether *we* ought to punish them or how.

One may protest here that it is generally not we as individuals who punish, it is public institutions. They, like gods or the Fates, can be required and expected to judge impartially, fairly.[21] If we

---

[21]Mackie explicitly associates "a morally respectable public" with "a morally respectable god," as if they were authorities with similar perspectives ("Morality and the Retributive Emotions," p. 4).

haven't got a just universe, well, government can act in some small way toward making it more just. The just universe is a sort of guide to what a just government should do. Such a connection is rooted in Greek thought, in Anaximander, whom Werner Jaeger describes as "projecting the idea of a political cosmos upon the whole of nature."[22] Government acts on the same rules as the Fates, acts as their surrogate, and while individuals are not justified in punishing one another, a government stands above them and beholden to none. Why can't it, like nature herself, act to give people what they deserve? It is simply a different agent administering the same program.

But nature isn't a good guide. As Lloyd-Jones observes, the justice of Zeus is harsh. Zeus, like Medea and Achilles, sometimes goes too far; while "the justice of Zeus is at all times recognisable as a kind of justice," it may also be baleful and horrible to contemplate.[23] How could such behavior be a guide for us?

We can't say precisely what the just universe should provide for a particular wrongdoer, or how we might shrink to see it. And since we have no model for what should be done, in the last analysis it is crucial that we agree among us that some treatment or other is just treatment for wrongdoing. We cannot institute a system to deal with wrongdoers and leave those judgments open. On the other hand, it isn't clear how we make judgments that *are* patently just.

The reason government cannot fill the role of the cosmos is therefore like the reason an individual can't do so. Even though an offender deserves to be roasted over hot coals or deserves a painful and humiliating death, having committed awful offenses—even though he deserves to be treated as he treated others—government still isn't justified in imposing such sentences. Therefore deserts do not provide a guide for our responses to injustice; and it follows that the misfortunes that would come to wrongdoers in a just universe fail to be a guide for political or judicial institutions. What is just when the Fates or the natural world brings it about is unwarranted—*morally unwarranted*—for human agents. No one and no

---

[22]Werner Jaeger, *Paedeia: The Ideals of Greek Culture* (New York: Oxford University Press, 1945), 1:110.

[23]Lloyd-Jones, *Justice of Zeus*, p. 153.

institution is morally justified in doing such things. Similarly the sins of pride and meanness and arrogance may lead a person to receive his due in a play or an epic, but not in a human court of law.

I admit that this conclusion is curious. One might reasonably expect that divine or universal justice is the *best* model for earthly justice, and the safest guide for human institutions. But there is an important difference: the Fates aren't accountable for their actions while humans are. The punitive actions of the fates don't make them in turn culpable. In a sense you could say that we cannot do the things they can, cannot do them in the same way, for we cannot avoid the implications of acting as human beings, possessed of human choices and framed in a moral perspective. Gods, Fates, nature, all fall out of this frame. They don't answer or need to answer to our code and moral standards. No wonder we would like to have their view and take their perspective, acting with abstract impersonality in a world of absolute values, where the relations and responsibilities of humans don't apply. But we cannot escape our conditions. So we cannot mimic supernatural actions, any more than we can take the role of wind or storms as they impersonally bring about consequences that are deserved. When humans act, their actions are bathed in a moral light that doesn't strike the wind or the sea. Thus it is quite possible to say of someone who harms another in righteous anger that we understand why he did it, how he was driven to do it, and agree that the victim had it coming—and still stop short of saying he was justified in what he did.

VII

It is still not tolerable or acceptable that the innocent should suffer and the wicked not pay for their misdeeds. As Dostoyevsky wrote, we refuse to accept such situations and would be morally corrupt if we did. So with Feinberg we may agree that there is something in Kant's position that we *must* punish wicked acts which reflects, "however dimly, something embedded in common sense."[24] A person who sees injustice done with complacency is morally deficient, not someone who has overcome a human weakness.[25]

But as we found in Chapter 6, there is a sense in which injustice cannot be obliterated. It continues to exist, it endures in a sense. So there is a question here as to what a person can possibly do about a wrong once it is done. And we came to the conclusion that the injustice itself may not and often does not point the way. The intolerability of wrong is not linked internally to action; action isn't part of its grammar. And so its expression may take the form of weeping and protest and angry demonstrations, which are a long way from what might be called corrective or restorative. However powerful as expressions, they don't serve to help the cosmic imbalance.

Such protests are nevertheless important, as I argued in Chapter 6. Their importance is emphasized by Feinberg, who sees punishment as having just such an expressive, condemnatory role. We punish as an expression of abhorrence, not in addition to such expression, and "certain forms of hard treatment have become the conventional symbols of public reprobation."[26] But even if punishment is one "conventional symbol," abhorrence may be expressed in many other ways. Thus the justification for punishing rather than doing something else is left open by his account.

Since a particular wrong doesn't itself dictate the right remedy or even a fitting response, the question of what to do with the wrongdoer is left open. Should he be punished? Should he be quarantined to protect the rest of society? And educated? Should he be made to work to repay the victim's loss? The choice of alternatives is much wider than we sometimes recognize. It is quite

---

[24]Joel Feinberg, "The Expressive Function of Punishment," in *Philosophical Perspectives on Punishment,* ed. Gertrude Ezorsky (Albany: State University of New York Press, 1972), p. 33. Feinberg's view is that the expression of the community's condemnation is one important function of punishment, and "to say that the very physical treatment itself expresses condemnation is to say that certain forms of hard treatment have become the conventional symbols of public reprobation" (p. 29). This view allows the condemnation of wrong and the role of punishment to be identified, which I think is mistaken.

[25]The roots of this idea are traced in Jaeger, *Paideia,* 1:124.

[26]Feinberg, "Expressive Function of Punishment," p. 29.

possible that we would choose one thing in one instance of a certain kind of crime and another in another, if we were dealing with matters case by case, as Godwin recommends, and not through general rules. And thus one might easily argue for giving impetuous offenders help and education, but requiring of practiced criminals hard work for the public benefit, and forcing wealthy offenders to experience life without the cushion of wealth, and so on. Here one could make the argument that rules that require the perpetrators of similar crimes to be treated alike obstruct and frustrate justice; yet many people believe that justice without such rules is an impossibility.[27] At this point, where we no longer find it necessary to search for a positive meaning of justice, it is also not necessary to decide between these views. The argument of a utilitarian that punishment adds more wrong and suffering to what has been done can be heard, as can the argument that offenders should be punished for some particular reason.

The intolerability of wrong doesn't entail a requirement that we must take any particular action against the wrongdoer, although human beings commonly assume that some action is called for. The wrong makes us angry at the offender; we would like to see him suffer. The reaction is understandable in a psychological way. It shows that we have a clear sense of the wrong and the need to condemn it, to express our opposition to it. But an appropriate action also has to be one that we can take without loss to our own credit.

If we have a hanging party to get rid of someone particularly awful, no matter how awful he is, our action is not creditable even though it is understandable psychologically. But if no way is available to us as people of moral substance to express our indignation, it would seem we are stuck. We're in a state of conflict. On the one hand we face a morally intolerable situation and need to express our abhorrence, our intolerance of wrong. One way to express it, as Feinberg says, is to punish the offender. But just as we are morally prohibited from taking the kind of action the gods may take, which most aptly express intolerance, we may not find other

---

[27]John Rawls, for example, defines justice in terms of rules or principles (*A Theory of Justice* [Cambridge: Harvard University Press, 1971], pp. 58–60).

justification for punishing. What can we do, then? Perhaps find another form of expression. To call something a "conventional expression" is not to give much justification for it, and imposing suffering is a serious matter. We need to look further as we view cases to see the range of our options. This is not an intellectual puzzle to be solved by philosophy, but is an aspect of the human condition.

VIII

The concept of justice shows us two sides of morality. On the one side there is the demand for cosmic justice—suffering of a sort appropriate to an offender. On the other hand, actions to harm an offender and make him suffer may not be morally possible. These are two complementary moral perspectives. Under the one we speak of what people have coming to them in the long run. Under the other we must take account of our actions as *our* actions, for which *we* are accountable. We cannot claim exemption because of our indignation. Actions that may satisfy us under the one view may not be justifiable under the other. So we speak of what people have coming to them, in life, in the long run, and in this vein we speak of a person's life showing a pattern: See, his misdeed has followed him all these years. Even accidental or apparently trivial events become important in this design. It is on such a stage that the Fates do their work. They give a person's life an overall moral coherence. They bring the chaos of momentary events into ultimate order, through winds and accidents and chance.

The other perspective is narrower. It shows a person in the context of his responsibilities, but as possessing a terrible indignation at what is wrong. What shall he do? Here we don't interest ourselves in the weaving of a pattern that will have symmetry and sense in the end. Who knows at this moment what such a pattern would look like? Our indignation and intolerance of wrong impel us to act now, they have to be expressed somehow, or our status as moral creatures is forfeit. That is the dilemma we find ourselves in.

Even if someone claims to be acting as the instrument of a higher power that is balancing things out and carrying out a plan, he cannot seriously be understood as acting on any stage other than the human one. Two figures who justified their actions by referring to divine powers were Socrates and Jesus. But their claims to have been guided by divine sources didn't exempt them from being viewed for the most part as human beings, acting in a human context and as exemplars for others to follow. Ultimately it is that context—the particular circumstances such figures are in, their human options, and their righteous objection—that illuminates their actions and shows them to be right.

Both of these frameworks are important to morality, but we can see why they lead us to puzzlement. It is perfectly natural to make the intolerability of wrong serve as a reason to harm the wrongdoer and bring him what he deserves—as if the job that the Fates and gods neglect to do we must take on ourselves. In such reasoning we try to bring the two frameworks together. We try to join them in one and let cosmic justice be a guide for our actions or our government's.

But the two frameworks aren't compatible in this way; they are separate and disjoint. While we view an action under one perspective we aren't seeing it under the other. We see it in a determinate framework and, like one of the illusions of perception, it appears now in one way, now in another, but never as both at once. We cannot use the reasoning of cosmic justice to justify human actions any more than we can call up the winds to express our indignation or blame someone who can't master the tides.

IX

The intolerability of wrong gave a plausible foundation for the institution of punishment, but only because it put humans and their institutions into the roles of superhumans and natural forces.[28]

[28]Nonetheless, we find superhuman or quasi-human figures (e.g., Superman) highly attractive, perhaps because they can be seen as correcting wrongs in a way that we cannot do. The possibility of taking a role in a cosmic activity has no doubt been attractive since ancient times, when humans were supposed to sometimes transcend their human limitations and gods to come to earth in human form. For ancient Greeks the Delphic oracle was a bridge between the two worlds and so a source of information from the one perspective to the other.

But this is a role they cannot take, not while they remain human. Human actions are seen under a different perspective, that of human morality and the human condition. Cosmic justice will not tell us whether humans are justified in making wrongdoers suffer as they do.

There is room under this view for choosing to isolate criminal offenders, in effect quarantining them from the rest of society. And in quarantine we find a whole range of options in regard to their treatment. We might consider this range. It isn't necessary to equate isolation and restriction with punishment.[29]

There is room here for the utilitarian argument that if it is wrong to cause suffering in the first place, we can hardly improve matters by causing more suffering. The issue between retributivism and utilitarianism, seen correctly, is never joined. The one side begins with the cosmic framework and is guided by deserts; the other side begins with human actions, for which we and not the cosmos are responsible. Both views show us something about how justice works. But it is a mistake to suppose that the cosmic realm can dictate what is justifiable for us to do.

In short, my argument doesn't prove whether wrongdoers should or should not be punished, or how, but only shows that their punishment at human hands is conceptually different from punishment by the Fates.

This recognition leaves our understanding of punishment incomplete, but it is nonetheless an advance. For to recognize the difference between human and cosmic agency is to see why punishment cannot be justified directly on the basis of wrongdoing. Thus if a tribe or any community chooses to punish wrongdoers, it has to make that choice on some grounds other than the wrongdoing itself. Ultimately it needs a background idea of the relations that hold between one member and another, and between any member and the larger world. It also, as I argue in Chapter 8,

---

[29]While one may protest that quarantine still makes the offender suffer, and so is tantamount to punishment, the fact that he dislikes confinement is irrelevant to the question of quarantine, and the imposition of isolation need not be seen as punishment. Surgery may be painful but nonetheless therapeutic; so may even education. Thus confinement can be justified as a means to protect society without being justified as punishment.

needs a conception of moral responsibility and the understanding of wrong.

We conclude temporarily that a community may justify punishment in any of various ways. We expect to find in the justification it chooses a distinction between what cosmic justice demands and what human institutions consider justifiable. The two perspectives on justice will not be merged. The gods will be seen as acting outside the human stage, and humans will be incapable of acting on theirs. The idea of cosmic justice and divine punishment are nevertheless ideas of paramount importance. To discuss wrongdoing and punishment without them would be to leave the design unfinished.

8

Punishing Our Own

Punishment of an offender is not justified by his guilt alone. Nor is it justified by our righteous anger, our need to respond and oppose the wrong rather than accept it passively. But if not in either of these ways, how can it be justified? There is another possible way that stems from a different perspective on punishment.

In philosophical literature, punishment is most commonly considered in terms of law violators, and the term's meaning is often crucially tied to that context as philosophers take legal punishment as the central case and regard punishment in a family or school as secondary, derivative, peripheral.[1] But despite this focus on gov-

---

[1]Hobbes, for instance, defines punishment as "an Evill inflicted by publique Authority, on him that hath done, or omitted that which is Judged by the same Authority to be a Transgression of the Law" (Thomas Hobbes, *Leviathan* [New York: Everyman, 1947], p. 266). J. D. Mabbott identifies the legal case as the only important one because it involves the breaking of a rule. He simply neglects the family case, as if in that context no rules are broken or no appropriate authority exists ("Punishment," in *Philosophical Perspectives on Punishment,* ed. Gertrude Ezorsky [Albany: State University of New York Press, 1972], pp. 167–68). Kurt Baier characterizes it in terms of a complicated game involving "giving orders or laying down laws, affixing penalties to them, etc."; punishment within a family has to "tacitly imply" the formal moves of the legal model ("Is Punishment Retributive?" in *Philosophical Perspectives,* ed. Ezorsky, p. 16). As will be evident, if we compare a parent's command with legislation, we overlook the instructive side of the parental model.

ernmental provisions and institutions, we don't first learn about punishment in this context. Our first encounters with it belong to a much earlier time, to early childhood—with the slap, the reprimand, and the moral lecture. When we take parental punishment of children as the central or paradigm case of punishment, we get an altogether different slant on its nature and point. And this perspective can then serve to illuminate the institutional case.[2]

I

A child is reprimanded and scolded for various things, some less wrong than dangerous. Thus the child is taught not to play with electrical appliances, but not because there is anything in principle wrong with doing so. And children are taught not to go bareheaded into wintry weather, again not because it is wrong but for their protection. In such cases scolding, reprimanding, and even striking are sometimes viewed as means of training the child in certain behaviors. The end desired is simple obedience and conformity to a rule, and if the child fails to obey, fears are awakened and communicated, but not moral concern. These are not the cases our discussion of punishment needs; what we need are behaviors that somehow call forth our moral disapproval, our intolerance of wrong, offenses that are distinctively moral.

There are also cases in which a child's behavior is "naughty" but not morally offensive, as when the child breaks something through carelessness. Punishment applies here again as a means of training the child to be more careful; such cases are again qualitatively different from those of stealing and lying.[3] What we need to focus

---

[2]If we view punishment entirely as a civil phenomenon, we may infer with Hobbes that "injuries of private men" cannot properly be called punishment (*De Cive* [New York: Appleton-Century, 1949], pp. 76–77). This view makes parental punishment a logical impossibility.

[3]Piaget proposes that a child's moral understanding begins with *material* wrong, such as broken china, and progresses to nonmaterial cases (Jean Piaget, *The Moral Judgment of the Child*, trans. Marjorie Gabain [New York: Macmillan, 1965], chap. 2). This formulation leads easily into the view, which Piaget also holds, that material restitution is a form of punishment. I argue that the treatment a parent gives to a moral offense is qualitatively different and distinctive; in general no restitution is possible in such cases.

on are unequivocal cases of moral offense.

Such a focus is more elusive than it may seem. If we look for instances of moral offenses by young children, we find that the very youth of the children makes it difficult to call their actions "moral offenses." Infants don't commit moral offenses; the idea is absurd.[4] Nevertheless, in our experience it happens that we come to learn about moral offensiveness by spontaneously doing offensive things. That is to say, our understanding doesn't begin with moral precepts that we *subsequently* violate; rather doing the wrong thing and learning that it's wrong are tied together logically and biographically. Awareness that he or she is culpable is something a child has to learn as part of understanding what a moral offense is, and this is one of the functions that punishment is supposed to serve.

Suppose a child steals from other children, taking whatever he wants and can get. What does a parent need to do to teach the culprit? The first consideration may be to stop the conduct and prevent its repetition: the *behavior* needs to stop. If this were all that is involved, however, teaching children not to steal would be no different from training them not to play with electricity. In both cases the sole object would be behavior training, or what you might term conditioning—similar to the training of a dog or a horse.[5]

Suppose someone objects that stopping the behavior *is* the main point of punishing a child and that further argument is required to show that any other factor is at issue. What we really want to do (it is argued) is to get the child to stop; why and how we get him to stop and whether he sees his action as morally offensive are either

---

[4]The same kind of absurdity is seen in talk of the infant's sexual impulses and sexual behavior and sexual attachments to adults. There is certainly continuity between the spontaneous responses of infants and the sexual adult and between children's early mistakes and their moral adulthood, but it is nonetheless important to try to distinguish the differences in the categories that apply to the various stages.

[5]Piaget's questioning of children six years old and under revealed the common attitude that punishment is per se behavior control, while older children expressed the idea that punishment is a less effective means to control behavior than explanation, understanding, and censure (*Moral Judgment of the Child*, pp. 201–17). This finding suggests to me that the older children understood the moral point of their punishment as the younger children did not.

secondary or irrelevant. This account might be used to represent the deterrent theory of punishment: what punishment is concerned with, that theory says, is the prevention of certain behavior.

Return to the view of a responsible parent. What is his or her attitude toward the child's stealing? Although it is imperative that the child not steal (the parent might say), of even greater concern is his moral development. Parents are responsible for the moral development of their children, and whatever they do in the way of punishment, this responsibility is never out of view. The location of responsibility is the more clear if we notice that the training of a young child is entirely in the hands of the parents or a parent's surrogates: anyone who punishes the child without authority delegated by the parents may be guilty of battery. The authority to punish and the responsibility for moral training are logically connected here: parents have punitive authority *in virtue of their moral responsibility* for the child.

If parents' authority to punish derives from their responsibility for a child's training and moral education, certain things follow directly. First and principally, it follows that punishment for moral offenses needs to carry a moral message. How can it do so? Here one thinks of Hegel's language: the point of punishment is to induce repentance, which works to reform the offender. A parent's indignation, shock, disapproval, and shame are potent expressions of the abhorrence intimately associated with injustice, and a moral lecture on why the action was wrong is part of that expression. Its aim is to get the child to *see* that what he did was wrong and thus to change his behavior. These two things—explanation and the recognition of the moral wrong—are often taken as inseparable.[6] Through expostulations, accusations, lectures, and implorings a child learns about the nature of the wrong and his parents' feelings and motives, and in the process gets glimmerings of the ultimate point of the procedure.

Other experiences fortify the meaning of moral censure. On occasion the parents and other adults express abhorrence and censure of others and sometimes even of themselves. What is ex-

---

[6]Some of Piaget's subjects made clear that the point of punishment was to "make [the child] good" (ibid., pp. 224–26).

pressed is intense feeling and criticism and condemnation of actions together with disapproval of a person's character. When such disapproval is directed against them, then, children naturally feel it keenly. Eventually they come to understand it as reflecting on their status in the family, and as affecting their parents' self-respect and standing among others.[7]

The ultimate point of parental punishment and the lecture and the expressions of censure is the moral development of the child. Whether these are good or necessary means to foster moral development we needn't decide now; it is enough to conclude that when we punish a child for a moral offense, we should keep this goal in view. Since punishing children in one way or another is a general practice in our society, one that many parents think good, our question is how punishment is conceived to perform this educational and developmental function.

II

We encounter problems when we tackle this subject. First, it is unclear when exactly punishment comes into the picture. Suppose a child takes another child's marbles and is told that he must return them. Is the return of the marbles a punishment? The case has its analogue in the adult world when a thief is told to return what he stole; the farmer who steals his neighbor's sheep, for instance, must restore them to the owner. Is the return of the sheep a punishment? It certainly is repayment, and thus fits the literal sense of the terms "retaliation" and "retribution"; but as we have seen, it hardly makes sense as punishment. Now change the case in this way: the thief has lost some of the stolen goods (some

---

[7]Piaget thinks, in contrast, that "parents [who] point out to the child that he has just done something very wrong . . . inculcate in him respect for [right behavior]" and that "commands [to do the right thing] . . . on the occasion of particularly strong affective situations are sufficient to arouse in the child's mind obligations of conscience" (ibid., p. 166). Although Piaget holds that "affect" and emotions are critical in the understanding of moral concepts, his account does not make clear how conscience becomes aroused by simple training and without the child's deeper connection with the parents.

sheep have died, say), so that instead of simply bringing back what he took, he now has to suffer a net loss. This case is like that of a child who breaks a window and is told to replace it at his own expense and trouble. Now is this a better case of punishment? One can still object that, insofar as the demand is simply for restoration of property, punishment proper is absent. There is no *moral* message in the necessity to make good the damage or loss, and personal censure needs to be part of whatever counts as punishment.[8] So if the family's insurance covered windows broken by children, the insurance company could be called on to make restoration without personal involvement of the child, and we wouldn't say then that he had been punished.

Somehow the culprit has to suffer personally, and to make losses good is not clearly to suffer. What further is required? Would the case be stronger if something of the culprit's were damaged in return for the damage he did? That is the logic of retaliation: equal suffering makes the point unequivocally. But this solution has the further difficulty that it is not the kind of thing that authorities can justifiably do, and punishment means punishment by an authority. That is, the government cannot justly insist that a person's nose be broken to punish him for breaking someone else's nose, nor can it justifiably steal from a thief. And a parent who punishes is not engaged in retaliation or retribution; if the parent struck a child who had struck him, the situation is one of combat, not of punishment. Retaliation is something that peers engage in, not something authorities administer.[9]

When, then, do we come to punishment proper, avoiding repayment on the one side and retribution on the other? The thief who simply returns stolen goods may look at it as a loan repaid. If this interpretation is to be avoided, some further and more person-

---

[8]Patrick Devlin makes this point: tort law "as a whole is without any consistent moral purpose. It does not stand in an auxiliary relationship to the moral law. . . . Its attitude is: 'You can do what you like so long as you pay for it'" (*The Enforcement of Morals* [Oxford: Oxford University Press, 1965], p. 39).

[9]The objection that God, who is the model of a punishing authority, is capable of retribution needs to be answered by the argument that in acting retributively, God is revealed as a personality and not as an impersonal governing force. For some of the difficulties in seeing God as an agent, see D. Z. Phillips, *R. S. Thomas: Poet of the Hidden God* (Allston Park, Pa.: Pickwick, 1986), pp. 81–83.

al charge against him is needed and punishment needs to carry that message. A variety of things may be done to convey it—punitive charges, sentences, humiliation, physical suffering—but without this message one hesitates to call something punishment. As I said before, however, it is not necessary to punish in order to convey this message; a scolding or demand for apology or penance will often do the same work.

Next, though punishment needs to be designed so as to carry the message of censure, we need to notice that other interpretations may be given, some of which miss and altogether defeat the moral lesson. If the child who suffers punishment thinks that the misdeed is completely paid for in this way, then he has learned no moral lesson. He takes punishment simply as the cost of offending and nothing more, just as the cost of candy is what is required in exchange for it. He may be deterred, judging the risk and the penalty to be too great; but nothing in this reasoning requires acknowledgment of wrong. The success of the deterrent may have nothing to do with a grasp of the moral lesson.

In addition, if the child stops doing what he did *because it was wrong,* we would be mistaken to speak of deterrence. For now the child sees what he didn't see before, understands something new, and it is this insight that makes his attitude and behavior change, not punishment per se. To call the moral lesson deterrence is to suggest that the situation is one of cost and benefit, and that the child decides the penalty is not worth the pleasure; but the moral lesson is different. The moral and the deterrent interpretations are therefore incompatible. A child who interprets punishment as the price of wrongdoing may conclude that everything amusing has a price and that some kind of punishment goes with every pleasure. And a parent who takes the deterrent view may think that most childish offenses can be deterred if the penalty is severe enough, in which case severe penalties will be good ones.[10] But this view does not give punishment a morally educative role.

The interpretation the child gives to punishment raises interesting

[10]Piaget's small children (6–8 years) tended to believe that severe penalties were justified. Piaget considers this response proof that they conceived of punishment as "expiatory," but the inference could as well be that they saw it simply as a deterrent (*Moral Judgment of the Child,* pp. 204–5).

problems here. While a punishment may be meant to carry a message, whether it is conveyed depends on the child's understanding rather than on what the parent does. A parent may *say* that punishment is a painful responsibility, but if the child understands it to be a deterrent, its moral role is lost. That is one problem.

There is a second hazard. When we condemn and censure, we often express our feelings with great power and effect. The child may think of such censure solely in terms of the parent's anger and its considerable power, but when only the anger of the parent is seen, the moral message is again ambiguous. Once the anger has passed and dissipated, the slate may be considered clean, like air after a storm; the anger may be viewed as fortuitous when it conveys no moral message.

If punishment is justified morally and has an important role to play in moral education, then its justification should take these problems into account.

III

If we suppose that punishment has a part to play in moral training, what distinguishes this role, and under what conditions can punishment be expected to succeed in it?

Several things must *not* be the case. First, the offender should not perceive his punishment simply as repayment, restitution, or compensation. Second, the culprit should not see the punishment simply as the expression of anger, which is a disturbing transitory state that eventually gives way to one of tranquillity and amicability.

We come upon a curious inversion here: when we specify the message of punishment, the perspective of the one punished appears more important than that of the punisher. The child may sometimes grasp the intended message and the parent may see that the child has understood, but even when the intentions of punishment are clear, the interpretation is not under the control of the punisher. It is not for the parent or other authority to define the meaning of the message and determine how it will be interpreted.

What is involved when the child gets the moral message right? Some features seem obvious. The child who sees punishment as a kind of moral teaching already sees the parent as a moral teacher.

He sees the parent as having the status, as J. D. Mabbott might say, required to punish.[11] Parents are seen to have the responsibility to punish, much as a judge has the responsibility to sentence. Second, and relatedly, the child sees himself as morally imperfect, as capable of mistakes in judgment and in need of correction.[12] So that even though he doesn't understand why what he did was wrong, he understands that he needs to learn why in order to conduct himself more acceptably in the future.

The role of understanding here is crucial. Socrates made understanding the prerequisite of virtue; one needs to understand virtue and have a grasp of it, he argues, in order to be virtuous, for only then does one understand the reason for acting or refraining from acting in a given way. Only with understanding will one's moral action be secure and really moral.[13] The other side of the coin is at issue here: in order to be morally corrected, one has to have an understanding of one's wrongdoing and the reason it is wrong, for without understanding punishment cannot carry a moral message. Plato develops this claim in the *Gorgias,* where he argues that one who does wrong and feels guilty about it will seek punishment for his own good, because punishment rids us of injustice in the same way that medicine rids us of sickness and moneymaking rids us of poverty.[14] The intelligent wrongdoer sees that he will benefit by

[11]Mabbott, "Punishment," p. 167. Mabbott, however, restricts the notion of "status" to institutional contexts and maintains that there is no such thing as punishment apart from a system of institutional rules: "The only justification for punishing any man is that he has broken a law," he writes, contrary to common usage (pp. 171–72). Mabbott is concerned to deny not familial punishment, however, but the existence of punishment for a moral offense: for that "God alone has the *status* necessary" (p. 168).

[12]Nietzsche is right, it seems to me, when he says that consciousness of one's guilt and capacity for wrongdoing should be at the ground level of any account of morality. See Friedrich Nietzsche, "'Guilt,' 'Bad Conscience,' and the Like," in *On the Genealogy of Morals,* trans. Walter Kaufmann and R. J. Hollingdale (New York: Random House, 1969).

[13]Alexander Nehamas explores this part of Socrates' ethics and defends him against intellectualizing morality in "Socrates' Intellectualism," a paper read at the University of California, Berkeley, in November 1986, to appear in *Proceedings of the Boston Area Colloquium in Ancient Philosophy, 1987.*

[14]Plato, *Gorgias,* trans. W. D. Woodhead, in *The Collected Dialogues of Plato,* ed. Edith Hamilton and Huntington Cairns (Princeton: Princeton University Press, 1961), p. 478.

being punished; on the other side, if he sees no benefit, he will receive none.

Now this seems paradoxical: the man whom punishment can benefit is the wrongdoer who appreciates punishment and even seeks it. It seems paradoxical that while he has committed a moral offense, the wrongdoer understands a good bit about morality, and his understanding enables him to feel guilty; and in this context punishment seems good to him and purifying. It seems paradoxical because under such conditions punishment doesn't really teach him about wrong, for he already knows about it.

The paradox is worked out in three dimensions by Dostoyevsky in *Crime and Punishment,* where the chief of police appears to play a game of cat-and-mouse with Raskolnykov, who has justified his murder of an old woman on a sophisticated philosophical view of good. The police chief, though convinced of Raskolnykov's guilt and possessed of evidence against him, declines to close in on the culprit; he seems to be waiting for something. What does he wait for? We discover that he is waiting for Raskolnykov to recognize that what he did was wrong. *Then* his criminal apprehension will have its right meaning and will be viewed in its right light, then it may carry its moral message. Reformative punishment rests on a culprit's moral understanding: that is the paradox Dostoyevsky presents.

Discussing Hegel's view, McTaggart writes: "The object of punishment is that the criminal should repent of his crime, and by so doing realize the moral character . . . which is, as Hegel asserts, really his truest and deepest nature." But this, he adds, is not the same as the "reformatory" view of punishment: "The reformatory theory says that we ought to reform our criminals *while* we are punishing them. Hegel says that punishment itself tends to reform them."[15] We have found, however, that reform requires that the

---

[15]McTaggart, "Hegel's Theory of Punishment," in *Philosophical Perspectives on Punishment,* ed. Ezorsky, p. 41. McTaggart considers the punishment that reforms to be an impossibility. "Can [an offender] ever be reformed simply by punishment? Reform and repentance involve that he should either see that something was wrong which before he thought was right, or else that the intensity of his moral feelings should be so strengthened that he is enabled to resist a temptation, to which before he yielded. And why should punishment help him to do either of these things?" (ibid., p. 484).

offender regard his punishment in a certain way, and a theory of punishment cannot make such a requirement.

Now we come to the question: What does the case of the child have to do with criminal punishment? McTaggart puts the difference this way: "A child, while it is young enough to be treated entirely as a child, can and ought to find its morality in the commands of others. . . . But a man is not a child." An adult lacks the relation to the state that a child has to his parents, a relation of moral subordination. "The state is not God, and the surrender of our Consciences to the control of others has become impossible. A man may indeed accept the direction of a teacher whom he has chosen. . . . But then this is by virtue of his own act of choice. We cannot now accept any purely outward authority as having, of its own right, the power of deciding for us on matters of right and wrong."[16] Having reached adulthood, an individual has moral autonomy, which he cannot relinquish. He is no longer in a position to be taught about morality by an authority. There is no room for moral education of an autonomous adult.

If this argument is right, then there is no point in talking of institutional punishment as a means to moral reform, for although punishment may have served that purpose in childhood, it cannot do so in adulthood. A paternalistic moral role for the state cannot be justified: this is roughly Kant's position.

It is nonetheless true that punishment sometimes brings about a change in moral perspective and thus in a sense reforms. Dostoyevsky gives us the impression that such a change occurs in Raskolnykov, for while originally his view was that punishment was something a clever person might and should avoid, his view undergoes a change. Persuaded to confess and turn himself in to the authorities, he remains rebellious for some time; but in prison he comes to see things differently. What brought about the change?

The change, one speculates, had something to do with his sentence to hard labor and the rough conditions of his life, and had much to do with his faithful friend Sophie. Yet by the present argument repentance requires another condition without which

[16]Ibid., pp. 54–55.

Raskolnykov's conversion is finally unconvincing.[17] If punishment is to do an offender good, the ground must be prepared so that he can interpret punishment to his moral benefit. He must, then, already have an awareness of morality and responsibility and he must respect the authority that punishes, not view it as arbitrary or prejudicial. Given these conditions, punishment might be understood as expressive of the community's condemnation; and under these conditions a responsible person may understandably feel ashamed and humiliated.

Feinberg emphasizes the "expressive" function of punishment, as we have seen, saying that "punishment is a conventional device for the expression of attitudes of resentment and indignation, and of judgments of disapproval and reprobation." But one wants to know precisely what the connection is between this symbolism and the suffering that punishment imposes. According to Feinberg, the connection is simply conventional: "certain forms of hard treatment have become the conventional symbols of public reprobation . . . [just as] certain words have become conventional vehicles in our language for the expression of certain attitudes."[18] This account suggests that an offender, being familiar with the conventions and practices of his society, will understand the message, which is one of censure and disapproval. But it also allows the possibility that no moral lesson may be grasped, and in that case punishment can't be the direct vehicle for moral reform. This argument is in keeping with my own.

If punishment is to help an offender, a necessary condition is that he be prepared and already have a sense of responsibility for his actions. He has not only to feel the condemnation of the community but to acknowledge its moral authority and its claim to his uprightness; thus he has to be able to see for himself the wrongfulness of his action. Under such conditions a culprit may, as Raskolnykov does, benefit morally, be repentant and reformed.

This conception is related to Plato's view that punishment is

---

[17]It is arguable that Dostoyevsky is simply unconvincing on the change Raskolnykov is supposed to undergo. I owe to Jo Anne Shea an interesting and persuasive argument to this effect.

[18]Joel Feinberg, "The Expressive Function of Punishment," in *Philosophical Perspectives,* ed. Ezorsky, pp. 27–29.

valuable as an antidote to guilt, and to Kant's and Hegel's view that punishment is *respectful* treatment of an offender, that it is what he has a right to. For punishment is now really an instrument of reform and moral teaching. But the conditions necessary for this function still lie in the offender and cannot be presumed to be general.[19] Can we be sure they are satisfied? Often we can't. Like some children, adult offenders may take punishment in a sense other than the one intended no matter what we do. It is not qua punishment, then, that punishment is educational; it is instructive for someone ready to learn, who already has moral understanding.

This analysis shows that the "reformative" view of punishment depends on having a certain kind of offender.[20] The assignment of such a role to punishment encounters precisely the same difficulty as does parental punishment, that is, no moral lesson is conveyed unless an offender is ready to understand it. An expression of condemnation may satisfy the community but do nothing at all for the one who needs moral correction.

The comparison of criminals with errant children changes our perspective on the subject. Instead of focusing on the punisher and his choice of punishments, we now put the offender in a central position and raise the question the utilitarians raise: What is the point of it? When an offender stands behind his offenses, the point is lost. Consider Thoreau's interpretation of his imprisonment. "As I stood considering the walls of solid stone, two or three feet thick, the door of wood and iron, a foot thick, and the iron grating which strained the light, I could not help being struck with the foolishness of that institution which treated me as if I were mere flesh and blood and bones, to be locked up. . . . I could not but smile to see how industriously they locked the door on my meditations. . . ." This prisoner has no lesson to learn. His moral compass is set, and consequently he sees his punishment as pure

---

[19]Mabbott ("Punishment," p. 165) cites the comments of W. F. R. Macartney, an ex-prisoner, who writes: "To punish a man is to treat him as an equal. To be punished for an offence against rules is a sane man's right" (*Walls Have Mouths* [London: Gollancz, 1936], p. 172).

[20]I am using "reformative" more loosely than MacTaggert in the quotation cited earlier, for he characterizes the reformatory view as the judgment that an authority should reform *as well as* punish, while I am discussing the power of punishment itself to reform.

foolishness, a mistake of lesser people. It expresses their anger at his stubborn noncompliance (as Feinberg requires) but in doing so it fails to merit his respect. "As they could not reach me, they had resolved to punish my body; just as boys, if they cannot come at some person against whom they have spite, will abuse his dog."[21] They punish what they can get at in stupidity and spite, Thoreau thinks. This is a paradigm of ineffectual and pointless punishment if punishment is supposed to be morally instructive. What makes it pointless, however, isn't the law itself, or the authority that enforces it; what makes it pointless is the attitude of the prisoner.

IV

I have argued that the ability of punishment to carry a moral message depends on the attitude of the punishee; it's thus a chancy kind of communication. The message won't be understood any more than the explicit message of a moral lecture, which might in any case be substituted for it. Walter Moberly says that "the proper attitude towards flagrant wickedness is robust and militant." Nonetheless, "we do not feel this of the misdemeanours of small children, or of the feeble-minded, but . . . we feel it especially of deeds of cruelty or heartlessness, for here, most manifestly, the offender punished is reaping what he himself has sown."[22] The hardened criminal is the target of our fiercest wrath. Besides taking a retributive stance in punishing him, we condemn him further by saying that he doesn't even mind being wicked! But that complaint tells a tale: if he lacks moral awareness, then he is beyond our means to help him even while we condemn and punish him. His position is a little like that of a creature from another country or another planet. Would we punish such a creature, and if so, why? In the absence of the offender's understanding, punish-

---

[21]Henry David Thoreau, "Civil Disobedience," in *Walden and Reflections on Civil Disobedience* (New York: Signet, 1960), p. 233.

[22]Walter Moberly, *The Ethics of Punishment* (London: Faber & Faber, 1968), pp. 81, 82.

ment lacks its moral meaning, and thus lacks its strongest moral justification.[23]

An offender's moral understanding needs to be seen, then, as an aspect of his membership in the community that he offends.[24] If he is to feel guilt and to see his punishment as justified, he must see his actions from the viewpoint of others, including those who are offended by them. Thus taking punishment morally is linked to seeing oneself as a member in a community. Some writers on punishment refuse to give this linkage any importance. Mabbott, for example, writes: "I have treated the whole set of circumstances as determined. *X* is a citizen of a state. About his citizenship . . . I have asked no questions. About the government, whether it is good or bad, I do not enquire. *X* has broken a law. Concerning the law, whether it is well-devised or not, I have not asked. . . . It is

[23]Joel Feinberg makes an important distinction between penalties and punishment. Punishment involves reprobation, censure, condemnation; penalties don't. Using this distinction, we can say that while in legal punishment the reprobation comes from the community, in parental punishment it comes from the parent. Feinberg thinks that imposition of hardship expresses such condemnation, and he adds: "To say that the very physical treatment . . . expresses condemnation is to say simply that certain forms of hard treatment have become the conventional symbols of public reprobation. . . . Particular kinds of punishment are often used to express quite specific attitudes. . . . Note the differences, for example, between beheading a nobleman and hanging a yeoman, burning a heretic and hanging a traitor." The symbolism of punishment expresses a fusion of resentment and a "stern judgment of disapproval" ("Expressive Function of Punishment," pp. 25–34). In my terminology, it expresses our abhorrence of the wrong done and serves as a language of moral censure.

This account is right so far as it goes, for there is an important difference between payment for damages and punishment. But it doesn't go far enough. In a sense we cannot *impose* shame on an offender—either adult or child—who doesn't already understand something about morality. The Raskolnykov who didn't see his crime as morally wrong cannot be shamed, no matter what the police inspector does or says to him. Similarly Thoreau answered the question "Aren't you ashamed?" with a vehement "No!" Under such circumstances, the symbolic value of punishment would be confined to its value *to us*, to the rest of the community, the punishers—who are then communicating less with the offender than with themselves. Therefore my conclusion stands: if the punishment is to have moral value to the culprit, he must himself recognize its legitimacy and value.

[24]Piaget treats all moral offenses as the breaking of the social bond; see, e.g., *Moral Judgment of the Child*, pp. 208–9. But it is evident that no bond is broken when a child offends and a parent punishes; whatever bond there was remains and is not vitiated. On the contrary, one might say that punishment is in a sense dictated by it.

the essence of my position that none of these questions is relevant. Punishment is a corollary of lawbreaking by a member of the society whose law is broken." Mabbott thinks that he has shown that punishment is justified solely by the violation of some law that pertains to the lawbreaker. The law itself, not membership in a community or a sense of it, is correlated with punishment in its full sense. It is evident, however, that the law violated has its status as a law of a community that includes the offender at the same time that it punishes him. A wrongdoer is a part of a community, not an enemy or adversary, and it is simply as a member that he is punished. Mabbott should therefore think of the offender as related not only to the law but to the law *in virtue of* his membership in the community. And how does his membership in that community affect his relation to those who punish him and ascribe responsibility to him? If, as Mabbott says, "it takes two to make a punishment," in what relation do the parties stand?[25] That is the question that needs to be answered.

V

Some writers have dealt with punishment simply as a practical necessity in the maintenance of social order. In this light it is not understood as treatment of individual offenders but as part of the larger machinery and practical functioning of the community. Moberly writes, for example: "The main purpose of penal law is not to be found in the actual infliction of punishment on the few convicted criminals, but in the operation of the threat of punishment on the far larger number of potential criminals."[26] The weakness of this treatment lies in the way it morally neutralizes punishment. It may be practically necessary to punish people in order to maintain society, making it an instrumental good to the

[25]Mabbott, "Punishment," p. 174. Edmund Pincoffs presents a valuable discussion of the issue whether people cannot generally be held responsible for what they do, arguing that ascriptions of responsibility constitute a variety of related processes (*The Justification of Legal Punishment* [New York: Humanities Press, 1966], pp. 106–7).

[26]Moberly, "Ethics of Punishment," p. 62.

end of something good in itself. But if this is the only or main
justification of the institution of punishment, then its moral significance is frail; its justification must rest on something like deterrence. Limited in this way, punishment would be a tool of social
behavior training and its interest to ethics minimal.[27]

The social need for conformity can, however, be connected to
morality, as it is in Devlin's view that "the criminal law as we
know it is based upon moral principle . . . [and] in a number of
crimes its function is simply to enforce a moral principle and nothing else. . . . A common morality is part of the bondage" necessary for a society, he argues, and "society may use the law to
preserve morality in the same way as it uses it to safeguard anything else that is essential to its existence."[28] Here we have the
practical aim, to bind society together, furthered by the moral one,
to bind it with moral rules. On Devlin's view, the law, which
creates and imposes penalties for immoral conduct, is essentially a
tool of morality and an extension of it, and therefore the conformity it imposes has the same justification as a moral rule.

But this view raises a very interesting point. The law may compel behavior that is morally acceptable insofar as the disincentives
to crime are effective. By means of draconian measures, theft and
embezzlement, for example, might be controlled. But to compel
behavior that is morally acceptable is not to compel citizens to be
moral. There is nothing particularly moral in obeying a law whose
violation subjects offenders to harsh punishment, even though the
law is founded on a moral injunction, since the reason for obeying
may still be prudential and, as Kant would say, thus lack moral
content. This is basically the point made about deterrence: even
when the motive for promulgating a law is to express the moral
commitment of the community, its ability to express and impose

[27]Pincoffs argues, for instance, that the justification of *legal* punishment has to
satisfy two conditions: "that under the circumstances, *a* practice is necessary,
called for, or would be useful; and that of the alternatives available and acceptable,
the practice in question would likely be the most effective" (*Justification of Legal
Punishment*, p. 116). It is clear, however, that the public debate over forms of
punishment invariably involves moral elements and moral reasons, and that the
justification of legal punishment is not easily separable from the way it is seen
morally.

[28]Devlin, *Enforcement of Morals*, pp. 7, 10–11.

morality is limited in precisely the same way as punishment's ability to express a moral judgment: in both cases the moral force is conveyed only when the law and the punishment *are seen as having moral force*.

When we deal with the community instead of with law or rules as such, we get a deeper, more complex view of punishment. When we take the community as the context of both offense and punishment, with its institutions serving as the machinery for dealing with both, it becomes clear that even an offender who is "put away" in a prison and cut off from his normal community and activities is nonetheless in the community. A prison is not somewhere outside the society, a kind of purgatory or exile; it lies in and is governed by the community to which the offender belongs.[29]

The importance of this fact is made clear when we compare the actions of a school in punishing a child and in expelling him. Punishment can be regarded as part of the student's school life, but expulsion brings that life to an end. In the same way when we punish a criminal we keep him—through the penal institution—in the wide communal circle, just as a parent keeps a punished child within the family while confining him to a room. In neither case is expulsion an aspect of the confinement. But to impose exile is really to sever the bonds of responsibility and obligation, and this action goes beyond the strictest sense of punishment.[30]

The significance of this distinction is large. Since an offender remains part of the community that punishes, it has not only to accommodate his presence but to deal with the fact that punishment is not interminable, boundless. Thus it has to face a prisoner's eventual reentry into the normal currents of social life. Does this eventuality affect, or should it affect, the punishment im-

---

[29]On the tendency to remove offenders from society into a separate environment with its own code, relationships, and institutions, see Michel Foucault, *Discipline and Punish: The Birth of the Prison,* trans. Alan Sheridan (New York: Random House, 1979), pt. 4, esp. pp. 292–93.

[30]An indication of the difference is seen in the differential treatment of aliens who break the law and offending citizens. The alien is treated like an enemy for whom one lacks responsibility; his treatment may be brutal and ferocious even when treatment of citizens is relatively humane. This distinction has been observed from ancient times. For a modern discussion, see Sissela Bok, *Lying: Moral Choice in Public and Private Life* (New York: Random House, 1979), pp. 141–53.

posed? One can hardly answer no. The former prisoner W. F. R. Macartney, reflecting on what prisons may do to offenders, makes the point often made by utilitarians: "To keep a man in prison for many years at considerable expense and then to free him charged to the eyes with uncontrollable venom and hatred generated by the treatment he has received in gaol, does not appear to be sensible."[31] The analogous meaning for the child's case is also clear. If the net result of punishment is to harden the child's negative attitudes and raise the intensity of his anger, something is not right. For there is a future for offenders just as there is for victims, and the community that serves as the background for that future has every reason to be concerned about whether its actions foster hostility. But further, as parents are concerned with their responsibility as moral teachers, the community should be concerned with its responsibility to preserve a healthy moral community. Incarceration needs to be shown to have an intelligible relation to that end.

Godwin and other utilitarians argue that as we are all members of the same community, we are responsible for dealing humanely with others even though they offend, since their actions in future will necessarily affect us. But my point goes further: the offender remains one of us even in prison. And regardless of good or bad consequences, we cannot pretend that retribution for wrongdoing is the end of the story, since the retribution comes to an end within the same social setting where punishment is imposed. The community is morally involved with the offender even while he is imprisoned; it continues to live on some moral basis with him. Exile, which may be imposed for similar reasons, puts a person beyond punishment. It puts him where he may begin again with no connection to his past community, the society that he wronged. Here forgetfulness has a palpable form.

This discussion reflects again how mistaken it is to think of punishment in terms of abstract formulas, as if justice had a definite form under the gaze of eternity. For the community that punishes can be seen as shaping the offender's character and the extent of his understanding in countless ways, and even in punish-

---

[31]Macartney, *Walls Have Mouths,* p. 152, quoted in Mabbott, "Punishment," p. 179.

ment it participates in his life. How can it pretend detachment when an offense has been committed? The culprit's punishment necessarily takes place in the same context as his youth and training, not in a world of abstract concepts and principles.

VI

I have pursued the assumption that there is an important similarity between a family and a community in regard to punishment. Both are possessed of authority and both have some kind of responsibility for the moral environment of their members. In both cases, members are knitted together by moral bonds. Socrates expressed his obligation to the community in this way: "Bad people always have a bad effect, and good people a good effect, upon their nearest neighbors. Am I so . . . ignorant as not even to realize that by spoiling the character of one of my companions I shall run the risk of getting some harm from him?"[32] We set examples for one another; but even more important, we have to live with others in the environment that we help to create. In the light of such interdependency, the roles of victim and offender are not so easy to distinguish. All suffer at the hands of all. Not only the character of the offense but the character of the community should be a guiding consideration for punitive policies.

In the *Crito* Socrates imagines the laws of Athens speaking to him when his friends urge him to escape execution. The laws say: "You did not have equality with your father, or your employer . . . to enable you to retaliate. You were not allowed to answer back . . . or to hit back. . . . Do you expect to have such license against your country and its laws that if we try to put you to death in the belief that it is right to do so, you on your part will try your hardest to destroy your country and us its laws in return?" They pursue the analogy: "Compared with mother and father and all the rest of your ancestors," the laws tell Socrates, "your country is something far more precious, more venerable, more sacred." And

---

[32]Plato, *Apology,* trans. Hugh Tredennick, in *Collected Dialogues,* ed. Hamilton and Cairns, 25e.

violence, which is a sin "even against your parents . . . is a far greater sin against your country."[33]

Likening one's community to one's parents may be hyperbolic, but its main features are sound. There is reciprocity in both relationships; in both there is care and responsibility for a person's welfare on the one side and respect owing on the other. In both cases responsibility and respect seem to derive simply from the fact that both, community and parents, are one's own. This analogy then shows how to answer the perennially interesting question why we should obey the laws: we should obey them not because they are good or just but because they are the laws of our own state. At the same time the duty to obey the law (and by analogy one's parents) is rebuttable by more powerful moral considerations, as Thoreau gives striking witness.

It follows from this relationship that the state's use of punishment needs to be seen not only in terms of an abstract equation of suffering to wrong, or in terms of a moral notion of desert, but in the light of other values. For if we imagine the state concerned with moral education, then other measures, besides or in addition to punishment, might better further that aim. This possibility becomes more reasonable when we recognize that the offender remains part of the community and thus potentially an active citizen even while he is being punished.

Offenders who are thoroughly unconscious of their guilt, unconscious of the moral bond between themselves and the community that punishes them, pose a serious problem. They need to be dealt with somehow; but if they are not morally educable, how can they be dealt with? The question is profoundly troublesome. On the one side the question is how to approach them so as to improve their moral awareness; this is a concern not only because the community is responsible for what it does but also, as Socrates says, because their good or bad characters affect the rest of us. On the other hand, there is a clear need to put them out of circulation, separated from the rest of the community, to be monitored and regulated so as not to endanger others again. But when the han-

---

[33]Plato, *Crito*, trans. Hugh Tredennick, in *Collected Dialogues*, ed. Hamilton and Cairns, 51a–b.

dling of offenders is described in this way and as having this purpose, it clearly amounts to quarantine, which we have seen is distinguishable from punishment and lacks its troublesome moral features. One suffers in being quarantined, but not in the manner of punishment.[34] In any case, one question that confronts us is: How important is it to express censure and condemnation by punishment rather than in some other way? For if the expression of condemnation is what punishment is primarily expected to do, it is a particularly powerful and hazardous form of expression. A second question is what form punishment, if it appears justified, should take. There are many options here which are for the most part unexplored in the literature on punishment.

To see what one did as seriously wrong is to be in a wretched state. If an offender has this awareness, then punishment is only an additional, and perhaps even a minor, imposition. For such offenders its moral message is not needed; it is not an instrument of education, though it may be one of atonement; and such an offender may agree it is just and even welcome it as purification; but he will not be morally improved by it.

But if an offender cannot see that he is responsible for a serious wrong and punishment cannot carry its moral message, the question then is: How does it help him? It cannot, without a change in him, though that change may come nonetheless, fortuitously. Of course in the meantime something must be done to protect the rest of society from him. But punishment is not a form of protection from an offender; it is something directed specifically at him. How can it be justified in the present case?

VII

An examination of the punishment of children sheds light on the debate between retributivists and utilitarians. The utilitarian

---

[34]Durkheim writes that originally incarceration was instituted so that the criminal could be detained until his punishment was determined, and only later did incarceration become itself a form of punishment ("Forms of Social Solidarity," in *Emile Durkheim: Selected Writings*, trans. and ed. Anthony Giddens [Cambridge: Cambridge University Press, 1972], pp. 125–26). Foucault is very informative in tracing punishment through various phases to the modern "correctional" prison; see *Discipline and Punish*, esp. pt. 4.

would punish only for future good results. Now punishment is part of many children's training, and in the context of a family, it often serves to express moral censure and parental concern for character. But it is also part of children's training in everyday practices and manners; so there is a potential difficulty in separating the moral connection from the more arbitrary nonmoral one, where censure of a deep kind is absent. The fact that punishment is thus an unreliable way of expressing a moral message needn't bother a utilitarian, however, since if it works to achieve good results, those results justify it in any case. In short, the utilitarian declines to give punishment a moral role as opposed to a deterrent one.

The retributivist, however, often sees punishment as educational, as does Moberly, who argues that in administering retributive punishment the community is exercising its moral role and giving moral education, for the punishment serves "to deepen the horror with which certain types of action ought to be regarded." The general aim of punishment, he says, is "always to *vindicate* the moral order."[35] Thus he appears to see all punitive authorities, from parents to states, as bringing home the moral lesson. In considering the harshness of punishment as instructive, Moberly seems to see it from a divine or cosmic perspective, as exemplifying a cosmic order of justice, and, as we have seen, this perspective is in general an inappropriate moral guide. We may therefore try to take a more mundane view, like that of a responsible parent or the concerned head of a school, and ask what results we want punishment to achieve in the long run. But now our approach resembles the utilitarian one.

We can combine the two approaches if we suppose that one of the good results punishment may have is to foster moral development, carry a moral message. Such a position would be distinguished from Bentham's, which declares that the end of law is to augment happiness, from which it follows, he says, that "all punishment itself is evil . . . and ought only to be admitted in as far as it promises to exclude some greater evil."[36] We can look at

[35]Moberly, *Ethics of Punishment*, pp. 95, 96.
[36]Jeremy Bentham, *An Introduction to the Principles of Morals and Legislation* (New York: Hafner, 1948), chap. 13, sec. 1; chap. 14, secs. 1–2.

moral training and moral awareness as one point of any response to wrongdoing, and if an offender's understanding is necessary for interpreting our response, then any avenue to that understanding is also an appropriate response to his wrongdoing. At the same time, places of confinement can be justified not as institutions of punishment but as places of quarantine. What an offender may do while he is there, what useful work or community service, and what he may learn for his moral or other benefit are areas for development in a nonpunitive framework.

Mabbott poses the following intriguing issue: "A Headmaster launching a new school must explicitly make [two decisions]. First, shall he have any rules at all? Second, what rules shall he have? The first decision is a genuine one. . . . Would it not be better to have an 'honour' system . . . ? Or would complete freedom be better? . . . Or should he personally deal with each malefactor individually, as the case arises, in the way most likely to improve his conduct?"[37] This example can serve to expand our sense of the options we have in both the family and the community. A parent may choose the last alternative, as the person most concerned to instill moral training in whatever way is likely to be understood and effective and the one least concerned with order and conventions of equity. What works for one child may not work for another, and distinctions of treatment can be made if the family isn't large. A smallish school can manage without most rules fairly well, leaving most moral training to the family and legal discipline to the state. Yet the headmaster is also to a degree both "moral physician" and legal authority. Can a community take a similar approach? In a small community governed by a revered elder, each case might be considered without concern for precedent, for what was done the last time. But we have as part of our heritage respect for each person's moral autonomy and a mistrust of claim to authority. As a consequence we believe we must have rules that are applied impartially, without concern for individual differences, even without regard for unfortunate moral consequences. So moral atomism is at work here. One might say that under it the chief problem for the theory of

---

[37]Mabbott, "Punishment," pp. 177–78.

punishment is how to deal with the moral anomalies of egalitarian punitive institutions and policies.

The main conclusions of this exploration are that, whether in the context of a community, a school, or a family, punishment needs to be evaluated partly as an instrument of moral education, for that is its most powerful justification. Given the fact that offenders are, even in prison, members in the society for whom the rest are in some way responsible, the challenge is to conceive of prisons in some nondestructive and perhaps positive way.

Most of us are unwilling to concede that punishment may be at bottom, as Durkheim says, "a mechanical and aimless reaction . . . an irrational need to destroy."[38] Nonetheless, as we have seen, the proper response to wrongdoing *is* indignation, intolerance, anger, and the impulse to do something in response. That is part of the dialectic of wrong and justice. Thus indignation ought not to be derogated, as it is by utilitarians, and made something to be ashamed of. At the same time, as we saw in Chapter 7, it is often difficult to find any right and satisfying response to wrong. Sometimes all options are morally flawed, and in such cases our anger finds no justifiable expression in action and may go unassuaged.

Wrongdoers provoke deep indignation; that is as it should be. But precisely because they do and because we have impulses to act against and hurt them, we must exercise care and caution in adapting punishment to human frailties. We need in the end to concern ourselves not only with the frailties of offenders but with those of punishers as well.

[38]Durkheim, "Forms of Social Solidarity," p. 125.

9

Justice and a Form of Life

I argued that the concept of justice is rooted in a sense of injustice, a felt indignation, and that abhorrence of wrong is the foundation of all talk about justice—just remedies, just punishments, and so on. But what is the moral significance of this abhorrence? It is not reasonable that moral judgments should turn upon uncultivated, "natural" feelings, variable and personal as they may be, and uncontrolled by reason. And it should be clear that I do not mean by abhorrence of wrong a "cool sentiment" in the fashion of Bishop Butler; a concern about injustice is powerful and passionate, typically angry and impatient, and sometimes able to move one to heroic efforts. But being thus connected to intense feeling, beliefs about what is just and unjust may seem to have neither a general basis nor any objectivity. They threaten to be as unpredictable as matters of taste. Thus an emphasis on the role of passion in such moral judgments puts them in danger of seeming subjective and relative. This issue needs to be faced.

I

How do people ever come to understand and make moral judgments—how do children, for instance, learn this part of their language? To answer we need to imagine the kind of context—

that is, a family—in which a child grows, and need to imagine a parent who says such things as "You didn't do *that,* did you?" and "How *could* you?" and "That's a *terrible* thing!" and "You *know* you shouldn't do that!" For these are a few of the direct ways in which a child learns the language of morality: "bad," "wrong," "ashamed," and the like.

When children are scolded, they learn what they are allowed to do and simultaneously learn one segment of the language, the part that deals with disapprobation and blame. So in much of a child's early training a pattern emerges: doing things right prompts praise, doing them wrong evokes criticism. Doing nearly anything incorrectly—using words, counting, tying shoes, dressing—typically evokes an expression of disapproval, while doing something right often evokes no comment. It may seem merely curious that such training typically involves more criticism, condemnation, and censure than praise, that this is an area of language with a peculiarly negative bias. But this fact is not so mysterious if one sees here a grammatical connection between making mistakes and the intolerance of wrong. Negative judgments—in particular expressions of abhorrence at wrong—are at the heart of moral discourse.

In censuring children's conduct by saying "You ought not" and encouraging it by saying "You ought," parents teach children not merely language but behavior. But how can this be? Without first understanding expressions of disapproval, how does a child know what she should do? Understanding the meaning must come first; only after that can we speak of obedience and disobedience.

This point can be compared with the point made by Wittgenstein about how we come to obey and understand orders. It seemed logically necessary to Bertrand Russell that we must first understand each word in a command before we can either obey or disobey.[1] Wittgenstein expresses the idea this way: "There is a gulf between an order and its execution. It has to be filled by the act of understanding."[2] Against this appearance Wittgenstein argued that

---

[1]See in particular Bertrand Russell, *Problems of Philosophy* (London: Oxford University Press, 1912), pp. 58–59.

[2]Ludwig Wittgenstein, *Philosophical Investigations,* trans. G. E. M. Anscombe (New York: Macmillan, 1953), I, 431.

knowing what commands and orders mean *is* knowing what one should do in response to them. We understand the order *when* we know what is expected of us. An intellectual grasp of meaning does not occur first, followed later by our application of that understanding to some concrete situation, an application that itself may be right or wrong. The understanding and training are not distinct; the two processes merge—there is only one.

In a similar way, learning the name of an object may mean learning what to do with it. I have already referred to Wittgenstein's dramatic assertion that "it is part of the grammar of the word 'chair' that *this* is what it is to sit in a chair."[3] His point here is that language "meshes with our life," as he says in another context; its use "is part of our life," and "commanding, questioning, recounting . . . are as much part of our natural history as walking, eating, drinking, playing."[4] For all of us the processes of learning our native language as children, learning how to do things, and learning how to act are woven seamlessly together.

Thus a young child who hears "Did *you* do that?" hears the tone of censure and disapproval and feels the sting of reproach. And how does the child know the meaning of that tone of voice? Where did she learn it? Was that meaning also taught in some particular way? Surely something lies behind the child's understanding of the reproachful tone, and that's what we want to clarify.[5] But the question "How does she know?" taken concretely in this context is very strange. The child *lives with* her parents. She is accustomed to their expressions of mood and feeling, including those of shame, regret, condemnation, and criticism of others. Moreover, such expressions *matter* to a child, as the feelings of people to

---

[3]Ludwig Wittgenstein, *The Blue and Brown Books* (New York: Harper & Row, 1958), p. 24.

[4]Ludwig Wittgenstein, *Philosophical Grammar*, ed. Rush Rhees, trans. Anthony Kenny (Berkeley: University of California Press, 1974), 65; *Philosophical Investigations*, I, 25.

[5]As the language of morality essentially involves expressions of feelings, the question here has a parallel in the question of how a child can learn the language of sensation. Norman Malcolm writes that "the gestures, facial expressions, words, and activities . . . that constitute pitying and comforting . . . are, I think, a good example of what Wittgenstein means by a 'form of life' " (*Knowledge and Certainty* [Ithaca: Cornell University Press, 1963], p. 119).

whom she is attached by bonds of many kinds, whose love and trust are important for many reasons. As a child observes her parents and lives with them, she gradually senses the feelings that go with these characteristic expressions, including expressions of condemnation.[6] Her parents are moved and upset as they speak in tones of passionate censure; something important has happened; in some cases the child's own behavior is the cause of their unhappiness. So the censure of others and censure of self become intertwined in the process of learning what one should do.

To say that understanding "dawns," to use Wittgenstein's expression, is to imply that it doesn't come in a flash—as one can sometimes grasp a mathematical truth—and also that it doesn't arrive by way of a proof or an explanation. To understand what this experience is for a child, think how we observe and interpret a person speaking a language that we don't understand at all. We watch the features, listen for the tone of voice, see what will occur next, how others react, and so on. In the child's case, what dawns is an understanding of what it is to censure, the emotions that go with censure, and the things that are censurable—a whole gestalt

---

[6] I emphasize tone of voice here because it is often more powerful than the precise words of censure. In his lectures on aesthetics Wittgenstein also emphasizes the role of tone of voice and gestures in some judgments. He asks of Macbeth's statement "Duncan is in his grave": "Can I describe his feelings better than by describing how he said it?" (according to his student Yorick Smythies, whose notes are also given, Wittgenstein's answer should go "than by imitating the way he said it?"); and in the same series of lectures he speaks of "This is fine" as "being used something like a gesture, accompanying a complicated activity" (another student, James Taylor, reports Wittgenstein as saying that the judgment "is on a level with a gesture, almost—connected with other gestures and actions and a whole situation and a culture") (*Lectures and Conversations on Aesthetics, Freud, and Religious Belief*, ed. Cyril Barrett [Berkeley: University of California Press, 1967], p. 33, and see nn. 2 and 11). Gestures, tone of voice, and judgments of commendation and censure are joined together, Wittgenstein appears to say in all versions; and often one can serve the purpose of the other. In this respect aesthetic judgments and moral ones are alike. This interpretation conflicts with J. F. M. Hunter's, who infers from Wittgenstein's remark that an order "may be spoken in a *variety* of tones of voice and with various expressions of face" (*Philosophical Investigations*, I, 21), that "tones of voice and the traditions associated with language are not necessary for learning it" ("'Forms of Life' in Wittgenstein's *Philosophical Investigations*," *American Philosophical Quarterly* 5 [October 1968]: 242). What I mean here is that understanding the tone of voice is part and parcel of understanding what is said in judgments of praise and censure.

of expressions and actions. In the present case it includes the relation in which the child stands to her parents.

In describing how some very basic kinds of learning take place, Wittgenstein said that the child *grows into a form of life.* "My life," he observes, "consists in my being content to accept many things"— among them accepted ways of acting. "We don't start from certain words, but from certain occasions or activities"; we learn how things are done and how to act in certain situations. Thus many things that seem subjective and private have expressions that are learned. The point can be seen in regard to intentions: "an intention is embedded in its situation, in human customs and institutions"; it isn't purely and irreducibly subjective, but embedded in external things, institutions, and customs. And these things and their connections have to be learned. Similarly with "commanding, questioning, recounting, chatting"; they are learned and at the same time natural, "as much part of our natural history as walking, eating, drinking, playing."[7] We learn them as basic elements in the context of a human life.

The child learns day by day a pattern of life, a pattern that has many dimensions. Children learn manners, but also learn appropriate ways of speaking and acting when they stub their toes, when they are frustrated with a problem or puzzle, when they are impatient, bored, and so on. And they learn expressions for intentions, wishes, expectations. Such learning does not proceed by methodical steps; rather it is often absorbed without being taught, without investigation, without verbal explanation or description.

If the child were reared in an environment where wrong was never spoken of or condemned, could she understand this part of the language? Examples of censurable behavior would be missing, she would have no acquaintance with expressions of righteous indignation or censure or guilt. In such circumstances it is difficult to see how morality could mean anything; good and bad, right and

---

[7]Ludwig Wittgenstein, *On Certainty,* ed. G. E. M. Anscombe and G. H. von Wright, trans. Denis Paul and Anscombe (New York: Harper & Row, 1969), 344; *Lectures and Conversations,* p. 3; *Philosophical Investigations,* I 337, 25. For a good account of Wittgenstein's view on the elements of learning in the subjective and private, see Norman Malcolm, "Wittgenstein: The Relation of Language to Instinctive Behavior," *Philosophical Investigations* 5 (January 1982): 3–22.

wrong would be altogether mysterious. But the circumstances here are inconceivable. It is not imaginable that a child should really never hear actions condemned or people censured, never be scolded for doing wrong.

Without examples, it seems clear that a child could hardly judge anyone, including herself, in moral terms—couldn't claim to have acted well or confess to having done wrong, for instance. These terms lie outside her experience. To carry the point one step further, mastery of a full moral vocabulary with its fine distinctions would also be impossible except as the child learns responsibility and grows in her relationships with others. For if she doesn't recognize certain things as responsibilities, she cannot understand their recognition as a motive for others. Understanding and moral development, like the understanding of commands and of the proper response to them, are woven together. These interconnections explain Aristotle's curious remark that only a person of virtue is competent to discuss ethics.[8]

The understanding of morality thus requires acceptance of a role and a moral status. To master the moral part of language is to grow into a set of practices and ways of dealing with others, into a respect for responsibility; and in the process one comes to abhor wrongs. These are features of an adult life toward which one is pointed by the moral experiences of childhood. We can call such a process training, which suggests some need for conformity, but it is a very deep kind of training involving the shaping of important life attitudes and relationships.

II

In the context of a family where a child is scolded and censured, *why* should the child be motivated to change her behav-

---

[8]Aristotle says, "Now each man judges well the things he knows"; thus in studying ethics, "*we* must begin with what is known to *us*. Hence any one who is to listen intelligently about what is noble and just and, generally about the subjects of political science must have been brought up in good habits" (*Nichomachean Ethics,* trans. W. D. Ross, in *The Basic Works of Aristotle,* ed. Richard McKeon [New York: Random House, 1941], 1095a–b).

ior—why should she learn to behave? One wants to supply a motive here.

This question seems very hard and at the same time very fundamental, a version of the question why anyone should be moral. But in a real setting it's nonetheless strange. How could the child *not* be motivated, given her connections of love and trust with her parents?[9] Not only is the child subjected to her parents' censure, but her behavior is the cause of *their* guilt and shame. The child's actions reflect on the parents, on their moral character and acceptance of responsibility. So with regard to children's behavior, it is as if parent and child were one gestalt, one complex form, the offense of one tied to the shame of the other. Thus one might say that the child's motivation is really an extension of the parents' concern, concern focused on her, but also on her *in relation to them*. The question why a child should want to behave better and avoid parental reprimand cannot be asked in an atomistic context, where children are independent and autonomous. And if the question is asked in the context of a normal child's upbringing, it hasn't any clear sense.

This account may be seen as psychology or autobiography of a particular kind, and such characterizations would be right insofar as they correct the assumption that first we learn about morals intellectually, and that this understanding motivates us to do what we should. For it's not a process in which prior understanding comes at some point to engage, like a separate wheel, the motive to do right. Rather the point of moral teaching is to get the child to do what is right and respect what is right within a framework of concern and responsibility and the love of others. The importance of good behavior is thus revealed by the multitude of ways we relate the good things the child does—and the bad ones—to our own lives and our own example.

This account is contrasted not only to those that maintain that a child first learns intellectually what is right and then does it but also to Piaget's empirical studies of children's behavior and talk.

9John Rawls views "authority guilt" as a product of the "love, trust, and faith" of children in their parents. The feeling of guilt at one's disobedience is logically connected with such love and trust, he argues ("The Sense of Justice," *Philosophical Review* 72 [1963]: 281–305).

Piaget believes that children first learn to follow rules given by an unquestioned authority and thus first associate what is right with following such rules to the letter. Their sense of wrong stems from "constraint and . . . primitive forms of unilateral respect" for authority.[10] But a child's early experience with right and wrong is not quite so simple or so dominated by rules. The connection of a young child with her parent is not simply that between an authority and an underling; it is a complicated, reciprocal relation in which the child's behavior reflects back on the parent both as parent and as person, and the parent's example, both in expression and in action, serves as a pattern for the child. Morally speaking, you might say that they are mutually dependent and symbiotic, even though the child is in other ways dependent and immature.[11]

On this account we have no serious reason to wonder why a child should bother to be moral, any more than we would wonder why she should learn her mother tongue. So to ask about a particular child why *she* wants to be good is to imply that the child isn't normal; it's like asking why she has *this* physical shape or *this* attitude. Of normal children there is nothing to explain. That children learn from the example and the concern of parents is not surprising: animal and bird offspring learn their practices in much the same way.

We are inclined to begin a subject by asking how crucial terms can be explained or defined, and that approach in turn leads to a separation of understanding and doing, between comprehension and motivation. What we need is a better way to begin. Wittgenstein's detailed discussion of simple languages lead to his use of "language games," which are "meant to bring into prominence the fact that the *speaking* of language is part of an activity, or of a form of life."[12]

Wittgenstein's term "form of life" has puzzled many philosophers and has been variously interpreted. Some readers have taken

---

[10]Jean Piaget, *The Moral Judgment of the Child,* trans. Marjorie Gabain (New York: Macmillan, 1965), pp. 135–36; see also pp. 11–12.

[11]This kind of symbiosis sometimes characterizes the relation of teachers and students, leading students to feel a responsibility to reflect credit on their teachers. The respect here is clearly more than respect for authority; it is respect for the relationship itself.

[12]Wittgenstein, *Blue and Brown Books,* p. 23.

it to mean an overarching system, like a system of religious beliefs; others take it to mean simply a language game. Still others think it finally comes down to our character as a species, that is, our form of life is the form of humans as a lion's is that of the larger felines.[13]

I propose that "Which is the right meaning, the biological or the cultural?" is the wrong question, that Wittgenstein means to include some biological capabilities, such as the capacity for speech, as well as things that develop out of these capabilities as a person grows, that is, learned behavior and expressive language. The term "form of life" thus contains both things organically united; and their unity in Wittgenstein's writings reflects, I believe, their unity in a person's training and growth. We have a human set of capacities and endowments, yes; but they are trained, guided, and developed not by biological programming alone.[14] The training can theoretically be separated from the individuals who are trained, but the fact that they become the individuals they do can be attributed in part to their upbringing.[15] It is the "unencumbered self" of atomism that is the myth, not the individual who grows into a form of life.

I propose, then, that the term "form of life" is useful to Wittgenstein and useful for the present subject *because* of these ambiguities and not despite them. It's useful because in that concept the various strains of meaning, the "natural" and what is imposed, don't bear separation but are permanently fused.

III

An expression of moral objection is a passionate expression, and such expression is a central feature of moral existence. We can hardly imagine moral discourse without expressions

[13]The first interpretation can be found in Patrick Sherry's *Religion, Truth, and Language Games* (New York: Barnes & Noble, 1977). The second view is J. F. M. Hunter's, in his "'Forms of Life,'" pp. 233–43. The third is the line of reasoning in Newton Garver's "Form of Life in Wittgenstein's *Investigations*" (unpublished manuscript).

[14]Mary Midgley, *Beast and Man* (Ithaca: Cornell University Press, 1978), is very good on this point; see especially chaps. 12 and 13.

[15]For an account of the way ancient Greeks acknowledged this connection and the way it becomes developed as part of a theory of human nature and of society by Plato and Aristotle, see Werner Jaeger, *Paideia: The Ideals of Greek Culture* (New York: Oxford University Press, 1945), 1: chaps. 3–6 and 8.

of censure and abhorrence: "It's terrible," "How could he?," "It's beyond comprehension," and so on. Without the expressions of abhorrence and disbelief, what would judgments of right and wrong sound like? Even natives of a very different culture will have ways of expressing abhorrence which are part of their discourse about wrong.

The feeling we have as we contemplate an action of immorality or virtue is, as Hume said, an essential feature of a moral judgment. The feeling that is expressed in and served by a moral judgment *must* precede that judgment. In this respect I don't deny the charge of subjectivism. For as we saw, we do not pronounce moral judgments in the same way that we speak about the price of oil or the distance between planets; that way of speaking is inconsistent with their correct use. Their use gives moral judgments very great significance, conveying an atmosphere both serious and intense. That is what their emphatic character shows.

To call something unjust is to take it out of the realm of disinterested reportage. But how is this effect achieved? After all, "unjust" is simply an adjective, and there is no hierarchy of adjectives. The answer is that saying that something is a wrong or injustice *marks it* for moral indignation and moral concern.

Nonetheless, calling something wrong does not *only* express indignation. What else, then, does it do? The line between description and expression needs to be considered here.

The child does not develop and grow through sitting quietly and receiving instruction. Nor is learning a language simply learning a skill, such as calculating. Countless things go on around a child, many incomprehensible, some only vaguely understood. Think, for instance, of the kind of altercations adults sometimes engage in, one party denouncing an action while the other defends it. Voices rise in vehemence, in passion, frustration, and anger. Righteous indignation is anger. Now while it is clear that what is being discussed is an intensely felt concern, at the same time no one need infer that it is a matter of *personal interest*. The subject may be public policy, or the actions of another person or of one of the disputants: any of these things may be discussed with fervor but at the same time disinterestedly with respect to the parties' personal desires or points of view.

Now this passionate interest in certain actions but not in others may be regarded by a child, or by a Martian, as simply curious. What does it signify? the Martian asks. What is the great interest these beings find in *this* action or *this* policy? How curious, this intensity!

It is tempting to think that, in order to understand the difference, the child or the Martian must already have some conception of moral judgments and their justifications: one must, or this performance couldn't possibly be understood. But now we have put the cart before the horse. The child *is learning about moral judgments* while she watches this dispute. She is also, like the Martian, learning about human beings.

What does the child learn? She can be compared here with a rather naive anthropologist, one who already has some experience and feeling for this culture. The child doesn't share the intense feelings she observes, but her intimate acquaintance with one or both parties casts some dim light on the exchange. She must suppose that there is something about the question that makes it so passionately interesting. But what?

This questioning curiosity of the child is sometimes mimicked in the attitude of certain moral philosophers. How, they wonder, can we be so concerned about matters that don't directly concern us, our welfare or well-being? Under atomism our concern is mysterious and hard to account for; perhaps at bottom self-interest can explain it. But such philosophers act as if they had no acquaintance with the life of their surroundings, their community and culture, as if they had totally forgotten their early connections with blame and accusation and punishment. In this regard their naiveté is far greater than that of the child.

The child of our example knows that this is a passionate dispute, and though she hasn't learned how to form her own moral judgments or exactly what things are abhorrent, she understands vaguely the place of such feelings in a person's life, and how they relate to what follows. Justifications are given, plans of action outlined, alternatives explored, and all in a tone of impatience and urgency. She has learned, then, about how a person views and is shaped by moral matters. But even knowing these things doesn't bring them into the child's life as completely understood.

But now let us suppose the child finds herself deceived by someone she trusts, and consequently feels taken advantage of. She becomes angry—not as she would if she had been hurt in a fall or been frustrated in doing something. She is angry *at being deceived*, injured at the hands of another, the butt of ill will. What happened was not only hurtful; it was wrong, mean, contemptible.

"Deceived" and "injured" as well as "contemptible" belong to the passionate moral vocabulary. But how did the child acquire this vocabulary? Common sense would find the answer obvious: the child expresses in a similar way the feeling that others do when they have suffered wrongs similar in some way to this one. She sees herself wronged as others have been wronged, and expresses the feeling appropriate to one who is mistreated.

A philosopher asks: But how did this child know that *this* was the right kind of occasion to make this particular judgment, feel this feeling? What indicated that *this* feeling was righteous indignation? What puts her feelings in tune with others'? The case here is parallel to Wittgenstein's classic discussion of pain, which asks, "*How* do I use words to stand for my sensations? . . . Suppose I didn't have any natural expression for the sensation, but only had the sensation? And now I simply *associate* names with sensations and use these names in descriptions."[16] We have the "natural expressions" for sensations, but what significance does "natural" have in this context? What determines that some expression is the "natural" one of a feeling?

We can imagine an animal to be angry, frightened, unhappy—but hopeful? "Can he believe his master will come the day after tomorrow? And *what* can he not do here?" Wittgenstein asks. "Can only those hope who can talk? Only those who have mastered the use of a language. That is to say, the phenomena of hope are modes of this complicated [human] form of life." Humans have dimensions to their lives that animals don't have, Wittgenstein seems to say. Take the *simulation* of a feeling. The reason a dog can't simulate pain isn't that it hasn't been taught or isn't bright enough. "The surroundings which are necessary for [its] behaviour to be real simulation are missing."[17]

What surroundings? One thing missing is what allows us to say,

---

[16]Wittgenstein, *Philosophical Investigations,* I, 256.
[17]Ibid., II, 1; I, 250.

sometimes, "I was only fooling." Now why can't a dog make that move? If not because it's insensitive or dense, then why? We don't know how to answer this question. *Our* ability to dissemble is connected with our use of language, our use of facial expressions, and with the way they allow us to relate to others. Such various abilities open up a wide range of ways we can deal with other people. The dimensions of these possibilities cannot involve only the capacity for language; they require a whole way of life that includes language. Even "way of life" is not adequate here, since we want to say *all* humans with their very different ways of life have the same wide range of options, which they develop differently.

How do we know dogs can't communicate with other dogs? We don't, and on the contrary may find occasions on which we like to say they do communicate, in the manner of dogs, that is. But we cannot speak of occasions on which dogs express hope or expectation that something will happen tomorrow. The dog's lack of language imposes a *logical* limitation on what can be attributed to that kind of being.

A dog can't express hope; what kind of assertion is this? One less about dogs than about hope: that we cannot attribute hoping or dissembling to a dog is a grammatical observation. Wittgenstein's point is that there is no one thing—a certain *feeling*—that's lacking in a dog; it isn't as if the lack were identifiable. What's lacking is rather the "surroundings" in which hope can be spoken of, the whole frame of reference, of circumstances and possibilities, in which we determine that hope is what is expressed. Hope has a grammar *for us* in the context of lives like ours. Could it have a grammar for other beings, in lives of other kinds? We cannot say, and if we try to say, the meaning fails. How can we conjecture what grammar "hope" *might* have if it didn't have the grammar it has? The strange thing about asking this question is how little one *can* say. We've run out of road to drive on.

These remarks are meant to show why Wittgenstein speaks here of a form of life. We are past the point where we can indicate reasons for either affirming or denying that the dog hopes. We are past saying even where the difficulty lies; we are in a kind of no-man's-land. All we know is that we can't fit any behavior of his—however hypothetical—into the grammatical form of the concept of hope.

IV

   Some philosophers, among them Reid, Shaftesbury, and Adam Smith, treat moral feelings as part of our natural constitution, arguing that we are by nature benevolent and sensitive to others. According to them, this feeling for our fellows is as much our destiny as being carnivorous and bipedal. Thus Reid could write: "To reason about justice with a man who sees nothing to be just or unjust, or about benevolence with a man who sees nothing in benevolence preferable to malice, is like reasoning with a blind man about colour, or with a deaf man about sound."[18] Such a foundation for morality is needed, they reasoned, if morals are to be more than merely conventional. Robinson Crusoe, the "wild boy of Aveyron," or any solitary primitive will be endowed with the same passions as we, for they are inherent in human nature. These philosophers were laying the groundwork for the kind of moral and social atomism that influenced the early Americans. *Everyone* is equally deserving of respect, equally capable of moral judgments, for all people are equally endowed in respect to being human.

   Although I stress the importance of revulsion at wrong, I do not claim that it belongs to our nature in the way being bipedal does. On the contrary, it is certainly educated, and it belongs to certain surroundings, the surroundings of a human community. I further argue that it is a mistake to try to separate what is biological from what is social; that too invokes an atomistic picture in which each individual can be seen complete in himself, in isolation. With Aristotle, I believe it is impossible to see a developed human being in this way. The study of any species in terms of a single isolated member 1 call the "zookeeper view," for a zoo is an artificial setting where individual animals are taken in order for people to see "what they are like." Whatever they are like really and in their habitat, however, in the zoo they are examples of how creatures of their species look and behave in unnatural conditions of captivity, isolation, and dislocation. Thus there is no need to decide whether humans are social "by nature" or only by conditioning. The sense

---

   [18]Thomas Reid, *Inquiry and Essays*, ed. Keith Lehrer and Ronald Beanblossom (Indianapolis: Bobbs-Merrill, 1975), p. 322.

of revulsion at wrong belongs to our upbringing, our upbringing as human children and not as children of some other kind. I think this is part of the importance of the term "form of life," that it signifies some complex of which biology forms an essential but unanalyzable part.[19]

V

After Protagoras makes the brash claim that "if you come to me, . . . the very day you will go home a better man," Socrates states his opinion that virtue "cannot be taught nor furnished by one man to another." When it comes to matters of government, he says, "the man who gets up to advise [the Assembly] may be a builder or equally well a blacksmith or a shoemaker, merchant or shipowner. . . . No one brings it up against any of these . . . that here is a man who without any technical qualifications . . . is yet trying to give advice. The reason must be that they do not think this is a subject that can be taught." The same skepticism applies to the idea that any teacher can reliably make people good. Even the venerable Pericles, who gave his sons the best education that teaching could provide, did not train them "in his own special kind of wisdom" or hand them over to an instructor: "they simply browse around on their own like sacred cattle, on the chance of picking up virtue automatically."[20]

Protagoras responds that when we punish offenders, we show that we believe "that virtue can be instilled by education," for punishment is imposed "for the sake of the future, to prevent

[19]Edmund Cahn, in contrast, believes that the sense of injustice must have a biological foundation—an explanation in terms of survival—to be palpable. That biological purpose, briefly, is "the repelling of assaults, sometimes immediately experienced, sometimes brought to immediacy by the miracle of imaginative interchange" (*The Sense of Injustice* [New York: New York University Press, 1949], p. 186). On this view, the capacity imaginatively to identify one's own fortunes with another's is the bonding material of any human society and the sense of injustice is an expression of this imaginative capacity.

[20]Plato, *Protagoras*, trans. W. K. C. Guthrie, in *The Collected Dialogues of Plato*, ed. Edith Hamilton and Huntington Cairns (Princeton: Princeton University Press, 1961), 319e–320a.

either the same man or, by the spectacle of his punishment, some-one else, from doing wrong again." We wouldn't punish, he in-fers, without believing that it's possible to teach goodness. A sec-ond proof has particularly to do with children: "As soon as a child can understand what is said to him, nurse, mother, tutor, and the father himself vie with each other to make him as good as possi-ble . . . pointing out, 'This is right and that is wrong, this honor-able and that disgraceful, this holy, that impious. . . . If he is obe-dient, well and good. If not, they straighten him with threats and beatings, like a warped and twisted plank."21 The child's recogni-tion of what is right and wrong is the responsibility of the parents, and later of school authorities, Protagoras says. That parents treat this kind of learning as an important part of a child's education shows that people believe virtue must be teachable. Otherwise indeed children would be left to browse around on their own, finding what morals they needed by luck.

Contrary to Protagoras, I believe that the process by which a child learns to be good and to respect goodness requires an element of luck, though not the kind he speaks of. What is needed is some happy rapport between child and parent, giving to the parent a place of moral authority and to the child a measure of understand-ing. For if parents aren't seen as moral authorities and understand-ing is lacking, then, as we have seen, the moral message may be lost. For the teaching is ambiguous in the same ways that punish-ment is, and a child may easily get things wrong. Moral education is even more ambiguous than teaching a child the meaning of "purple" by pointing to a vase, in which case the child may think that "purple" is a container for flowers. Some amount of chance and a great deal of background and surroundings are needed if the moral teaching is to take hold.

Look again at what Wittgenstein means by "surroundings." In the case of moral teaching, the surroundings need to include rela-tionships of trust and respect. Other relations and institutions could be mentioned, such as those of property or commerce; but one can imagine enormous variation in the institutions a society might have while trust and some close familial relationships re-

21Ibid., 324a–d, 325c–d.

main central.[22] We are content to say that there needs to be some kind of community with some kind of institutions.[23]

VI

In *On Certainty* Wittgenstein emphasizes that many things aren't learned through explanations. We are shown and told how to do something, then we do it as we are shown. Explanations and justifications may come later if they come at all. In speaking of the "foundation" of some of our beliefs about the physical world, he says that "at some point one has to pass from explanation to mere description" and the description says what we do. "In the end is not an ungrounded presupposition: it is an ungrounded way of acting." To quote Goethe, "im Anfang war die Tat"—in the beginning there were deeds, not words—and to say this is the beginning signifies that there are no deeper beliefs that could be invoked.[24] With them we have reached rock bottom.

These remarks about certainty can shed some light on morality. At the bottom of propositions about morals—what people should and shouldn't do, what things are wrong, what unjust—is a description of what people *do*. Among these actions are the response of shock at certain things, indignation, and the impulse to recrimi-

---

[22]It is easily overlooked, especially on the assumptions of atomism, that institutions of commerce and contracts are a locus for a good deal of our talk about ethics. Some such institutions will exist in even the simplest society, providing the setting for judgments of censure and praise.

[23]If we wanted further to specify conditions for laws and legal institutions in a society, we might follow A. M. Honoré, who sketches some. Law, he says, must pertain to a *group*, and that is not a "mere collection of individuals." What else is needed? For one thing, a "shared understanding" among the members. And he describes a shared understanding as follows: "In the first place, each member must understand what the others profess to regard as the proper thing to be done in given conditions. The prescription . . . must be communicated by word, example, or attitude to others, or to one's own conduct." "Such a shared or common understanding, or a number of such understandings is a defining characteristic of a group." However, he exempts morals from this requirement: "There can be private morality, but no private law" ("Groups, Laws, and Obedience," in *Oxford Essays in Jurisprudence*, 2d ser. [Oxford: Oxford University Press, 1973], pp. 4–5). It is interesting that Honoré does not believe that morality requires a group; some of the same conditions seem clearly relevant.

[24]Wittgenstein, *On Certainty*, 189, 110, 402.

nate. It is not some "ungrounded presupposition" about morals but an "ungrounded way of acting" that forms the beginning. Justifications will be considered later, and then they have to come to an end somewhere: "If I have exhausted the justifications I have reached bedrock, and my spade is turned." Wittgenstein writes, and "then I am inclined to say: 'This is simply what I do.' "[25] In morality, too, justification comes to rest in what we do.

What we do is show revulsion at wrongdoing; but this fact is not bare or self-explanatory. Wittgenstein says, "Imagine that the people of a tribe were brought up from early youth to give no expression of feeling *of any kind*. Let the training be severe. 'Pain' is not spoken of. . . . If anyone complains, he is ridiculed or punished." In such a tribe or culture there is no shamming of pain because expressions of pain are themselves taboo. Wittgenstein draws this conclusion: "an education quite different from ours might also be the foundation for quite different concepts. For here life would run on differently. What interests us would not interest *them*. Here different concepts would no longer be unimaginable. In fact, this is the only way in which *essentially* different concepts are imaginable."[26] If we imagine a very different upbringing for children, we must imagine moral concepts that are different, for ours go with our surroundings: we learn to abhor certain wrongs. Nonetheless, the abhorrence or revulsion we feel at wrongs is a kind of bedrock, the point where the spade of inquiry is turned.

If we weren't horrified, disturbed, moved, offended by injustice. then it wouldn't be injustice we reacted to but something else. A being who couldn't feel and express those feelings couldn't master the idea of injustice, couldn't understand that concept's grammar. Still we can imagine learning that people in another kind of culture felt abhorrence at different wrongs; indeed, their reactions would give us the cue to their different morality.[27]

---

[25]Wittgenstein, *Philosophical Investigations,* I, 217.

[26]Ludwig Wittgenstein, *Zettel,* ed. G. E. M. Anscombe and G. H. von Wright, trans. Anscombe (Berkeley: University of California Press, 1967), 383, 387–88.

[27]Are there conditions for the capacity for abhorrence? Imagine a dog: can it be moved by the sight of an injustice, such as another dog being cruelly hit with a stick? How would he show that this was what impressed him? How would we know that his flinching was flinching at the injustice and not at the possibility of

The question, raised so often by moral philosophers, as to the real foundation of morality asks for something impossible—that we supply a foundation to morality as if it were *not* part and parcel of our lives and the process of learning our language. We learn morality and the moral vocabulary together, and come to have a sense of injustice at the same time. Is that sense altogether learned, then? All of culture is learned, and all language; but that doesn't mean that all culture and morality are "conventional," if that means they are part of life's superfices. On the contrary, they belong to our life's *form*, not to its matter, and in the deepest sense.

The profound and puzzling character of moral concepts, religious concepts, and some psychological ones derives from the fact that we not only learn behavior and meanings together but learn them very young. Wittgenstein says that "the word 'God' is one of the earliest learnt—pictures and catechisms, etc."[28] Learning the practices of religion and learning the terminology were bound together with what we call learning to believe. This is much like the way that learning the meaning of an order is bound together with doing what it commands. Showing we understand it, we do what we're told; learning the meaning of religious terms, we learn to behave in certain ways, perform certain rituals. When did we begin to accept the propositions? At no particular time. D. Z. Phillips compares religious belief to dance, calling attention to Wittgenstein's observation that "the origin and the primitive form of the language game is a reaction; only from this can the more complicated forms grow." "What is primary is active response rather than reflection," Phillips writes. One learns to dance, and the belief becomes incorporated in the action; there is "a fusion of 'dance' and 'thought.' "[29] That is how rituals work.

---

being beaten himself or something altogether different? The answer is that we cannot say how he would show indignation at an unjust beating, which is also to say how we could read this response. Then do we say that the dog has no sense of injustice, that he is morally calloused or amoral? These inferences don't make sense. To say that the dog has no sense of injustice goes beyond the grammatical setting of injustice and into a nonsense realm. The dog can't *lack* a sense of injustice for the same reason that he can't *have* one: because we have left the region where the concept functions and does its work.

[28]Wittgenstein, *Lectures and Conversations,* p. 59.

[29]D. Z. Phillips, "Primitive Reactions and the Reactions of Primitives," Marratt Lecture, Exeter College, Oxford, 1983, pp. 16–17, 15.

The question what is human nature really, apart from the training and influences of family and society, is inherently strange. Think of the question "Is its song natural to a song sparrow?" Here one wants to speak of instinctive responses; yet the song that is characteristic of this species is not sung by birds that haven't heard and learned it while they are young. Such birds have a coarser call, with intermittent croaking sounds. Then is that the "true" song sparrow call, natural because it was *not* learned? Yet one might say no; that's the call of a bird deficient in one respect, a kind of cripple of its species. Why take it as a species exemplar?

The same point applies to humans. The person who is untaught and untrained, like the "wild boy of Aveyron," is a human anomaly.[30] Would we take such a one as showing us what human nature really is, as giving us a natural, Archimedean point for moral and social theory? That would be a strange strategy, like taking an autistic person as representing human nature. When we speak of humans, we mean humans as we know and recognize them, and that means humans with their form of life intact.

Religious beliefs and religious practices, moral beliefs and moral practices, are pairs that belong in one fabric. Taken together they help make certain aspects of people's lives comprehensible, while any attempt to separate them makes the same lives incoherent. I have argued that analysis will not reveal to us two independent things and the glue that holds them together, will not allow us to see how the whole is made. Analysis wrenches apart what grows as one thing. Analysis suggests that there are independent entities that could exist alone—the feeling apart from its expression, the religious belief apart from its practices, the concept of injustice without the practice of condemnation and expressions of abhorrence. The problem here is not to analyze but to understand the grammar of our concepts, to see the whole not in pieces but in its various aspects.

[30]For an excellent account of this child, the role of "natural man" given him by French academics, and his anomalous place in society, see Roger Shattuck, *The Forbidden Experiment* (New York: Farrar Straus Giroux, 1980).

Index

Abhorrence of wrong, xii, 46–47, 128, 139, 144, 146, 150, 163–64, 172, 193–94, 203
  as fundamental, xii, 48, 139, 193–94, 211
  and learning language, 142–43, 199
Affirmative action, 39
Agamemnon, 136–37, 154–55
Agency, 167
  and good deeds, xii, 77, 81, 83–86, 93–94
  and government, xii, 77, 91–94
American Bookseller's Assn. v. *Hudnut,* 118n
American political tradition, 17th-century origins of, xi, 2, 6–7, 22, 207
Anti-authoritarianism, 2, 3, 12
Antigone, 136
Archimedean point, x, 2–3, 8, 57, 59, 68, 213
Aristophanes, 51, 54
Aristotle, 9–10, 21, 24–25, 67, 84–86, 91–92, 94–97, 122n, 139n, 199, 207
Atomism, 25, 50, 66, 202
  and anti-authoritarianism, 2, 19
  and autonomy, 3, 192, 207
  and babies and children, 31, 38, 40, 200
  and competition, 18–19, 57, 60
  and democracy, xi, 51, 55–56, 59, 75, 97

difficulties of, xi–xii, 17, 26–27, 35, 38, 40, 43, 50, 59
  and egoism, 19, 56, 59, 66, 76, 204
  ethical, 6, 7
  and individual freedom, xii, 98
  and pregnancy, 39, 40–43
  and rights, 31–32, 36–38, 46, 49, 98
  as scientific theory, 7, 20, 68
  social, xi, 4–5, 7, 12, 97
  and U.S. Constitution, 7, 19
  virtues of, 3, 4
Autonomy, 2–3, 5–6, 11, 15, 25, 61, 63–64, 119, 179, 192
  difficulties of, 41

Babies, needs of, 39–42. *See also* Children
Bentham, Jeremy, 55–59, 65, 80n, 82–83, 87, 89, 91, 191
Berger, Fred, 100n, 102n
Blacks, 14, 116–18
Bradley, F. H., 147–48, 160
Brown v. *Board of Education,* 116–17
Burke, Edmund, 24n
Burkert, Walter, 134n
Butler, Bishop Joseph, 14, 194
Butler, Samuel, 33

Cahn, Edmond, 108n, 129, 132n, 138, 142n, 149n, 208n

Library of Congress Cataloging-in-Publication Data

Wolgast, Elizabeth Hankins, 1929–
    The grammar of justice.

    Includes index.
    1. Justice.   I.   Title.
JC578.W65   1987   320'.01'1   87-47608
ISBN 0-8014-2081-4 (alk. paper)
ISBN 0-8014-9402-8 (pbk. : alk. paper)